NO PICNIC
ON MOUNT KENYA

Felice Benuzzi (Bartolini, Paris, 1949)

Felice Benuzzi

NO PICNIC
ON MOUNT KENYA

MACLEHOSE PRESS
QUERCUS · LONDON

First published as *No Picnic on Mount Kenya* by
William Kimber, London, 1952
"The Unknown" first published in *Fuga sul Kenya* as "L'ignoto" by
L'Eroica, Milan, 1948
First published in Great Britain in 2015 by MacLehose Press
This paperback edition published in 2016 by

MacLehose Press
An imprint of Quercus Publishing Ltd
Carmelite House
50 Victoria Embankment
London EC4Y 0DZ
An Hachette UK company

Published by agreement with Agenzia Letteraria Roberto Santachiara

ISBN (MMP) 978-0-85705-377-0
ISBN (Ebook) 978-0-85705-375-6

10 9 8 7 6 5 4 3 2 1

Designed and typeset in Adobe Garamond by Libanus Press, Marlborough
Plate section designed by Richard Carr
Printed and bound in Great Britain by Clays Ltd, St Ives plc

CONTENTS

LIST OF ILLUSTRATIONS

PREFACE

I would like to thank:

First of all my companions Dr Giovanni Balletto, Dodoma, Tanganyika Territory, and Mr Enzo Barsotti, Mombasa, Kenya, who appear in this book as Giuàn and Enzo, and without whom neither our adventure nor the writing of this book would have been possible.

All our fellow prisoners of war of P.O.W. Camp 354 who assisted us in the actual escape and gave us their generous and silent assistance during the period of preparation and organisation.

Mr R. M. Graham, Acting Conservateur of Forests, Nairobi, Kenya, not only for having assisted me with invaluable information but also for having attempted to convert my English into a more readable language, and Mrs Graham, Dr J. D. Melhuish and Mr E. Robson, M.P.S., for having assisted me with much advice.

The Mountaineering Club of East Africa for having given permission to quote some extracts from their Journal *Ice Cap*.

F.B.

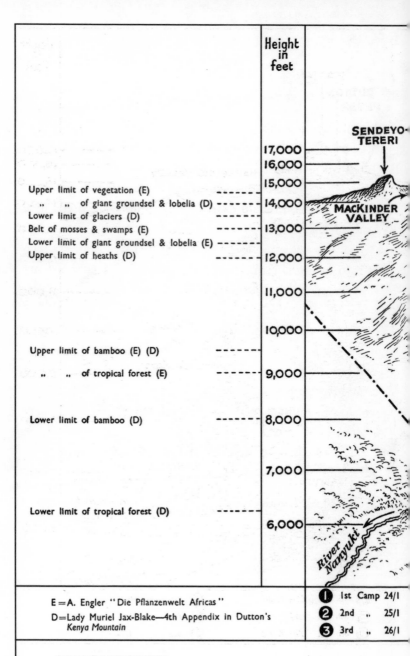

	Height in feet	
		SENDEYO-TERERI
	17,000	
	16,000	
Upper limit of vegetation (E) ------	15,000	
„ „ of giant groundsel & lobelia (D) ------	14,000	**MACKINDER VALLEY**
Lower limit of glaciers (D) ------		
Belt of mosses & swamps (E) ------	13,000	
Lower limit of giant groundsel & lobelia (E) ------		
Upper limit of heaths (D) ------	12,000	
	11,000	
	10,000	
Upper limit of bamboo (E) (D) ------		
„ „ of tropical forest (E) ------	9,000	
Lower limit of bamboo (D) ------	8,000	
	7,000	
Lower limit of tropical forest (D) ------	6,000	*River Nanyuki*

E = A. Engler "Die Pflanzenwelt Africas"

D = Lady Muriel Jax-Blake—4th Appendix in Dutton's *Kenya Mountain*

❶ 1st Camp 24/1
❷ 2nd „ 25/1
❸ 3rd „ 26/1

SUMMARY OF THE TRIP

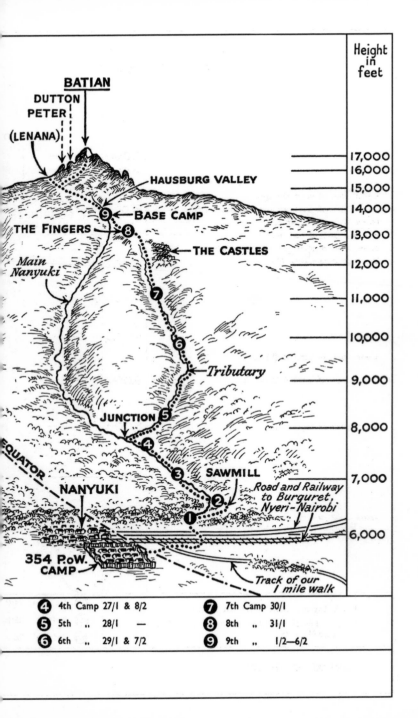

Height in feet

BATIAN

DUTTON
PETER
(LENANA)

HAUSBURG VALLEY

17,000
16,000
15,000
14,000

BASE CAMP

13,000

THE FINGERS

THE CASTLES

12,000

Main Nanyuki

11,000

10,000

Tributary

9,000

JUNCTION

8,000

SAWMILL

7,000

Road and Railway to Burguret, Nyeri–Nairobi

EQUATOR

NANYUKI

6,000

354 P.o.W. CAMP

Track of our 1 mile walk

④	4th Camp 27/1 & 8/2		⑦	7th Camp 30/1
⑤	5th ,, 28/1 —		⑧	8th ,, 31/1
⑥	6th ,, 29/1 & 7/2		⑨	9th ,, 1/2—6/2

CHAPTER I

The Mirage

*Of life in prisoner of war camps on the Equator,
and of the organising of a mountaineering expedition
towards a 17,000-foot peak, despite difficulties over
the question of stores and equipment.*

P. O. W. Camp

After a thirty-six-hour journey, the long train stopped outside a little station, the name of which I could not read from our cattle-truck "coach".

On our left there was a wood of strange thorn trees with smooth green stems; on the right a vast plain where the corrugated iron roofs of hundreds and hundreds of barrack huts shimmered in the midday haze. Between the guard-towers one could make out the barbed wire fence.

The very sight of this encampment tumbled one's heart into one's boots. We stared as though mesmerised, but nobody dared to utter aloud the question each put to himself: "Yes, inside there: but for how long?"

A dead silence reigned in the waggon while each man gathered up his few belongings. An equally silent column of prisoners from the first waggons was already assembling outside, alongside the rails. We were surely more than a thousand on this train, yet not a word was spoken.

Flies buzzed in the heavy air. In the nearby wood, doves cooed with ironic indifference.

Having travelled in the last waggon, we were the last to start our slow march and in the meantime, the head of the column had covered a good half of the distance between the railway and the camp. In doing so it had raised such a cloud of dust that we were deprived of the depressing sight of our goal.

At last our turn came and we started too, mechanically four by four, heads drooping in the midday heat. The huge snail, slow and dumb, crept forward through the dust cloud as though marching towards infinity.

At the threshold of the camp we were halted and then we entered the gate one by one. It was at last, we had been told, the "definitive" camp. What a horrible word, "definitive"!

There was no vegetation to conceal or in any way soften the crudeness of the barbed wire fences. Starkly, almost desperately it seemed, the gallows-like poles supporting the wires reached towards the empty sky.

Fig. 1. P.O.W. Camp 354, Nanyuki, in 1943.

"Why have you woken me up?"

"It's half-past seven."

"But roll-call is at half-past eight. You've tricked me out of an hour!"

"Tricked?"

"If you had left me asleep, I should have avoided one hour of captivity . . ."

A voice from the upper end of the barrack: "A four for bridge wanted."

Answer from the far end: "For half a loaf of bread you can have *me.*"

The poster on the door of a barrack: "Do you want a long and happy captivity? Do as my grandmother did. She lived for 110 years because she minded her own business."

People in prison camps do not live. They only vegetate or as a Russian writer puts it: "they live at the level of physiology".

From the *Polar Diary* of Umberto Cagni, referring to life during the long Arctic night: "The spirit gets blunted more and more and the mind of everybody is invaded by an odd indifference for everything not material and not present."

"In spite of the communal life each man feels strangely isolated from his fellows."

"Every remembrance of the time when we led a less animal-like existence engenders longing, and with it a remote kind of suffering. While forgetting everything and living like a bear one does not feel moral needs which cannot be satisfied."

These truths apply perfectly to our prisoner of war life.

But Admiral Cagni wrote also: "I should like to emulate a Spartan and lose all my bad habits. Never in my life shall I have a better opportunity for doing so."

You can never be alone.

You open a letter (if you are lucky enough to get one, once in a blue moon) and ten pairs of eyes gaze at you and ten mouths bombard you with questions: "Any news?" "Good news?" "Alright?" "Are they all well?"

"Thank you very much," you would like to answer, "for your kind interest, but couldn't you leave me alone to read, at least now?"

You open your suitcase (if you are lucky enough to have one) in order to air your rags or to chase off those black beetles that infest our barracks in legions. Immediately your "friends" gather round you and exclaim: "Look! You've still got a spare pair of socks!" "What book is this?" "May I have a look at this photo?" and so on.

You cannot even whistle a tune (if by any chance you get up in a cheerful mood) without hearing another prisoner at the far end of the barrack joining and whistling the same tune.

At night you fall asleep immediately, but after a few hours you wake again. You feel so tired that you do not even want to open your eyes; but you feel an appalling lucidity of mind.

You just lie there and remember. Slowly you begin to "see" episodes lived through years and years before; phrases, inflections of voices, countenances appear again as clearly as though you were able to recall the film of your own life; as though you were present, spectator and character at the same time, in the making of a talking and musical picture. It really is "musical" too, because many episodes have a sort of musical background, even if this consists of the most plebeian songs fashionable for a brief moment. Thus for me, 1934 is connected with the song "Why", the summer of 1938 with "Following the Fleet" just as other years and seasons are unalterably identifiable with other songs.

Slowly the grey dawn comes and at last you drop into a short, restless sleep, which does nothing to restore you.

To remember is far worse than to forget. This is not a discovery of mine. It was an old truth in the times of the Greek statesman Themistocles. Once he was approached – so the story goes – by a schoolmaster who asked him for a reward because he had thought out a system of teaching that greatly improved the memory of his pupils. Themistocles answered: "I shall give you a reward if you invent a method of enabling mankind to learn how to *forget*, not how to remember."

The sole activity for this host of people is to wander round the camp – this camp has accommodation for ten thousand people, it's a regular town – the whole day. They just walk and stop where they see other people talking. There they stay for a while and join in the conversation.

What are they talking about?

A pessimist used to say: "Seventy-five per cent of the subjects talked about in the camps are lies and twenty per cent are stupidities. Only the remaining five per cent are matters worthy of being discussed." Sometimes I wonder whether he was not an optimist, rather than the pessimist he professed to be.

No wonder the camps are the breeding ground of the most fantastic rumours, which are spawned mysteriously, thrive in the unwholesome atmosphere, are discussed avidly and, inevitably, are at last firmly believed.

Every distraction, every spectacle is welcome.

Once I saw a few hundred prisoners gathered between two barracks. I approached them, curious to see what held their attention.

They were watching a cat playing with a mouse. They were prepared to watch for hours.

*

Sometimes, at the moment of *reveille*, when you open your eyes once more only to find yourself still a prisoner, you have not the courage to accept the day. You close your eyes again, hoping to snatch a few more moments from the land of dreams.

It's impossible. Your fellows are already up. Carlo, shaving, whistles Saint-Saëns' "Danse Macabre"; people slam doors and snap suitcase catches. You are compelled to summon up your strength, to jump out of your bunk and accept captivity.

At this time there are still few books circulating.

When any rag enters the barrack, it is assaulted by ten, twenty men, each hungry for reading matter. "What's this?" "Let me have a look." "Only for a moment, please."

If it appears to be a book – a book in dreadful condition, of course – a struggle for "rights" of priority begins.

"When you have finished the first hundred pages would you mind giving them to me?" "I'm second." "Oh please, I was first, so *he* is second and *you* only third."

An endless argument follows.

The reader usually objects: "How can I lend you the book if I have to give it back at 9.00 a.m. tomorrow?"

"It doesn't matter. I'm a quick reader."

"I've found half a pint of cooking oil for my lamp. I can read the whole night long. Give it to me."

After all, it is a pleasant struggle; as long as it lasts, time has value again.

Concentrated humanity

"Naturalists in charge of zoos have noted – if I am rightly informed – that captivity provokes considerable alterations in the character of animals. It would be foolish to deny that captivity exercises a still greater influence upon human character, infinitely more complex than that of animals."

Starting from this premise, some of us spent a long, idle evening half-seriously debating the question: "What is the main difference between *Homo Sapiens* and the subspecies, resulting from years of captivity, *Captivus Vulgaris*, or expressed mathematically *P.O.W. No. 00*?"

I cannot remember the whole course of the discussion at this amateur psychologists' meeting, but from among the answers I liked most, I recall this one:

"*Captivus Vulgaris Kenyensis* is not a subspecies of *Homo Sapiens* but a super-species. Here one finds concentrated humanity. Every character becomes saturated, that is to say concentrated, both in its better and worse aspects, to an extent that could not occur in free life. *Homo Sapiens* thus appears in its synthesis – *Captivus Vulgaris*, as nowhere else in the world. You will find here, as though assembled for scientific study, every human type. Nowhere else in the many camps born out of this Second World War will you find, as here in East Africa, so complete an assortment of all ages and trades. Remember that here are not only captured soldiers but also a whole European male population, deported from Ethiopia."

There was indeed every kind of person in the prisoner of war camps in East Africa: old and young; sick and healthy; crazy and sensible; people from every part of Italy and Italians born in every part of the world, of every trade; optimists and pessimists; silent people and irrepressible chatterers; generous minds and those which seemed to personify meanness; men who minded their own business (alas! a minority) and those who for the life of them could not do so; people who gathered commodities left and right (called by us "hunting dogs", for this animal is perhaps the most voracious of African mammals) and those who were happy with nothing; true gentlemen and irreclaimable villains.

Between these extremes there were the usual intermediate types, but a mere description of them all would fill a book.

There were the fanatics of sunbathing and gymnastics; boxers; volleyball players and footballers; people who worked with make-shift tools for hours in the sun until exhausted in order to make a tennis court, only to be transferred to another camp before they could enjoy the fruits of their toil. On the other hand there were human specimens who never got up from their bunks for fear that they might waste energy and who, if this were possible, would have sent someone else to settle even their most private affairs.

There were people who studied the whole day and for them captivity was, in a way, bliss.

I have read somewhere that Disraeli, writing about Hugo Grotius, who like Marco Polo, Cervantes, Bunyan, Silvio Pellico and many others, wrote his best work while a prisoner, stated: "Other men, condemned to exile or captivity, if they survive, despair; the man of letters may reckon those days as the sweetest of his life." I am not a man of letters and therefore I do not consider the five years I spent as a prisoner of war as the sweetest of my life; but, when all is said and done, I can at least bear witness to the difference between my mental state in the years "before Mount Kenya" and those years "after Mount Kenya", when I was busy writing these lines.

People who spent their time studying had my full approbation. Some of them, by preparing for exams or actually learning a science or one or more languages (we had teachers among us who held lessons on almost every possible subject), not only improved their education, but above all prevented their minds from getting stale and warped.

Sketching, drawing and painting were extremely popular subjects, as soon as we were able to get the necessary materials through parcels and later through the kind help of the Y.M.C.A. of East Africa. High prestige was enjoyed by artists able to enlarge the most faded and smallest photographs of girlfriends or relations.

Then there were the actors, entertainers and musicians: they deserve a chapter on their own, because they really worked wonders. Their ability and ingenuity helped us to pass many delightful evenings.

There were those artists in tin – no mere tinsmiths – who out of empty containers created lamps, dishes, paraffin boilers, frying pans, mugs, toys and models of every description. Woodcarving was also very fashionable, the tools all being made from scrap material worked with the aid of camp-made forges. Repairers of watches and glasses attained the meridian of fame. Musical instruments were made from packing cases or from timber "borrowed" from the camp stores, and a few people achieved such perfection in this craftsmanship – I mean the building of instruments, not the "borrowing" – that whole orchestras were equipped with beautifully toned instruments. For instance, the orchestra that later became the Central Italian Orchestra of Nairobi, which gave concerts all over East Africa, was equipped mainly by this means.

Then there were the card-players and gamblers: lots of them.

O mighty Ely Culbertson, every P.O.W. camp should erect a marble monument in your honour, for without you how would thousands of people have passed their years of captivity? Fifteen or twenty rubbers per day were not records but only the average of games played by at least twenty people I could recall by name.

Of course, the stakes were mainly cigarettes; but I knew people who quite literally lost their last shirt at poker or baccarat tables, and others who, after having sold everything available, were compelled to wash linen and clean boots for their creditors in order to make good at least a part of their debts.

Superstitions of every kind flourished like the green bay tree in the camps for a while. Chiromancers, astrologers and destiny-diviners enjoyed their short periods of glory. Spiritualism too was fashionable for a short time. The great spirit of Napoleon him-self was evoked in order to tell those who believed which side would win the war, and when. The innocent shades of maiden aunts – those rigid custodians of family morals – were kept work-ing overtime; through them alone it was felt, would it be possible to get news of possible infidelities on the part of wives and fiancées.

There were hard-faced traders and usurers who organised busi-nesses and banks, leases and sales and who accumulated hundreds of shillings which were often confiscated by the searchers when prisoners were being transferred from one camp to another.

There were people with a variety of imaginary ailments crowd-ing the sick bays, begging the doctors to give them priority over people who were in genuine need of medical treatment.

There was a fanatic hygienist who spent a fortune in buying toilet paper, which he used to wrap around door handles before grasping them. He hoped in this way to avoid being infected, but I do not know – and I doubt if he knew himself – what disease he feared. On the other hand there were certain well-known prisoners who were never seen at the shower baths even at Christmas or on Bank Holidays.

Some built brilliantly functioning wireless receiving sets in secret, and there was a whole organisation of shorthand writers to distribute news bulletins.

Not even common criminals were absent, as some three hundred "guests" of Akaki jail had been freed by the occupation authorities of Ethiopia and subsequently impounded in the Kenya camps. Judge Pace of Addis Ababa slept – I repeat *slept* – in a double bunk in Compound E, Camp 354, with one of his "customers", whom he had recently sentenced to ten years seclusion for manslaughter.

The strangest trade I came across in my prison life was perhaps that of a mesmeriser whose subjects were animals, mainly chickens. Perhaps I had better explain. Towards the end of our long captivity, in Camp 356, Eldoret, we enjoyed a three-mile walk, during which we were sometimes able to buy chickens from Africans. The mesmeriser, who ranked high among the bridge stars of the camp, was asked to remain close to the buyer and while the bargaining proceeded he quietly mesmerised one of the chickens, which immediately dropped asleep.

"And what do you want for this one?" the buyer would ask the African, pointing to the mesmerised bird. Without hesitation the African would say: "Five shillings, the same as the others."

"But don't you see it's sick? It looks as though it might be dying."

The African, afraid of losing his money, would be happy to sell the bird for a shilling or two. The only reward the mesmeriser claimed was to be asked to dinner to help eat his "subject" roasted with potatoes.

There came a day when we were transferred to Camp 354, Nanyuki, at the foot of Mount Kenya. Our carriage – not a cattle truck this time – watched by sentries, remained in Nairobi station from 5.00 a.m. till 11.00 a.m., being shunted up and down in order, presumably, to comply with mysterious railway exigencies.

After about a year of incarceration we were able to see people living in freedom, coming and going as they liked. We gazed with fascinated eyes as though witnessing miracles.

A man stepped out of a train and bought a newspaper and a packet of cigarettes at the tobacconist's. He paid with clinking money and went off. Just like that! Soon we heard the sound of the engine of a car starting up. The very idea of steering a car gave me a dizzy feeling.

We saw women, young and good-looking, middle-aged and elderly. Among them were undoubtedly fiancées, wives, sisters and mothers, all real, alive, not mere phantoms as were ours in our dreams. We saw children, sweet little ones among them; one wanting to collect that empty red cigarette packet on the platform, another throwing his round arms about the neck of his daddy who was just stepping out of a train. No doubt the few words they were able to stammer were spoken in English, but from a distance they might as well have been speaking in Italian. Their expressions, their gestures were the same as those of our own children, now interned in the camps of Ethiopia and Somaliland.

It was torture. One could have jumped out of the train for no other purpose than to mix for ten minutes with free people. I would bet that every one of us, looking from our carriage windows onto that crowded Nairobi platform, was busy with thoughts of escape, soon repressed.

The idea of escaping is a vital factor in the mind of every prisoner. On our arrival in East Africa I had, as a matter of course, carefully considered the chances of reaching the nearest neutral territory, Portuguese East Africa, but I had concluded that, for me at least, this would be impossible. The distances one had to cover were enormous; one needed a frightful lot of money, the opportunity of

credi tu ancora?

credi
tu alle poltrone
ai tappeti egli arredi!
ai bei letti per una o due persone?
al piumino sui piedi!
tu alle poltrone
credi!

ancora
credi al campari
al ramazzotti al cora
e a quella strana storia da giullari
della birra che odora?
credi al campari
ancora?

non credo
io più all'abbacchio
o al cacciucco nè credo
a quell'altro discorso falso e racchio
del porchetto allo spiedo
io più all'abbacchio
non credo

gnocchi?
chianti e barbera?
ciliegi ed albicocchi
di tutte queste non ce n'è una vera!
favole per gli sciocchi
chianti, barbera,
gnocchi!

donne?!
e tu ancora
credi ch'asistan gonne?!
solo esiston kikuyu, alla buon'ora
snebbiati o insonne
che sogni ancora
donne!

disegni di crivelli

sicelio

From camp comic 365, November 1941

getting a car, knowledge of the country and of the main languages, and faked documents. Even if one reached Portuguese East Africa the problem of getting home from there presented still greater difficulties. As a matter of fact, out of all those who attempted to escape during our five years of captivity in order to reach Portuguese East Africa, only a group of four officers succeeded.

Mount Kenya

In the low barrack of tar-painted hessian the night had closed in quickly. The wind whistled and rain thundered on the corrugated iron roof. Outside, throughout the camp, the ground was a swamp. At every step, one raised several pounds of sticky mud on one's shoes.

At a small makeshift table placed between two bunks, four prisoners sat playing bridge around a flickering oil-lamp fashioned from an empty meat tin.

"One down," remarked a player, sadly putting down his last few cards.

"Of course," his partner said acidly, "if you insist on not drawing trumps . . . "

"But listen. Had I found the ten of spades on my left instead of my right . . . "

The argument carried on endlessly. It is impossible for a bridge party in a prisoner of war camp not to degenerate into an argument.

On another bunk two men sat, wrapped in their blankets, sharing a single light while they read.

At the far end of the barrack, a dead silence reigned. No lights showed, yet it was too early for anyone to have gone to sleep. People just lay on their bunks busy with their own thoughts.

On my bunk, two men sat beside me, one of them playing chess with an opponent sitting on the opposite bunk, the chess-board on a stool between them.

A train whistled lamentably.

One of the chess players shook his head: "I'm going to lose the queen. There's no other way."

The other fellow sitting on my bunk bent over the chessboard, closing his book but keeping a finger between the pages.

"Let me see," he said, studying the strategic situation.

The train whistled again. The flame of the oil-lamp smoked and flickered.

From the bunk opposite the chess players, Umberto, whom I had thought to be asleep, called me and whispered: "I'm frightfully hungry."

"You're telling me!"

The next morning, May 13, I was shaken out of my sleep by Umberto: "Quick. Get up. Come and look at Mount Kenya!"

"What's it like?"

"You'll see. It's like Monte Viso, but so much more impressive."

Owing to the rainy season we had so far had no opportunity of seeing anything of the mountain but the huge forest-clad pedestal. I was so anxious to see it now that I almost got entangled in my bootlaces while dressing.

"Hurry up!" Umberto shouted from the door, "or the peak will be covered with clouds again."

I emerged at last, stumbled a few steps in the mud and then I saw it. An ethereal mountain emerging from a tossing sea of clouds, framed between two dark barracks: a massive blue-black tooth of sheer rock, inlaid with azure glaciers; austere yet floating fairy-like on the near horizon. It was the first 17,000-foot peak I had ever seen.

I stood gazing until the vision disappeared among the shifting cloud banks.

For hours afterwards I remained spellbound.

I had definitely fallen in love.

Day followed weary day and the mountain remained blanketed under a pall of mist and cloud. The one glimpse I'd had of it days before gradually became a half-remembered dream. Prison life fastened on me once more like a leaden chain. Future prospects were not even considered and only the present existed for us, dark and dismal.

For three months, I had had no news of my family and, to add to my anxiety, there were rumours of a fatal epidemic of measles raging amongst the children in the evacuation camps of Ethiopia. Nerves were near breaking point. The maddening worries which one could do nothing to alleviate, the passivity to which we were condemned, the deadly monotony of the rains and above all, the communal life one was forced to lead in a small barrack with twenty-five or thirty similarly irritable people, seemed likely to drive one mad.

Never being alone for one moment was perhaps the worst thing for us in our state of nerves. Those with whom I shared a barrack were well bred and equitable by temperament; all nice lads individually, but how they racked one's nerves as a mass! Their most trivial activities, like knocking a nail into a pole to hang up a towel, or pulling aside a bunk to look for a missing clog, made one irritable.

Forced to endure the *milieu* we seemed almost afraid of losing our individuality. Sometimes one felt a childish urge to assert one's personality in almost any manner, shouting nonsense, banging an empty tin, showing by every act that one was still able to do something other than to wait passively. I have seen normally calm people suddenly rise from their bunks and climb the roof poles of the barrack, barking like monkeys. I felt I understood them, and they had my full sympathy.

On this particular evening, even the last resource of the prisoner, a remnant of sense of humour, had left me and I felt only a dreadful emptiness, as if I had lost contact with the very ground beneath my feet.

The past was finished; there was nothing more to think about, to grasp. A normal life in the future seemed so far off, so impossible, that I did not even long for it any more. Only the present existed, unavoidable, overwhelming. Time stood still. It was easy to understand how people go mad.

There was no oil left in the lamp and even if there had been, I had no desire to read. I got up from my bunk and went slowly out of the barrack.

Umberto was on his bunk playing his thousandth game of patience. He raised his head as he saw me:

"If this one comes out, we shall be free this year."

I could not even smile. I went out.

It had stopped raining and a chorus of crickets sang loud in the night. A prisoner walked with heavy steps towards the latrines and comprehensively cursed the quaggy mud.

I met another friend and accepted his invitation to play chess. I lost all three games, and as I tramped towards my barrack in the darkness, I was in no better mood than before, though normally I am not a bad loser. I was as tired as though I had marched for miles and miles. I did not even feel hungry.

As I approached my barrack, I heard the noise of hammering. I wondered who was busy at that hour of the night and what he was doing. A strange sense of envy crept into my mind. That prisoner had set himself a task, whatever it was. For him the future existed because presumably he meant to finish his job. For the moment he had found a remedy against captivity.

The night sky was clear. There was a smell of good earth in the air such as I had seldom noticed in Africa. I was thinking, the future exists if you know how to make it, and it's up to you, as I turned the corner of my barrack at the exact spot from which I had seen Mount Kenya for the first time, and from which I had always cast a look in the direction of the peak since that first view.

Now it was visible again and in the starlight it looked even more tantalising than in daylight. The white glaciers gleamed with mysterious light and its superb summit towered against the sky. It was a challenge.

A thought crossed my numbed mind like a flash.

"What are you doing there?"

"I am waiting for midday. And you, what are you waiting for?"

"For the end of the war."

Nobody laughed at this sort of joke any more, because it had ceased to be a joke. It was a real expression of feeling. Time was no longer considered by the average prisoner as something of value to be exploited; time for them was an enemy, but for me this was no longer so.

I was already busy with a secret plan, a plan that was slowly taking definite shape.

A prisoner of the last world war wrote in his memoirs: "At the front one takes risks, but one does not suffer; in captivity one does not take risks but one suffers."

In order to break the monotony of life one had only to start taking risks again, to try to get out of this Noah's Ark, which was preserving us from the risks of war but isolating us from the world and its deluge of life. If there is no means of escaping to a neutral country or of living under a false name in occupied Somalia, then, I thought, at least I shall stage a break in this awful travesty of life. I shall try to get out, climb Mount Kenya and return here.

I realised from the start that I could not do this single-handed; I should have to find companions. As proof that we had reached the summit – if we ever did – we would leave a flag there.

In a torn copy of Steinbeck's *Grapes of Wrath* I found the following paragraph underlined:

"When I was in jail I never thought of the moment of liberation. I thought only of today, perhaps of the football match to be played on the following Saturday, never beyond. I took the days as they came."

An anonymous prisoner of war had written in the margin, "Good advice".

But, anonymous brother, have you ever thought of one difference between the conditions of a man sentenced to jail for an offence and those of a prisoner of war? The former, however long his sentence may be, has a precise knowledge of the date of his liberation; we on the other hand have not. No one can foretell how long this war will last, how long our sentence will be.

The more I considered the idea of escape, the more I realised the magnitude of the task I had set myself. Should we be able to climb without a long period of acclimatisation in the thin air of 17,000 feet? How should we make the actual climb? Whom should I ask to accompany me? How could we get out of the camp and in again?

"Fig. 2. "It's like Monte Viso, but so much more impressive."

These and other problems kept my mind fully occupied. I found it fascinating to elaborate, in the utmost secrecy, the first details of my scheme.

Life took on another rhythm, because it had a purpose.

Silent Preparations

I started my preparations.

First, I wrote to my family asking them to send me my boots and any woollen clothing that had not been sold: vests, shirts, jerseys, and so on.

I stopped smoking. As cigarettes were the normal currency in the camps, I could use my weekly ration of thirty-five in this way together with those I was later allowed to buy from the canteen.

I sold what few of my belongings I could spare in order to get the cash I needed for buying various items of necessary equipment. The system I followed was this: some prisoners inside the camp who retained cash in spite of the severe rules against it feared that it would be confiscated at the first search, and tried to convert it into food and clothing. Therefore from time to time they sent their commission agents through the barracks, as they wished to avoid doing business in person. The agents, neither unobtrusively nor tactfully, went around the barracks asking: "Who wants to sell anything?" and appeared with clock-like regularity at the bunk of anyone who had just received a parcel. Not a hard job this, as the names of the lucky addressees of parcels would appear on the compound noticeboard, with the hour at which the parcels would be distributed after they had been opened and searched under the eyes of their owners.

The problem of whom to select as my companions was the most pressing and the most difficult to solve. I reckoned that a party of three would be the best, which meant that I should have to find two men willing to take the risk. Of these, one need not necessarily be a mountaineer because the actual climb could be attempted by two, while the non-mountaineer could stay at the base camp. His main job would be to assist in keeping watch in the forest on our way up. A party of more than three, I thought, would enable us to keep shorter watches, but on the other hand it would increase appreciably the amount of stores and equipment we should have to collect and carry.

By chance I learnt that a man I already knew was a mountaineer who had to his credit several first climbs in the Alps. One evening, when Mount Kenya showed clear and majestic half an hour before sunset, I approached this man and pointing to the glorious mountain I remarked, as though making the most natural suggestion in the world:

"Have you ever thought about escaping and trying to climb it?"

"If they would feed us on beefsteak," he answered, laughing, "we might consider it."

I pressed him to enlarge his point of view and he carried on by saying that in our condition of under-nourishment, it would be impossible to carry out the serious training which the climbing of such a difficult peak would necessitate; that at high altitudes the craving for highly nourishing and variegated food was a well-known fact; that it would be impossible to get the necessary stocks of food and equipment and even more impossible to carry them up without porters. Anyhow good ropes, good crampons and good ice axes were not available to prisoners. And so on. The word "impossible" was his long suit. He concluded: "It looks tantalising, I agree, but it would be sheer madness to think of it seriously."

I broke off the conversation. We were speaking different languages. He was a realist and when all is said and done it was he who was right; I, an incurable idealist or possibly a madman, as he had it. I realised then that I would find companions only among "madmen" like myself.

For a week or two I studied my companions from a "Kenya" point of view. I made confidential enquiries about anyone who claimed to have been a mountaineer. I could of course not ask openly: "Who would like to make up a party for climbing Kenya?"

It seemed hopeless. Those who appeared to have some of the essential qualifications lacked others. At last I confided my secret to Giovannino, an Alpini N.C.O. who had been in my unit in the Abyssinian War but who had been badly crippled in a motor-car accident in 1938 and was now in captivity as a civilian. He was an utterly reliable fellow and more than anything he regretted that with his lame leg he would never again be able to climb mountains.

Together we prepared a list of indispensable tools and he put me on the track of a flag hidden in the camp, brought by a friend of his from Harar in Ethiopia to Kenya. Above all, we studied our companions and he became my confidential agent in investigations into the mountaineering records of prisoners. We were completely unsuccessful.

Without abandoning what we called in fun, "plan two" – to find a mountaineer – we were eventually successful with "plan three" – research aimed at finding a non-mountaineer to be "number three" in the party.

We concentrated our attention on a Police Lieutenant who was a fairly good football player and who had earned a high reward for a gallant exploit with a small band of Askaris in the rear of the enemy's lines. No one doubted his outstanding courage and endurance, and he had the reputation of being extraordinarily lucky.

I approached Mario, and opened my heart to him. He welcomed the prospect with enthusiasm. Being from the Abruzzi, the highest mountain region of the Apennines, he was a born mountaineer although he confessed to not having had any experience of actual rock and ice climbing. He would very much have liked to join the "top-party", but at last he agreed to be "third man" and to serve at the base camp.

Unfortunately he was unable to make any suggestions as to who might act as the second man we so badly needed. He would have to be a good mountaineer, a man of endurance, silent and reliable. After all I should have to link my life to his on the same rope. As I became better acquainted with Mario I realised too that our "second man" should, if possible, be of a calm and reasoning temperament; because if Mario had a fault it was his over-enthusiasm. The "second man" should, I thought, tend to counterbalance Mario's character.

With Mario I explored a rubbish heap situated near our one-mile walk by a signpost marking the Equator. There, one might find iron and aluminium scraps of every kind.

We had decided to make our ice axes from hammers, which we had so far not been able to "acquire", and our crampons of material from this rubbish heap. Therefore we concentrated our attention on the remnants of a motor-car running board and pieces of mudguard, which, little by little, we brought into the camp. A motor-car axle, we thought, would make a useful anvil as we had decided to make crampons by "cold working" the metal ourselves.

What we needed badly was a cold chisel and a hammer, which, together with the two hammers to be transformed into ice axes, meant that we should have to find three hammers. We only needed two ice axes, as the third man would not carry one. Indeed Ugo de Amicis states that "an ice axe, put into the hands of a would-be mountaineer, often represents the only danger in a climb."

At last an opportunity arose for getting what we needed.

The minor works of maintenance in the P.O.W. camps in Kenya were at this time carried out by Indian artisans, barefooted chaps with dignified beards, whom I watched with particular interest. I soon discovered that during the lunch interval they put their tools in a store, the door of which was sometimes left open.

It was an easy matter to enter the store one day, to collect two hammers – there were only two to be found – and a chisel, to conceal them in my shirt and to saunter off nonchalantly. It was the first theft I had so far committed and it seemed so marvellously easy that I wondered why the fruitful profession of thieving was not even more popular in the world.

One hammer was transferred by night into Mario's barrack and from thence to the P.O.W. blacksmith, an old acquaintance of

Mario's, who transformed it on his forge into an ice axe resembling a rough sketch I had drawn for him. We could not start making the crampons immediately as we had till then found no suitable room in which to work undisturbed.

Time passed quickly. The end of July had arrived, and with it several cloudless days on Mount Kenya. The sight we enjoyed every day was grand. We already knew every feature of the rocks and glaciers on the north and north-west faces, and every gap in the cockscomb ridges had been investigated by studying the trail of shifting clouds. It looked as though it would be difficult, very difficult, to find a route up there, but for all we knew the other faces might prove to be even more challenging.

We had considered the possibility of a flag not surviving for more than a few weeks or perhaps days, if exposed to the heavy blizzards raging on the peak. Accordingly, I concocted a message to be left in a bottle at the foot of the flagpole.

I bought with cigarettes unwanted fragments of bread with which I increased my rations, and I followed a detailed routine of daily exercise. Mario carried on playing football and walking. We avoided being seen together and met only by night. It was good fun.

The stores we collected piecemeal accumulated steadily under our bunks. We had decided to start in September, as soon as the rains stopped, if our tools were ready, and provided that by then we had found our "second man".

At about this time – the end of July – I was transferred to a newly enlarged compound and it became more difficult to meet Mario. I was able to see him only during the day, for at night the compounds were shut off from one another. My contacts with him therefore lessened.

In my new barrack I met a doctor whom I had not noticed

before as he lived very much on his own, being intimate with few people.

One day someone, I do not remember who, brought into our barrack a book which gave me a few bits of precious information about Mount Kenya. It was Father F. Cagnolo's work *The Akikuyu*, dealing with the folklore and the country of the Kikuyu, a native tribe occupying land in the central Kenya highlands and as far to the north as the western slopes of the mountain.

The most interesting items I learnt from the book itself and from its map (scale one centimetre = eighty kilometres) were the following:

1. The great pedestal on which the highest peaks are based has an average radius of some twenty miles. That was more or less the distance as the crow flies that we should have to cover when escaping first through farmland and then through thick forest, before starting the actual climb of the peak. In these twenty miles we should have to ascend some 11,00 feet.

2. There were two peaks mentioned in the book: Batian (17,040 feet.), the higher, was the one we could see from the camp; and Lenana (16,300 feet) was lower and invisible from Camp 354, being obscured by Batian.

3. On the attached map only one route was shown through the forest towards the peaks. It started from Chogoria on the eastern slopes, just opposite Nanyuki. This route had been taken by some Italian Fathers of the Consolata Mission at Nyeri who on January 31, 1933, had climbed Lenana and had there left a cross, the gift of the Pope to the Mission.

   The reason why the Fathers had erected the cross on Lenana rather than Batian was not mentioned in the book, but it seemed to me to be obvious enough; Batian was far more difficult to climb than Lenana. This supposition was confirmed by a photograph in the book, which showed Lenana and Batian from the east. The slopes of Lenana were gentle, although even an easy climb would prove extremely tiring at that height on the Equator. Batian on the other hand was a huge compact rock wall, seemingly more impregnable than the Nanyuki face. I decided that we should attempt Batian, but that in the event of failing in our main programme we should "do" Lenana.

4. The map showed the sources of a number of rivers rising from the glaciers of Kenya, diverging like spokes of a wheel from the hub. One of these, the Tana, is one of the most important rivers of East Africa. The scale of the map was too small to show whether the river Nanyuki, bearing the same name as that of the village near our camp, actually rose in the glaciers near the summit of the mountain; but it seemed to me that this was very probable.

   As we should not be able to use known paths during our ascent, I thought it would be worth trying to follow the river Nanyuki upstream toward its source. The route might be long but by adopting this plan we should at least avoid the main headache of escapees in Africa: the necessity of finding water.

5. The main rains in this part of East Africa lasted from the end of April to the beginning of September; the short rains from the beginning of November to the end of December. That was why the Fathers had chosen January for their ascent of Lenana.

   It seemed reasonable to follow their example and to alter our plan accordingly. This would allow us six months in which to perfect our equipment, the first insurance against complete failure.

6. Many of the beliefs of the Akikuyu were connected with Mount Kenya. This of course did not affect the programme of our

proposed trip but it was, to me at least, very interesting. The Kikuyu believe Mount Kenya to be the throne of God whose bed is made of a very fine white powder called "ira" – the snow. White is therefore the "sacred" colour used by medicine men when adorning themselves on ceremonial occasions and by children during initiation ceremonies.

I observed that my new barrack mate, Giuàn the doctor, displayed a great interest in the book and above all in the photographs of Mount Kenya.

While I was making a copy of one showing Lenana and Batian from the east, we started talking about mountaineering. Little by little I began to realise that Giuàn might be the man I had so far sought in vain.

I spoke to him about our plan and I observed his reactions with keen interest. Unlike Mario, he displayed no extravagant enthusiasm at first; he merely asked searching questions about the details of the scheme. I did not press him to join us but, as I hoped, he himself led the conversation around to his possible participation in the trip a few days later. I was greatly pleased and relieved, although at that time I did not realise just how lucky I had been in contacting him. I know now that not only had I found the best companion imaginable for the adventure that lay in store for us, but also a friend for life.

Together we studied the mountain again and again, and he agreed that it would be a difficult climb. From the east it looked still worse, according to the photograph I had copied from Fr. Cagnolo's book. The southern face remained unknown to us until we obtained information about it from a very strange source.

We were accumulating as much food as possible from our

rations – and from those of other people. One day we were issued tins of "Kenylon" preserved meat and vegetable, not previously supplied to this camp. On each tin was gummed a label depicting as a trade mark a view of Mount Kenya from another aspect unknown to us. We guessed it could only represent the mountain from the south or more likely from the south-south-west. We were disappointed to see that the peaks looked just as formidable from this new viewpoint, with even more glaciers than appeared on the northern slopes.

We continued to train and to collect stores and equipment and at the same time, we began to consider how we should find our way to the Nanyuki River, which we proposed to follow until it led us to the glaciers.

Once a month a party consisting of those in need of dental treatment was sent over to Camp 359 at Burguret, some twenty miles from Nanyuki. I happened to be suffering from a bad tooth and as I wanted to have this attended to before escaping, I applied to be allowed to accompany the next party.

I was put into an open lorry with several other people and an escort, and off we went. During the whole trip, I studied the landscape carefully and tried to memorise the main landmarks. I was even able to plan out an escape route from our camp to the edge of the forest.

At Burguret Camp, while awaiting my turn in the dentist's torture chair, I met a few fellows I had known before and I questioned them about the forest on the mountain, as Burguret Camp was much closer to it than Nanyuki Camp.

The stories I heard made me shiver. Prisoners of war are notorious for distorting most plain facts and for inventing fairy tales, but even after allowing for this, it seemed that our progress through the forest would be a dreadful business. The gardens outside the camp,

I gathered, had been visited several times by rhinoceros and buffalo. A fuel party of prisoners in the nearby forest had been attacked by a troop of elephants on transfer, and a prisoner who had been rash enough to approach them in order to see some baby elephants had been caught up by a mother, smashed against a tree, and killed on the spot.

A few days after my dental trip to Burguret, an article was published in the *East African Standard* partially confirming the stories of the number of wild beasts to be found around Mount Kenya.

The short report in the paper stated that an unnamed major had tried to reach the northern glaciers of the mountain with a view to taking photographs. With another officer, he had set out from Brigands Retreat Rest Camp – which sounded sinister enough, although no explanation was given – and had followed an eland track. By midday, they had reached the snout of a glacier called Kolbe. There they were overtaken by a blizzard but managed to get back to their camp by 4.00 p.m. on the same day. Although they had been accompanied by porters, they were so tired that they slept for fourteen hours straight on their return. During their absence the porters left at the camp had repulsed an attack by a herd of buffalo and had shot two of them.

From the mountaineering point of view, there was nothing in this report new to us except the fact that at this altitude even people accompanied by porters and living as free men became victims of exhaustion. Not a pleasant prospect at all. But what we liked less was the story of the buffaloes. We did not want to meet them, as buffaloes are classed by many experienced sportsmen as being among the most dangerous of the African big-game animals. In a 1944 report by Hugh Copley, *The Game Animals of East Africa*, I later read that on the slopes of Mount Kenya a buffalo after a hard struggle had even killed a lion, reputed to be the king of animals. As a matter of fact, in Western Abyssinia the Galla esteem a man who has killed a buffalo more than one who has killed lion, and the tombs of their chiefs and famous hunters are adorned with buffalo trophies only.

No, the prospect of meeting buffaloes was not at all inviting, since we should be wholly unarmed.

In October, there arrived in our camp a copy of the *East Africa Annual, 1942–3*. In it we were delighted to find an article written by Lieutenant Colonel C. H. Stockley, which at last cast light on some features of the mountain we intended to ascend. It contained extremely useful information about the vegetation and fauna of these regions, and particularly about the flora zones, which we reckoned would enable us to estimate approximately what altitude we had reached from time to time:

"The violent storms which cover Mount Kenya's crags and barren screes with snow, drench open moors below the 15,000-foot mark; these are covered with great tufts of coarse grass which make walking just toil and misery, and which become four-foot solid lumps of roots and earth by the time that the tree line is reached. The moors are dotted with six-foot Giant Lobelias and still taller Giant Groundsels of several species, while at their lower edge comes a 500-foot zone of Giant Heather, up to fifteen feet high, containing clumps of six-foot everlastings. This belt of heather is the same as that from which briar pipes are made in Europe, but for some obscure reason the roots are here commercially valueless.

"Below the heather is a 1,000-foot belt of bamboo, then come the lovely camphor trees and, below, the cedars, with other forest trees whose undergrowth includes a six-foot nettle which is the champion vegetable pain producer if sat on: I know.

"Why Mount Kenya should produce such a profusion of exag-

Fig. 3. "The moors are dotted with six-foot Giant Lobelias and still taller Giant Groundsels of several species…"

gerated growths I do not know, though I have been told that they are the result of tropical light rays at high altitude – which leaves me just as ignorant as before.

". . . Of the largest beasts buffalo go to 14,000 feet on Mount Kenya, while the rhino likes lying up in the Giant Heather. When camped at the top of the tree line at 11,000 feet, a herd of twenty-five elephants spent an afternoon feeding on the opposite slope just across a little valley. In the morning they were still there, standing in an open grassy hollow which was white with frost: an incongruous sight, for elephants and frost do not go together."

A few days later, idly running through the advertisements of the *East African Standard*, I noticed one that gave me further food for thought:

46

"RHINO LOOKOUT MINIATURE TREE HOTEL IN MOUNT KENYA FOREST. RECORDS DIFFERENT NIGHTS: THIRTY ELEPHANT FIVE RHINO, FORTY BUFFALO, BEST TIME NEAR FULL MOON . . . NANYUKI."

One would look in vain for an advertisement of this nature in a European newspaper!

On the whole, it seemed to us that the stories told by the Burguret Camp prisoners I had interviewed were not entirely without foundation and that the most dangerous part of our trip would probably be in the forest zone.

At about this time, a friend of mine, Carlo, an ex-provincial Commissioner from Abyssinia who had been allotted a small room to himself in our camp, allowed us to use his cubbyhole so that we might make our crampons in privacy. To those who enquired about the strange hammering noises, he would explain that we were working on a secret wireless set.

In the meanwhile, I had confided my plan to Umberto, who had been my close companion since the first day of our captivity and who had drawn my attention to Mount Kenya on that May morning, which now seemed so long ago. He had at one time been a good mountaineer, but owing to his poor state of health I had never considered him as a possible partner. As he was of a mechanical turn of mind and was also utterly reliable, I thought that his assistance might prove to be invaluable to us.

I have already related how Mario and I collected steel from the mudguards and running board of a scrapped motor-car on the rubbish heap outside the camp. I had also "acquired" two half-inch steel bars from a consignment that had been brought to the camp for use in the concrete cover of a bakery oven. Hammer and chisel were at hand. Files and drills could be borrowed at the cost of a few cigarettes per evening from a man who had started making cigarette lighters in the camp.

Umberto and I started working on two pairs of crampons. With the cold chisel we cut four large and four small X-shaped plates from the steel sheets, the larger to be put under the soles and the smaller under the heels of our climbing boots. At the end of each arm of these X's we drilled a hole:

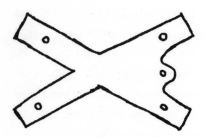 

The work was not performed without accidents. Twice we broke a drill and it needed all my powers of persuasion to induce the owner to lend us his third and last.

Another accident might have had more serious consequences: a tiny splinter of steel got into Umberto's left eye and I had to accompany him at once to the camp hospital to have it removed. Inflammation of the iris followed and Umberto had to stop working for ten days. I do not know if anyone else would have carried on working at our crampons after this accident; it seemed to me only logical that after such an experience, a man not actively interested in our expedition would have been justified in consigning Giuàn and me and the crampons to hell. Umberto did no such thing. As soon as his eye stopped paining him, and as soon as he had recovered his normal sight, he started afresh.

During Umberto's absence I had prepared thirty-six spikes –

one for each of the holes we had drilled in the arms of the X's – and had filed down the head of each spike as shown in the diagram (*left*).

Thus as soon as Umberto was able to work again we were able to assemble the various parts. The spikes were hammered cold into their holes and the ends of the arms were bent in order to take the connecting rings (*right*). These I had cut from the wires of the fences after removing the barbs. It was very appropriate – we remarked – that the same barbed-wire fences that enclosed us should provide material to be used during our escape.

Finally we fitted the rings, one to each arm of the X's and one to connect the sole and heel sections.

Through the rings we passed the laces that would fasten the crampons to our climbing boots. The crampons had been made to fit our boots exactly and everything went according to plan. We were so proud of our work that we regretted not being able to exhibit these masterpieces around the camp.

Prisoners of war count vanity among their other faults.

*

One day, while I was at the tailor's barrack having a fitting of the climbing suit which was being made for me from two blankets, a prisoner came in and shouted:

"They've all been caught. They are all in the cells now."

"Who?" I asked, as I did not know of anyone who had escaped in the past few days.

"Mario and his crowd."

"Mario!" I exclaimed, believing myself to be dreaming.

I soon learnt what had happened.

The previous night, ten people had sent a messenger to Mario asking him if he would like to escape with them. They alleged that ten miles from the camp a lorry was waiting for them which would take them to Mogadishu. Mario agreed and went off with them.

The party of eleven marched throughout the night. At dawn they stopped near a rivulet in order to have a drink and to await the evening before proceeding. They told Mario that the story of the lorry was an invention, and that they had "kidnapped" him in order to include a leader experienced in bush-craft in the party, but the whole story is none too clear to me even today. At about 8.00 a.m. they discovered that they had selected a spot just below a slope on which a unit of K.A.R. was encamped for their bivouac. They tried to move off, which was rather a difficult matter for such a big party. One of the last of them made too much noise and attracted the attention of an Askari who had come down to the rivulet to fetch water. The Askari called up some of his fellows and investigated. To cut a long and foolish story short, by ten o'clock Mario and his eleven companions were back at the camp.

I was mad with anger. How could Mario have believed the story of the lorry? Why had he decided in a matter of minutes to let me down and to go with people he hardly knew by sight?

On the following day, when I saw him taking his hour's exercise in the cell compound he signalled to me from afar. At first I ignored him but later I approached the wire. He apologised, telling me that the prospect of gaining complete freedom in Somalia had proved too great a temptation as it would have been far better than a mere trip up the mountain with the certainty of punishment on our return to camp.

It was no use crying over spilt milk and I asked:

"Do you want anything?"

"No, thank you."

"How many days have you got?"

"Twenty-eight."

"Would you like a book?"

"No thank you. I already have something to read. A friend sent me Leo Pollini's *Sapri: the Tragic Expedition.*

When Mario was returned to his compound he avoided answering my questions about the truck that was to have taken him to Mogadishu. I think he repented of having consented to being kidnapped and elected leader of his "tragic expedition" party.

Well, at any rate he had not taken away any of the stores which he had collected for Mount Kenya, he had shown a pronounced spirit of adventure – too pronounced in my opinion – and last but not least he was now striving to make us forget his peccadillo by working harder for us than ever before. In a few days' time he produced two workmanlike ironshod handles for ice axes and three iron-pointed staves, two to be used as tent poles and the third for the flag.

One evening when all the human inhabitants of my barrack had gone to a theatrical performance in another compound, Umberto and I fixed the ice axe, made from the hammer, to its handle.

In order to avoid arousing suspicions we had asked Giuàn to go to the theatre.

To be perfectly honest, there were occasions when the thought of our impending adventure made me frightened. Sometimes, returning late to my barrack on a cold and rainy night, I thought what it would be like lying out in the dark, wet forest; dead tired, exhausted by hunger, drenched to the bone, in imminent danger of being attacked by wild beasts. That prospect I compared with the warm blankets in my bunk, the familiar oil-lamp and the good book I was now preparing to read.

At such moments it was the thought of the security offered by a regular even though an unpleasant life, the spirit which dooms the canary bird to its caged existence, a natural tendency to follow the line of least resistance, that predominated.

On the other hand, standing in the ranks at morning roll call and seeing Batian beckoning me with its shimmering glaciers, I sometimes felt like running away on the spot, to seek and to meet adventure halfway.

We poor mortals are made like this, a mixture of contrasts, shade and light, fears and exaltations.

Listening to the platitudes of prisoners talking, I sometimes felt that I could not understand them any more. At other times I felt only pity that they should be content to endure this stagnating life without having a project like ours in mind.

Christmas arrived, our second Christmas inside barbed wire, and with it the December full moon. By the aid of the January full moon we should escape and make for the river.

I had received a few parcels I had asked for eight months before, and had sold or exchanged everything I did not need for the trip. All that we were taking had been carefully stored away.

The season had brought glorious weather. A fresh breeze blew from morning to night and for whole long days Mount Kenya was without a single cloud. I suspected sometimes that we were wasting the best climbing season.

In the large square of Compound C an altar had been erected. It was adorned with flags and green branches. Two powerful lamps shed a homely, gentle light on the scene of the Midnight Mass.

The crowd of thousands of people watched silently. An orchestra of instruments made from biscuit cases played Handel's Largo, Schubert's and Gounod's *Ave Maria.*

During the communion it happened that all three of us, Giuàn, Mario and I, found ourselves kneeling close together, although not one of us had known that the others were going to attend the Midnight Mass.

It seemed a good omen.

Wanted: Third Man for Trip to Mount Kenya

We had decided to escape on Sunday, January 24 but on New Year's Day we suffered a shock that almost caused us to cancel the whole expedition. An order was given to the effect that Police Officers would in future be considered as military and not as civilian personnel and that they should therefore leave at eight hours' notice for Eldoret Camp.

I asked Mario, who was gloomily preparing his kit for the transfer, to send someone else to Eldoret under his name. Things like this had been done often enough and sometimes it was possible to buy a substitute for cigarettes to the value of thirty shillings or two pounds. But Mario answered that it would not work. Since his October escape, he was known personally to the British Compound Officer.

"You see," I remarked pathetically, "that on account of that silly escapade you have really spoilt everything."

Mario bent his head, handed over the stores he had had in charge, including the second ice axe, which had been ready the day before, and joined the party due for transfer.

Giuàn and I, left behind twenty-four days from the scheduled day, with stores and equipment ready, were at a complete loss to find a substitute for Mario.

There was a noticeboard where the strangest appeals were wont to appear:

"Lost this morning at Compound A showers, toothbrush in a tin mug. Please keep mug and hand toothbrush to the owner, So and So, barrack number So and So."

Or: "Lost yesterday a towel which apparently flew away from the drying rope near barrack 23. Twenty cigarettes reward."

Or: "Should like to swap military jacket and trousers in fairly good condition for new civilian suit." (Close to this notice, some wag had put the following: "Should like to swap handkerchief in fairly good condition for St. Peter's Cathedral.")

We could have put on the board: "Wanted third man for trip to Kenya Mountain." Probably nobody would have believed that we were really preparing for this, but if suspicions were aroused everything would have been spoilt for us.

Again I resolved to apply for help to Giovannino, the lame ex-N.C.O. We held a long conference and reviewed barrack after barrack of his compound, but once again those who seemed to have certain qualifications lacked other essential ones.

Days passed. At last, on January 5, Giovannino sent a chit to my barrack:

"Please come with the doctor and have tea today soon after the wireless transmission."

We went. Rarely in my life have I looked forward to a tea party with more eagerness than on this occasion.

While Giovannino poured out the tea in our tin mugs (at camp tea-parties each man brought with him his own mug, spoon and sugar) I quietly studied the two other fellows he had asked. They looked fine, too fine. I wondered where we could find the food with which to maintain their athletic bodies without raiding the Quartermaster stores of the camp.

Giovannino passed the mug first to the one sitting near the window at the head of his bunk. As we had previously agreed, this was a sign meaning that he was to be considered as "the man".

"What is your favourite sport?" I asked, starting the conversation.

"Boxing."

I shivered. "Weight?" I asked.

"Middle-heavy," he stated proudly and sipped his tea.

His companion declared: "He was champion of Eritrea at his weight."

Our poor stores! I was thinking.

I carried on putting insidious questions. "He" was twenty-eight years old, shoemaker by trade, had been born in an Alpine valley of Veneto and had served in an Alpini regiment.

"As a shoemaker, my specialty is climbing boots," he declared, and I thought that Giovannino could not have been more clever. To have found a doctor who could look after our health was a good idea, but to take on as a third man a fellow who would be in charge of the health of our boots was the acme of good organisation.

We talked of sport. The man was training for a boxing competition to be held in March by the Welfare Section of the camp. He complained of being chronically hungry, although, being the compound shoemaker, he was drawing "worker's rations" instead of the normal prisoner rations.

After tea Giovannino held him up with an excuse, while the other chap went off without, I firmly believe, having noticed that in the meantime the destiny of his friend had been thought over and decided.

Giovannino kept guard at the barrack door. I whispered to Giuàn,

"Well?"

"Failing anyone better . . . "

"O.K. I shall speak to him."

While Giuàn and Giovannino pretended to be busy looking at a book, I threw my bombshell at the unsuspecting shoemaker. He bore the assault with a fortitude worthy of the best traditions of the ring. He agreed to come with us. He was ready to swear an oath that he would keep our plan secret and tell no one of our escape plan. He told us he had only the rags he was wearing and that he had not a penny. We should have to supply him with everything. True, we had Mario's stores left, but they consisted of foodstuffs only. They included no clothing and, of course, no shoes.

"Alright," I said. "We shall find everything for you. Come to my barrack tomorrow morning and we shall make together a list of what you need. Thank you very much, and, above all, *keep silent.*"

We had to run to our compound, for it was roll-call time. The next morning, as soon as the compounds were opened I saw with dismay the limping figure of the good Giovannino entering the gate. His whole attitude was eloquent with defeat.

"The shoemaker?" I asked as soon as we were alone.

"Gone," he said, in the tragic tone one might use to announce the death of a dear friend.

"Gone where? Speak, man!"

In his colourful Venetian slang Giovannino explained that the shoemaker had sent him, not daring to come himself, in order to tell us that he had "thought it over".

"But why on earth? Couldn't he have said at the time: 'Sorry, I can't'?"

"He says that he has too many shoes to repair."

"Did he get them all during the night?"

" . . . and a foot which pains him."

"But not when boxing!"

"You know what some people are like," he concluded, distressed at having put us on a false track.

I assured him that it was not his fault and that we were looking forward to another tea party, that he should continue his investigations and that his efforts were very much appreciated. Poor Giovannino, he was as upset as if he were himself to blame for having spoilt our plans.

*

Days passed uneventfully.

Giuàn and I were already debating whether to postpone the date of our departure, or whether it would be better for the two of us to make the attempt by ourselves. We seemed to be as far as ever from enlisting the support of a third man.

During this time we obtained further evidence to the effect that Kenya was a very difficult mountain to climb.

In a Christmas parcel a friend of ours had been sent a book published in 1942, *Escalatory*, containing a selection from accounts of some classic climbs made by Italian mountaineers. Among these was an extract from the story of the first ascent of Mont Blanc via Innominata Ridge, made in 1902 by the brothers G. F. and G. B. Gugliermina, accompanied by the guide Joseph Brocherel. In his report G. F. Gugliermina related how Brocherel, arriving at a particularly difficult pitch of ice-covered rock, exclaimed:

"This is worse than Kenya!"

And that, unfortunately, was all he did say.

What a pity it is that Alpine guides are men of so few words!

While Giovannino continued his efforts to find someone to invite to a tea-party, I fired a shot in the dark by approaching a prisoner who had at least two qualifications – physical fitness and a lot of money – because he was a "Red October" man.

This last statement needs some explanation as it refers to military and political matters which I have tried to avoid in this book, but which I must touch on briefly here, above all in order to explain the presence of some strange items in the kit of some of our fellow prisoners at that time.

The artisans of one of the great repair shops of Addis Ababa had volunteered to be transferred by the occupation authorities to a place in or near Nairobi where they carried on working for the

British army. There they enjoyed a certain degree of freedom and far better rations than those in the P.O.W. camps. I doubt whether they had even been searched. They were of course regarded by other prisoners as traitors or little less than that.

In the summer of 1942 as Axis troops pushed on as far as Stalingrad and El-Alamein, a hundred of these workers decided that it would be safer for them to be in a regular P.O.W. camp, and they were accordingly transferred to the Camp of Civilian Prisoners of War at Nanyuki. Again, either they were not searched or the searchers were very lenient.

They had luxurious kit and a great deal of money. In order to avoid incidents with prisoners who since the occupation of Ethiopia had lived inside barbed wire, they were put into a barrack of their own which was immediately named "Red October", after the famous factory at Stalingrad, stronghold of Soviet resistance. The men were commonly known as "Red October people".

How far their behaviour had been dictated by political feelings, as some of them claimed, I cannot say. Possibly they masked their desire to live well under a cloak of political ideals, but as I never talked politics with the few of them I met, I do not know.

One of them, a young mechanic in a splendid leather jacket whom I had known since his arrival as he was a good footballer, was my victim.

After having discussed the matter with Giuàn, I spoke to this man one evening and he agreed to come with us. He had almost everything, a rucksack, woollen underclothing, a torch and so on. He lacked only boots but was ready to buy these with his own money.

The next morning, the "Red October" mechanic came into my barrack early with a sulky look on his face that spoke volumes.

He had not told me the day before, he explained, that he had already given his word to some of his companions to escape with them to Italian Somaliland, where they hoped to be able to live under false identity. He had hoped that they would release him from his promise, he carried on explaining, but they had refused to do so. Now he was sorry, very sorry indeed, but he simply could not let down his companions.

I answered, comparing him with a certain shoemaker and boxer of my acquaintance who, having considered the dangers of a trip to Mount Kenya, had found similar excuses. The mechanic, perhaps a little offended by the comparison, said that in order to prove his good will he was ready to help us in every way. He was willing to give us financial aid to the extent of several hundred shillings and to lend us any items in his own or his friends' equipment that we might need.

We refused his financial aid immediately but said that we should be pleased to borrow equipment offered as a proof of his honest intentions, and we asked what sort of equipment was available from "Red October".

"My leather jacket," he offered first.

"No thank you, we have clothing enough."

"A few woollen jerseys."

We refused these too. Then he became mysterious and whispered:

"I could find you a 9 mm. revolver and a pair of binoculars."

Here we stopped our "No, thank you's" and asked for a few hours' time to consider the matter.

Both Giuàn and I agreed on the spot that we did not want the revolver even though there was, as the "Red October" man had put it, "plenty of ammo". The reasons for our refusal were many:

1. Against lion and leopard, not to mention buffalo, rhino or elephant, a revolver was practically useless. One should carry a rifle or nothing.
2. We were not proposing to escape in order to regain our freedom permanently. Our idea was to come back and to live again as prisoners. Therefore it would be foolish to use a revolver against patrols. Such an act would lead us into far more serious trouble than a mere twenty-eight days' confinement to cells.
3. If we carried a revolver, we might perhaps behave in a more foolhardy manner than we should without arms. Thus we might find ourselves in greater danger than would be the case if we simply marched with ordinary prudence.

We decided, however, to accept the offer of the binoculars and they were brought to us the same day. They proved to be Zeiss glasses with a magnification of six, in very fair condition. After the trip I gave them back to the owner who incidentally never tried to escape to Italian Somaliland at all. On the contrary, he with the other "Red October people" shortly afterwards started working in the Nairobi workshop again. By then Tripoli had fallen.

We could not be certain then whether the binoculars would prove useful or not on the trip, but on the assumption that we had secured a sort of magic key we were eager to look at the mountain through them. One chief difficulty was to find a place where we could use them in peace.

At last I managed to shut myself inside the office of the British Compound Officer while he was having lunch. I cut holes in the hessian wall of the room and focused.

What a thrill it was to see the Mountain of Mystery magnified six times! It appeared the embodiment of beauty, the smallest ice colours glistening in the midday sun. Most remarkable were the

Heim and Forel glaciers seemingly hanging on the west wall.

I had a great time examining and sketching the scene.

There again ensued an uneventful period. Not even the shadow of a third man was to be found. Giovannino gave another tea-party attended by a nondescript clerk, twenty-nine years old, who had climbed – as he alleged – a few peaks in the Western Alps, but after a short, desultory conversation I realised that he was by no means the man we sought.

We had already agreed that the two of us should make the attempt, when, seven days before the start, Giuàn decided, as I had, to make a shot in the dark. His victim was an old friend of his, whom we had never considered as a possible candidate because he was neither an athlete nor did he seem to be in hard condition. He had never climbed a mountain in his life. The only reason why we decided to try him was because he was universally thought to be mad as a hatter, and mad people were what we needed.

Giuàn anyhow shot and secured a hit.

When I spoke to him too, I noticed his sincere enthusiasm, but I was not at all sure how long this would last.

"I think it *will* last," said Giuàn, who knew the fellow. And right he was.

Enzo was thirty-five years old, married, a fairly good bridge player and a very heavy smoker. As it turned out, Enzo did not let us down. His endurance, his wit, his true camaraderie can never be praised enough. His health proved to be a serious handicap, but the memory of his cheerful presence remains one of the most pleasant souvenirs of the whole trip.

As it would have been impossible to break in a pair of new boots in seven days without getting blisters he had hobnails put on to the soles of a pair of his town shoes and sewed himself a pair of high gaiters out of a piece of yellow tarpaulin.

He got hold of an axe and a small knife, and managed to "acquire" from somewhere one of those big bush-knives called *panga* in East Africa and used in the camps for cutting the grass along the barbed wire fences. He made mitts, a cap and many other articles. In seven days he performed a miracle of organisation.

By the evening of January 23, we were ready. Only the morrow existed for us. The present seemed irrelevant, absurd. We had won the first round against *time*.

Out

The matter of getting out had been considered by us with no less care than that given to any other point in the organisation of the trip.

It was not very difficult to escape from a P.O.W. camp in East Africa, far easier probably than from any camp in Europe. On the other hand, in Europe an escaped prisoner was not unduly conspicuous among the indigenous white-skinned population, road and rail facilities were far better and the distances to cover in order to get, for instance, from any point in Italy to the nearest neutral country, Switzerland, were far smaller.

In East Africa the situation was reversed. It was extremely difficult to travel anywhere in a huge country where the European population before the war numbered less than twenty thousand, and where a white man walking along with a rucksack was as easily recognisable as an escaped prisoner as though he were labelled "Escaped P. O.W.".

The authorities knew this as well as we did.

The camps in East Africa were guarded by African troops. This was both a handicap and an advantage to the prisoners. Black sentries do not behave as white ones would; they have quite different reactions and a quite different sense of responsibility. Sad accidents such as happened in P.O.W. camps in East Africa would have been avoided by European sentries, who would have made life inside the fences less dangerous and escape far more difficult than it was.

The African sentries were often easy to bribe with a few hundred cigarettes, a bottle of camp-made brandy or a handful of coins. I know of instances where they even helped escaping prisoners to raise the wires in order to allow them to pass through without getting entangled in the barbs. With European sentries, the plan we adopted of marching out of the camp gate at midday would never have worked.

We rejected the easy way of bribing the sentry not only because it was a low method of escaping but also because it was not always safe. By chance we might have tried to bribe an honest sentry! Thus we decided upon a scheme which would leave no doubt in their minds about the legality of our behaviour – to open the gate leading from the compound to the vegetable gardens by means of a false key when the British staff were having lunch.

When I first became acquainted with Giuàn, he had just been given a plot thirty feet square where he grew tomatoes and other vegetables and on which he had been allowed to build a little tool shed where he could rest during the heat of the day. Inside this shed we dug a hole three feet deep in which we intended gradually to accumulate our equipment. Later we noticed a few white ants inside the shed so that we gave up the idea and simply hid our things in our tomato beds. There was one tomato bed for Giuàn's equipment, one for Enzo's and one for mine. Even at night we could get at everything in good order. We inspected our *cache* regularly. The white ants seemed to despise our stores and concentrated their attention on the wooden poles of the shed. As it was now the dry season we had no fear of a heavy shower drenching our buried treasures.

The key of the gate we intended to use was kept by the British Compound Officer. He opened the gate for any prisoner who produced a "vegetable garden pass". When the officer was not on duty the gate was watched by the sentry on the nearest watchtower. The sentries were accustomed to seeing prisoners opening the gate themselves and going out into the gardens as sometimes the British Compound Officer even passed the key to a prisoner to open the gate for himself.

The problem was to prepare a key with which to open the gate as soon as the British Officer in charge went off to have his lunch on Sunday, January 24. We chose a Sunday because there was no roll-call in the afternoon on that day.

It took us months to get this key made.

First I had to get an imprint of the key and I waited for weeks before I found an opportunity of doing so. At last one day when the British Compound Officer was busy elsewhere in the compound and had left the keys on his table. I entered the office and made several good imprints on pieces of tar.

A mechanic cut a key for us from the pattern of those imprints. This man was not the "Red October" man mentioned previously. I had known him before our captivity. He never asked me why I wanted him to make this key – he was a "walking miracle" of a prisoner of war.

When the time came to test the key I felt considerable emotion. It was a calm Sunday afternoon and there were neither British staff nor prisoners in sight. I leaned nonchalantly against the gate, manoeuvring the key with my right hand, which was hidden by my left elbow. I watched the sentry closely, ready to throw myself down in order to avoid the bullet if he should show any sign of becoming suspicious and opening fire. It was thrilling.

The sentry did not move; but neither did the key.

I sweated. I almost broke the key in the keyhole. It would not work. I had an idea that the teeth were too long.

The mechanic shortened them by a fraction and I tried my luck again. I was just as unsuccessful and the sentry was just as absent-minded. Altogether, I got plenty of excitement out of that key.

After four or five attempts, spread over a period of months, I at last had the brilliant idea of oiling the key. When next I put it into the keyhole I heard and felt with blissful satisfaction the "click" of a complete revolution. The key had worked. And it worked again when I locked the gate moving the key the other way around. The sentry watched me casually. Little did he realise the triumph I felt at that moment.

The great day, Sunday, January 24, had arrived. Our kit was outside. Ice axes, tent and flagpoles had been brought out, concealed in bundles of bamboo to be used in fencing the vegetable gardens.

At 12.05 hours, the British Compound Officer went off. At this hour the prisoners in the compound were all having lunch.

Umberto approached the gate with the key in his hand. He was dressed, as a precaution, in a khaki shirt, shorts and stockings. By chance he was about the same height as the B.C.O. If the sentry had not noticed the B.C.O. walking off, he would probably mistake Umberto for him. Had he, on the contrary, seen the B.C.O. walking off . . . well we had to take this risk.

"Come on! Quick!" Umberto shouted in English to three fellows dressed in prison clothing and carrying shovels. He opened the gate. The key worked splendidly.

Fig. 4. "Out marched the three prisoners . . ."

Out marched the three prisoners. Umberto closed the gate, locked it and went off.

We disappeared into the vegetable gardens. It had been so easy that we could hardly believe that we were out. We had still to pass, in the evening, the outer border of the gardens which was supposed to be watched constantly by patrols, but the main job was done.

We pretended to work in the gardens till one o'clock when the sentries were changed. Then we lay down in the shed and waited for evening.

The wait seemed interminable. We had plenty to eat and gallons of water to drink, although of course we did not break into the stores to be taken on the trip. We had books to read and during our eight months of preparation we had been able to select the most suitable ones. I was reading *Escaping Club*, by the R.A.F. officer Evans, while Giuàn was immersed in Tanesini's biography of the late Dolomite guide Tita Piaz, *The Devil of the Dolomites*.

Enzo slept or pretended to be sleeping. His behaviour seemed odd, not only to me but also to Giuàn, who at last particularly asked:

"Don't you feel well?"

At first Enzo maintained that there was nothing the matter with him but when Giuàn took a thermometer out of his pocket he confessed to having had fever for the last two days. He had taken so much quinine that he heard, as he put it, "the whistles of a thousand station masters" but the thermometer showed that he still had a temperature of 38°C.

"Do you realise that a trip to Mount Kenya in your condition might mean death?" Giuàn said.

"It's alright. I have left my will in my barrack," answered Enzo.

I smiled, thinking they were joking. But they were not, as I soon realised.

Giuàn went on: "You are old enough to make up your own mind. It is up to you to decide; both as a friend and as a doctor I advise you not to come with us."

"I have already made up my mind," Enzo answered. "I am coming."

After 4.00 p.m. when it got cooler, Enzo fell asleep.

"What shall we do with him?" I asked Giuàn.

"Well," he said, "either he will get better, or he will get worse and probably die. I think he will improve but we shall have to walk slowly tonight."

"That is impossible," I urged, "at least until we have reached the forest."

"Well then, he'll march. He will realise that if he does not, it means that he will be left behind."

Giuàn was right. Enzo marched.

Night fell and we unearthed our treasures and packed our rucksacks.

We were a little shaken to find that our stores would not fit into them and that we should have to carry a small but heavy hessian bag of foodstuffs in addition to our packs, but consoled ourselves with the thought that our adventure had really begun.

CHAPTER II

The Way

In which, after our escape from a P.O.W. camp,
a military car, a white cow, a sawmill
and a tractor are avoided.

Sunday, January 24

In inky darkness we started our march. I led, followed by Enzo and then by Giuàn, in his hand the bag of food for which room had not been found in our overloaded rucksacks.

"Off" was my only thought in those first steps of our adventure. The sooner we crossed the wide plain, still within rifle-range of the sentries, the better.

We tried to make as little noise as possible, and I hoped fervently that the cloudy sky would not clear suddenly. If the sentries had seen us, it would have resulted in complete disaster at the very beginning. Failure at this moment would probably have meant not only a well-aimed bullet but also eight months' preparations wasted, followed by endless, completely justifiable mocking by the majority of our fellow prisoners who considered every escape as an act of sheer madness.

As we reached the first thorn bushes, we relaxed and dropped our loads. The first step, and not one of the least dangerous, had been accomplished: neither shot nor alarm-whistle had been heard.

We adjusted each other's rucksacks, as they were too heavy and unwieldy to allow the carrier to do this himself, and were soon ready for a fresh start. A breeze coming from the camp stirred the scrub. The thorn rattled slightly and we heard the tune of a concertina playing the tango:

> Without a word –
> You have told me: I love you . . .

To us it seemed like a voice from another world saying "Goodbye" – a world from which we already felt isolated, of which we were no longer citizens and with which all communications had been cut.

The food bag passed from Giuàn's hands into mine. With the ice axe in my right hand, I tried as best I could to locate holes, tree stumps and branches of thorn trees, not always successfully as twigs often scratched my face or brushed off my cap.

The weight of my rucksack seemed unbearable, but we could not waste time settling our loads in a more rational manner as we were in a hurry. We wanted to cross the railway and the main road before the moon rose.

Poor Enzo! As he had insisted on coming with us in spite of his illness, we had ordered him not to cough, under penalty of getting his head banged with an ice axe. He had answered that this was a useless threat, as we were well aware that his stubborn head was far harder than our camp-made ice axes, which would only get broken. Now, desperately wanting to cough, he was grunting close behind me.

Emerging from the thorny scrub, we came to open grassland, which, according to our plan, we had to cross parallel with the railway line; but in the darkness the problem of proceeding on a parallel course with something we could not see seemed insoluble. Neither stars nor the Aberdare Range on the western horizon were to be seen.

Time and again a hare or a jackal would spring up right at my feet, making me jump in turn and causing Enzo, who followed very close on my heels, to bump into my rucksack. "Sorry," he would whisper, "I can't see an inch." "Hush," would be my standard reply.

Fig. 5. "We had to cross the grassland parallel with the railway line."

*

I had no bearing whatsoever and could not help being worried by recalling tales of abortive attempts to escape, told in the camp in the long evenings. Once, a party did run into the very arms of a patrol that they could not see in the complete darkness; another escaping party walked several times in a circle in the pitch black night and was caught at last at dawn, exhausted and startled, near the very point from whence they had set out. At the time of hearing them, I did not altogether credit these tales, but now I believed them all.

At last I felt smooth earth under my feet in place of the high grass. I knew then that we were on a path that crossed the railway at right angles and I was therefore able to correct our line of advance.

In due course, we crossed the track leading to a farm. On this we knew by heart the position of every stone, as it was here that prisoners were allowed to take their daily exercise. To our great delight nobody was on the road, in spite of the early hour and the fact it was Sunday.

As soon as we saw the telegraph poles against the sky we stopped for a rest, at a safe distance from the track. We were all in need of a break. Whispering, we at last exchanged first impressions of our escape. Enzo was given permission to cough "without making too much noise"; but perhaps as a form of sabotage of our orders, he did not cough at all. Giuàn told me that it was advisable to go a little slower.

During our rest, the sky cleared and stars appeared – just when we did not need them as guides any more. In the distance the roar of the evening train was heard. There was no time to lose; we wanted to cross the line before the train passed.

I handed over to Giuàn the hated food bag and approached the railway line. All three of us managed to jump the side drains without a fall and to cross the rails without the sound of nailed boots or ice axes rasping against steel. On the far side we reached a scrub-covered valley, from the shelter of which we planned to get on to the main road.

The roar of the train increased and at last it thundered across the valley. Presently, while still near to the line, we were bathed in the powerful beam of the engine searchlight. We stopped and slowly sank down until we lay on our rucksacks. I seized the opportunity to glance at my watch. The train appeared to be punctual to the minute, a matter of minor importance so far as we were concerned; but it appeared also that we had been marching for fifty minutes only, and I felt as tired as though I had walked for hours.

As soon as the red light of the train disappeared in the distance, and the roar had become a faint buzzing, we carried on.

The moon, according to our reckoning, was due to rise at 9.35

p.m., by which time we should have crossed the main road. There was no time to lose.

Amid the scrub in the black darkness our progress was a nightmare. Never in my life did I agree more enthusiastically with the English nickname of the thorn bushes, "wait-a-bit".

Apart from these we were confronted by traps of every size and kind, deep-trodden cattle tracks, holes of every diameter, thorny aloes and many other hindrances.

Luckily the sky cleared rapidly, and eventually the glacier-crowned Mount Kenya was seen clear-cut against the starry background. I was pleased to have a bearing through the scrub, but started wondering whether we should ever be able to carry our huge rucksacks up to those distant peaks.

Some twenty minutes after the train had passed, I noticed with growing unrest that the sky on the eastern side of the mountain was becoming lighter and lighter and there was still no sign of the road. To attempt to cross the main road on a Sunday night in brilliant moonlight before midnight might be fatal, and I accelerated my pace.

We had not gone much further when the moon rose. It was full and reddish, and I had the impression that its face looked at us with slight irony. I was startled. By my watch it was only 9.25 p.m. I wondered whether it was the watch or our calculations that had gone wrong, as I had to exclude any possibility of the moon herself making a mistake. And yet, I was busy thinking, our reckonings were childishly easy. We had observed that the moon rose fifty minutes later every night. Yesterday it rose at 8.45 p.m., thus today . . .

"Don't you hear me? A car! A CAR!" shouted Enzo behind me at the top of his voice. He had not finished saying this before a beam of light lit up the trees only thirty or forty yards to my left.

I threw myself down, scratching my nose on a thorny branch, as the big shiny eyes of a car fell leeringly upon us. A few yards from me – so near was I to the road without having noticed it – the driver changed gear, and I shivered, thinking the car was about to stop; but it dashed off towards Nyeri. In the bright moonlight I could read the number plate. It was a military car, and had not Enzo called my attention to it (entangled in semi-scientific considerations about watches and moon as I was), there would have been, in the records of A.D.P.W. Nairobi, the amazing and unprecedented case of a military car being rammed by an escaping prisoner of war.

The avalanche of contumely loosed against me by my companions was beyond description, Enzo's seeming especially inexhaustible. I myself would willingly have added a few epithets, so justified, I felt, was the anger of my friends; but this was not possible as they had left nothing unsaid.

When the well-deserved storm of wrath over my guilty head had cleared, I apologised deeply and reminded them that it was high time we got up and crossed the road. This we did with exaggerated care. The old proverb speaks rightly enough of shutting the stable door after the horse has bolted.

I might add here that when we returned to the camp eighteen days later, my watch was only thirty minutes slow. I had checked it the evening before we left the camp with the time signal on the wireless. It is possible that a fragment of grit caused it to lose ten minutes. Alternatively, as we had covered between two or three miles since leaving the camp, our horizon may have been altered a little. Otherwise I still cannot account for the error in our calculations.

At high speed we traversed a fairly broad clearing on the far side of the road, beyond which we collapsed as though we were sacks of potatoes under the covering shade of the first thorn trees.

It would have been sheer ingratitude to blame our luck; we had passed the sentries of the camp, the railway line and the main road complete with military motor-car, without being stopped.

Of course, Enzo was completely worn out. We wrapped him in a blanket and gave him a lemonade with plenty of sugar and two tablets of aspirin. He went to sleep immediately. Looking at the thermometer by the light of his torch Giuàn said: "His fever has dropped." Giuàn showed his habitual modesty, as he said nothing more; and yet he might have been proud of the results of the unusual treatment given to his patient in the form of a forced night march.

When at 10.30 p.m. the patient was rudely awakened to carry on with the treatment, he did not grumble. After all he had chosen to come with us of his own free will.

For a while we again passed through scrub, but the march was far easier, as the moon shone brilliantly and we could afford to advance at a reasonably slow pace.

Later we arrived at a flat plain where the grass had been burnt only a few days previously and we had no longer to trouble about where to put our feet. The air was fresh, we had before us the clearly visible goal towards which I was steering, the main dangers were passed; it should have been a pleasure to walk now, but it was not, because of the weight of our rucksacks. Every twenty minutes we had to rest. Enzo seemed to be about to collapse.

We did not even choose places for our rests; whenever I gave the longed-for signal "time!" we just let ourselves go wherever our loads dragged us down. Luckily we did not have any unpleasant surprises in this game of ours, such as that experienced by a fellow prisoner. During his escape, he sat down exhausted one night on a mound of earth hiding the entrance to the den of a wild pig. The ungainly beast charged out snorting and, more afraid than the prisoner himself, ran him over.

We continued to advance over the burnt ground for some time, following well-known landmarks, such as isolated trees, native huts and fences. At last we came to a wire fence. It was difficult for us to believe that the wire was not barbed! Apart from this peculiarity, the fence was remarkable in that it was so tightly strung that when touched by our rucksacks as we passed between the strands, the wires sang like plucked violin strings.

This unusual musical essay gave rise to a furious barking by a dog on our left, answered immediately by other dogs on our right. We were in the vicinity of a farmhouse.

First we had to cross newly ploughed land, but presently we stopped for a rest on the border of a pyrethrum field; the little daisies were open and shone snow-white in the moonlight.

When we resumed our way through the field, a buck stared at us for a moment, then dashed away uttering a cry like a frightened baby.

The air had grown chillier. Without noticing it we had gained height and the tops of the Aberdare Range were shrouded in silvery, shining clouds. I felt sleepy.

We passed another fence on the far side of the field and marched on over open grasslands for a further hour or more, resting at intervals as before.

"Are those native huts?" asked Enzo suddenly, pointing towards a group of black masses, in the vicinity of the forest edge. I stared until my eyes smarted.

"I should say they are the first clumps of trees."

"If you are right," added Giuàn, "we have almost arrived."

Indeed, like islands in the raw sea of elephant grass, the first spinneys appeared, huge olive trees surrounded by thick bushes.

They were the outposts of the forest, which clothes the lower slopes of the mountain to a depth of fifteen or twenty miles.

It was past midnight. We were quite content with having crossed in only four hours the danger zone in which we might have met men; but though we had passed through the "human" danger zone, we were now approaching the "beast" danger zone and we advanced carefully from the cover of one group of trees to the next.

Having reached a particularly hospitable tree clump, we decided to rest for some hours, instead of marching on the whole night as previously arranged. Giuàn said that Enzo definitely needed some hours of sleep. Towards daybreak we were to march on, seeking the river that would help us to find a way through the forest up the mountain.

It was arranged that I should have the first watch.

Slowly I walked around the tree.

My companions were asleep. I pressed the ice axe under my arm. It was my only weapon in a country to which, before the war, people came from everywhere for the best big-game shooting in the world.

The little leaves of the old olive tree trembled in the gentle night breeze, glittering like silver in the moonlight.

At three o'clock I woke Giuàn and we repacked our rucksacks so as to do away with the necessity of carrying that horrible extra food bag.

While I slipped into my waterproof sleeping bag Giuàn started his watch, clutching his ice axe, it seemed to me, with an air of joy and assurance. Thus I drifted gently into the depths of sleep, filled with cheerful confidence in the prospects of our strange expedition and in my fellows with whom I was to share the coming ordeals.

*

At 4.45 a.m. we were on the way. Enzo, completely without fever, felt pretty strong.

We continued advancing from one clump of trees to the next in order to expose ourselves as little as possible in the elephant grass plain, still lit by the moon.

In one of the glades I had to avoid a big hole, perhaps fifteen by thirty feet wide. We wondered if it was a trap, and if so for what species of animal. It might be for elephant, rhino or buffalo. However, this speculating did not stop us.

Further on we reached a track crossing our route. We noticed the deep imprint of motor-car tyres. To the left it led evidently to Nanyuki; but to the right . . .?

We turned right and followed it, as it seemed to penetrate more deeply into the forest. In order to leave no traces of our boots on the dusty road, we walked on the grass of the border.

It was rather chilly, although there was no sign of dawn in the sky.

A suspicious glitter among the trees about a hundred yards from the track stopped us suddenly. A corrugated iron roof shone in the moonlight. Approaching carefully we saw it was a bungalow surrounded by a fence of high, strong poles. Afraid of being heard by dogs that might betray us, we sped up the track.

Soon after passing the house, the road veered a little too much to the right to suit our taste, and as we were still hoping to reach the river before dawn we made up our minds to leave it and to enter the forest on our left.

While crossing the track we walked backwards. I confess that this perhaps exaggerated and surely infantile precaution was my own idea. I have to add too, for truth's sake, that my companions, although they followed my example, were hardly convinced of its utter necessity. But what fun it was to go through with adventure in all its most childish details!

After a short rest – we had been marching more than an hour – we entered the forest, which showed up before us like a black wall.

Our first encounter with the main tropical forest was disastrous. The undergrowth was so thick that it needed considerable exertion to advance a few yards, and worse, one could not avoid making a maddening noise. Owing to the complete darkness, we seemed to crush every dry branch within range of our feet, to slide into the deepest holes, grasping with our hands the ropes of countless creepers which, like alarm-signals on trains, transmitted their sudden motion to far distant fellow-creepers and branches. In a word we seemed to have started a sort of earthquake amid the sleeping trees. In a little while we were sweating buckets and so tired of extricating rucksacks, caps and above all ourselves from those thousand natural tentacles that we retreated ignominiously.

Thence we followed a series of much appreciated glades, leaving the forest on our left and the track on our right and fixing our bearing by the stars. We had no doubt that our course was correct, but when the stars began to lighten in the east we were still unable to hear the sound of the river. Still, we thought it could not be far away.

From bush to bush we scrambled on, in the dim half-light of dawn.

Suddenly, emerging from the cover of a bush, I avoided collision, by a hair's breadth only, with a quietly ruminating white cow. Judging by the reverse bound I performed, my fellows had every reason to believe that I had faced, if not Death in person, at least a pride of lions or a platoon of Military Police.

A short council of war followed. It was more than probable that the cow would not be alone, but one of a herd, watched by one or more local herdsmen, probably young boys or *mtotos*. The *mtotos* (or to be pedantic *watoto)* had among escape-loving prisoners of war the bad reputation of having spoilt more than one well-organised evasion. On the other hand, the cow or cows, with or without *watoto,* would almost certainly be close to water. Could we risk seeking it now?

Already it was light even in the undergrowth. We had been careful hitherto and we decided to carry on being so.

We sought a hideout where we might lie concealed the whole day, leaving at nightfall. We found one several hundred yards from the cow, well protected by thick bushes all around, and there we settled down.

The stars were no more. Here and there a bird started softly to rehearse its part in the coming morning symphony.

Giuàn and Enzo fell asleep. I watched.

A dim daylight filtered through the boughs. The dark mass of trees was already broken into branches of individual shape. Slowly every leaf became visible. The grey changed to violet, the violet to red and then to green. The birds with a powerful crescendo started their hymn in praise of a new day.

We had to face a whole day of time, to spend twelve precious hours lying down! This thought brought me to the very verge of repenting our decision to wait.

The speed at which the sun was climbing seemed unbelievable. One could follow the ever-changing play of light arrows piercing the slowly retreating shadows amid the thick undergrowth.

Why should I not try to portray these strange figures cast by light and shade upon the moss-covered stems and the curtains of creepers and twigs? I had time enough to do so. I sharpened my drawing pencil with a razor blade and leant back against a rotten stem. It was not comfortable. First I should have to pull away a thorny branch. I pulled, but the branch was mysteriously linked up with the bush under which Giuàn and Enzo were sleeping. The result was that the bush rustled and Giuàn awoke with a start:

"What's happening?"

"Keep quiet. It's me."

"You? Don't talk nonsense. How could you move this bush from where you are sitting?"

I explained things. Guiàn did not show much appreciation of my efforts to draw comfortably. At last, turning over on to his other side, he asked in a voice already sleepy:

"What time is it?"

"Eight o'clock."

"Only that?" he remarked, and covering his head with the blanket he went off to sleep again.

It was still wet down there. I could not settle into a convenient position to begin my sketch. Or was I too nervous? Or was the task I had imposed upon myself too difficult? As a matter of fact I gave up, and lay down again. Stretching out my long legs, I carefully avoided the springing of another alarm signal.

Time was passing desperately slowly. High above among the golden leaves a tiny bird with emerald-green feathers jumped from twig to twig. When he flew off at last, I could hear the flurry of his wings.

A dreadful sleepiness overcame me.

Another bird whistled a perfect chromatic scale of twelve descending notes. I counted them again and again. Then everything was silent.

Did I really fall asleep? What was that rustle of dead leaves and snapping of twigs? Was something afoot? Was it people or an animal?

Without getting up, I turned towards the direction of the noise, which suddenly stopped. I felt nervy. I could not see anything but stems, branches, thicket, shades and tongues of light, in which legions of midges danced. Time passed, but how long I did not know, as I did not want to look at the watch. Neither did I allow myself to drink, although I felt in my mouth the peculiar taste of "the morning after the night before". I did not want to sleep any more.

So it happened that my thoughts wandered to the camp. I endeavoured to imagine the face of the Italian Compound Liaison Officer when presented with the letter we left for him.

We had written:

> Sir,
> "We have not previously informed you of our inten-
> tions, sure that you would try to dissuade us. We are
> leaving the camp and reckon to be back within four-
> teen days. Then you will know and certainly approve
> of our action. We assure you formally that in escaping
> we have not misused the passes given to us by the Brit-
> ish Command. In order to avoid any such suspicion,
> we hand over to you herewith the above-mentioned
> passes bearing our names.
>
> We regret causing you this bother, and remain,
> Sir, etc. etc.

We were proud of our official red-tape style of address, but our main object in writing this letter was to ensure that our innocent fellow prisoners would not be deprived of the passes, which enabled them to walk for a distance of a mile from the camp and to work in the vegetable gardens. As we heard later, all passes in Compound A were withdrawn after our escape and we felt really sorry and culpable.

And what would our fellow prisoners say?

"I knew this would happen," the one-who-knows-everything-before-it-happens would say. "It could not escape *me* that they were up to something!"

The one-who-is-superior-to-certain-things would say: "What fools! Could they not find anything better to do?"

When it leaked out at last that we had escaped to Mount Kenya, more and still better remarks would be made. I enjoyed, in imagination, hearing this sort of thing: "Have you ever heard of such madmen? To risk catching a bullet in the ribs for the fun of dying of cold up there, or of being mauled by wild beasts?" At which the sentimental-one would add: "And all three are married and two of them have children too!" The very-clever-one would remark: "I can understand escaping with the purpose of reaching friends at Mogadishu or the neutral territory of Portuguese East Africa. Impossible? I quite agree. But at least one would live in the hopes of regaining one's liberty, not with the fixed programme of going back into the camp and the certainty of being punished at that."

So I amused myself, imagining people in the compounds commenting, criticising and condemning us. In a prisoner of war camp every sort of news is manna from heaven. A mysterious evasion like ours would be sweet cake in the mouths of the professional gossipers.

Suddenly I heard voices, human voices. Instinctively I tried to flatten myself into the soil. There were two different voices, talking a language which seemed to me to be Kikuyu. They could not be more than two hundred yards from our hide-out. They shouted, probably greeting one another. Then they left, one going towards Nanyuki, the other towards the mountain.

Evidently we were near a path, or a track.

Whither did this path lead after it entered the forest? Was it the "track of the gentleman" Guiàn and I reached in our preliminary exploration, carried out some months before?

Several months before, at the end of September, Guiàn and I had decided to "breathe the air of liberty" for a day and at the same time to have a look at the country we proposed to cross on the first night of our actual escape.

We happened to know that Camp Command had issued passes to two harmless prisoners of war, to allow them to cut grass for broom-making "in the swamps" – a wonderful vague term. For us it meant our river if it could be visited between the roll-calls of 8.00 a.m.. and 4.00 a.m. "In the swamps" became our motto.

For a few packets of cigarettes the owners of the passes were ready to lease them, provided that we brought back two big bundles of grass for brooms. Producing the passes we got through the main gate, and in the vegetable gardens we changed from P.O.W. shirts into khaki ones, previously sent out, and off we went. After crossing the road and the railway, we cut two sticks and fastened on them butterfly nets, made out of mosquito nets belonging to rich fellow-prisoners. Thereafter we strolled along openly as though we were two peaceful Kenya settlers on holiday stalking *Papilio Mackinnoni* or *Papilio Dardanus.*

After two hours' walk across the country, avoiding paths and tracks for safety's sake, we reached the margin of the forest, carefully noting on a sheet of toilet paper every landmark. (Following more or less the same route during our actual escape it took us by night, with a sick companion and encumbered with our beastly loads, just double this time.) Thence, after passing through the forest for more than half an hour, we reached a scarp at the foot of which we heard the river, overhung with entangled vegetation.

On the way back we hurried along so carelessly that, emerging from the thick forest on to a track, we found ourselves no more than fifty feet from a gentleman walking toward us. He was not alone but was followed by two locals, one – oh horror! – clad in the well-known blue jersey of the Kenya Police.

We were at first so astonished that we stopped on the track. Then, pretending to have seen a remarkable butterfly, perhaps a specimen which might revolutionise entomology, I stretched out my right arm with the net, and crossing the path a few paces in front of the gentleman, who was probably no less startled than we were, I ran off into the forest, closely followed by Giuàn.

No. We flew.

So early were we back, owing to this strange meeting, that we had time after changing our shirts to cut, near the camp fences, two huge bundles of coarse grass. With these in our arms, we entered the camp gate triumphantly in time for roll-call.

We forgot to inquire if the grass we brought back to the pass-owners was at all suitable for making brooms.

If the path near which we were hidden was the "track of the gentle-man", we could not be far from the river. But where did this track lead? Whence had the gentleman come? Probably from some inhabited place inside the forest; surely an obstacle on our route, which we should have to tackle that same night. It was useless to attempt to solve the problem theoretically.

Pigeons cooed. Life in the forest carried on as usual. Hours passed slowly. I became familiar with the various bird voices. There was one which reminded me of the staccato whistle of the time signal of Radio Rome; I almost waited for the familiar voice to add: "We have transmitted the time signal for eleven o'clock, middle-European time."

Another resembled the whistle of a man trying to imitate a bird note. Soon I had an opportunity of seeing the owner of this improbable voice. It was a wading bird with long legs and a long beak and it flew over us with slow lazy wing strokes. Its shape seemed to me as strange as its voice and it reminded me of the conventionalised, rather futuristic figures of herons on certain airmail stamps. I could not remember if they were Austrian or Czechoslovakian.

By noon I could endure this inactivity no longer and climbed an olive tree in order to have a look around, but only trees, trees and trees were to be seen.

Soon after this we had our first meal of the day. Having lost a whole day we tried to conserve as much food as possible. All that each man got was one hard-boiled egg, two tiny biscuits and one third of a tin of corned beef. We allowed ourselves to drink only a little water, because we did not know when we should reach the river nor if, at this dry season, it held water at all. This was the main problem with which my thoughts were busy, the river; but we did not discuss it together, partly because it was useless to discuss it, partly because as a precaution we spoke as little as possible.

Slowly the sun started its downward journey.

I darned a hole in my trousers and then emptied my rucksack in order to repack it rationally and to take stock of its contents.

(i) Mountaineering and camping equipment:
1. Sisal rope, some 70 feet long and 1/2 inch thick, i.e. too thin and too short to be reliable for a difficult climb. As we had not

found anything better we carried one rope each, in order to climb with the double rope, as we actually did.

The ropes were those issued in the camp for fastening bed nets on to the bed frames.

2. Thin rope, some 35 feet long and 1/4 inch thick, to be used for making rope-rings in case of double-rope descents.

   Originally this rope was a bed net. Only my barrack companions know what toil it cost me to unfasten the fifty – I repeat *fifty* – tight knots of the net.

3. Waterproof sleeping bag, lent for the trip by a friend.

4. British Army ground sheet, to be used both as a raincoat and as a tent floor. This was perhaps the only item of our equipment regularly issued, if not to me, at least to another prisoner of war who had been "outside" on road works. I acquired it by exchange.

5. Tent, complete with pegs and ropes. Our tent was originally a square Italian Army ground sheet acquired by exchange. After it had been folded across the centre to get two equal oblong sides, I sewed two triangular pieces to form the front and rear ends, made out of a second Italian Army ground sheet. The triangle at the back end was sewn into position all around but the other was to be used as a door. Along the whole inner side base I sewed a 10-inch wide strip from the second ground sheet, overlapping the floor, so as to make it weatherproof. I cannot remember the number of needles I broke in sewing the tent as I had to work in the quiet of the night by the flickering light of an oil-lamp, made from a corned-beef tin. The thread I was compelled to use proved to be so bad that I had to smear it with pitch. Unlike thread and needles I did not need to "acquire" the pitch, because we had it in plenty. During the hot weather it dripped down from the roof and through the hessian

walls of the barrack on to everything – blankets, sheets (not in my case, because I had none), clothing and hair.

The two ironshod tent poles were fastened together with the flagpole and were carried by Enzo, who had no ice axe. The dress rehearsal for erecting the tent, performed in the camp behind the latrines after midnight when it was of course pitch black, had provided a thrill of its own.

6. Aluminium waterbottle, containing about four pints, borrowed "for the duration" of the trip. The grey jacket for the bottle was made from the remnants of the blankets used for my climbing suit and mitts. The bottle had a fitting for a filter in the screw cap. We made a filter but it proved to be the only item of our whole store that was definitely useless. It consisted of two pieces of wire gauze found in the famous rubbish heap near the camp but boiled and otherwise disinfected, containing layers of compressed powdered charcoal and dressing muslin.

7. Italian Army cooking-pot with lid, which I had owned ever since the first transit camp.

8. Alcohol boiler, to be used only when no firewood was available. It had been built in the camp from empty jam tins and was carried in the cooking-pot into which it fitted exactly. The wicks were rags from an old towel.

(Items No. 3–8, together with the crampons, the story of which I have related elsewhere, were fastened outside the rucksack and were called "superstructure".)

9. Tin of two pints of denatured alcohol, "acquired" at the camp hospital by instalments and by the strangest ruses. It was to be used in the boiler. I am sorry to say that we did not realise, or we forgot, how rapidly alcohol evaporates, or we would have taken paraffin.

10. Tin containing solidified mutton fat, "acquired" in the camp kitchen for use as boot-dressing. During the boiling operation I managed, clever as I always am, to spill half the boiling, spluttering fat on my legs. I still bear the scars.

11. Seventy red paper arrows, to which, most probably, Giuàn and I owe our lives. I cut the pages of an exercise book that had been sent to me in a parcel, and painted them red, with enamel borrowed for a few hours from the camp store. How many times my fellow prisoners asked me what I meant to do with my bunk all covered with red paper arrows spread out to dry! "Put out more flags," I would answer and they would go off, shaking their heads in pity, deeply concerned for my mental welfare.

12. Rock-climbing shoes with rope soles. They proved useless on the rock, which was similar to the granite of the Western Alps, but extremely comfortable as slippers during the rest hours, once we had taken off our heavy and water-soaked leather boots. The climbing shoes were made as follows: first we unravelled some sisal bags, obtained from the kitchen for a few packets of cigarettes. The threads were twisted together into a rope that was soaked in water, beaten and straightened between two poles of our barbed-wire fences. Finally they were sewn together in the shape of a sole. The uppers were cut by a camp shoemaker out of a square yard of old tarpaulin. The latter we exchanged for a considerable quantity of cigarettes from a prisoner working at a salvage dump.

13. Torch with four spare batteries. Each of us had his own torch with spare batteries, which also came from "outside" but for which we had to pay cash. Having been lucky enough to get two or three parcels from home I was able to accumulate some cash for things to be obtained "outside" by selling everything I

did not need for the Mount Kenya trip.

14. Knife with tin opener and corkscrew. I'd had it from the beginning, retaining it through every search.

15. Odds and ends, like sunglasses, bootlaces, some fifty yards of string, five candles, iron and copper wire of various thicknesses and lengths for repairs; teaspoon and soup spoon but no fork, a mug, twelve boxes of matches, pencils, drawing and writing paper, a compass – a gift from a friend for the occasion.

16. The sketch drawn from a photograph in the book of the Akikuyu, which showed the peaks from the east; also the Kenylon corned-beef label and the sketch of the peaks drawn with the aid of the binoculars. I had copied out of the same book a map of the mountain, but as it was on the scale 1 inch:10 miles I considered that it would be as much use to us as, for instance, a directory of Rome or a copy of the Geneva Convention Rules about Prisoners of War. I left it at the camp.

17. The binoculars.

(ii) *Clothing*

Two vests, two jerseys, eight handkerchiefs, two pairs of cotton socks, one woollen scarf, all from a parcel from home. A light white cap, cut from an Italian Army towel.

Three pairs of woollen socks: one issued, one exchanged for a towel from a parcel and one exchanged for G. B. Shaw's *Saint Joan*.

Mitts cut and sewn by myself from the remnants of the blankets used in making my suit.

Odds and ends, like soap, washing and shaving utensils; white, black and khaki thread; buttons; needles; safety pins, some of which I happened to have in my pockets when I was declared a prisoner of war as they had been used for my daughter's baby linen;

Fig. 6. The peaks of Mount Kenya from the south.

anti-sunburn cream prepared by Giuàn who is a skin specialist, and therefore in the trade.

I wore my climbing boots (exchanged for a pair of high boots received in a parcel and which perfectly fitted a prisoner who was to start working on a farm), three pairs of ordinary socks, my P.O.W. shirt, shorts and my climbing suit, consisting of jacket, plus-fours, puttees and a cap with peak and earflaps. The suit was made by the man who was famed as the best tailor of Gondar, although for the time being his address was Compound D, Barrack 11. I had given him two of the three grey blankets with which we were issued, thread bought in the camp canteen and buttons taken from the Italian ground sheet used for the tent. For the pockets, he used linen from a pillowcase; a last glorious remnant of what had been my wife's trousseau. Not being able to afford any more material for lining, I did without. The tailor was paid with thirty shillings' worth of canteen odds and ends and a fair quantity of cigarettes.

(iii) *Food*

Our calculations were based on ten days for three men at about 2,000 calories per day per man.

Four tins of corned beef, saved from rations. Four other tins were carried by Giuàn and two by Enzo.

Four pounds of jam bought at the canteen in early 1942 when things were obtainable more easily.

About two pounds of rice, saved from rations. Giuàn carried a bag of about four pounds of oatmeal, bought "outside".

One tin of butter bought "outside". Giuàn carried a glass container with another half-pound of butter, which was to play a sad role in our story.

Some eight ounces of sultanas.

One bottle of Bovril meat extract, bought "outside".

Eight tablets of chocolate, bought "outside". Giuàn had a similar quantity of camp-made chocolate, concocted by a pastry cook from sugar, cocoa and milk.

Two pounds of biscuits, rations easily saved as they tasted rather mouldy.

Two pounds of sweet biscuits made by the pastry cook. Giuàn and Enzo carried about ten pounds of plain biscuits each, made by the same man.

One bottle of "brandy" distilled from pineapples in one of the many illicit stills in the camp. The bottle was to be left on the top of the mountain containing a brief message and our names.

Two pounds of sugar saved, with difficulty, from rations. Giuàn carried the same quantity.

Two pounds of sugar and peanut toffee made by the pastry cook.

Two pounds of barley sugar made by myself from rations. Enzo carried more than double this quantity of the same stuff.

Ten boiled eggs. Ten more were carried by Giuàn and twenty by Enzo. All the eggs were covered in a thin crust of maize flour. Boiling forty eggs would have raised suspicions, so we put a little maize meal into the water to cover the eggs when we were boiling them.

Giuàn carried also two pounds of powdered milk, one eighteen-ounce tin of Ovaltine bought "outside" and a tin containing about two pounds of olive oil obtained, by exchange, from a prisoner who got it in a parcel from Somalia.

I nearly forgot the final item. At the very bottom of my rucksack was a black beetle, one of the thousands and thousands which infested our barracks and which we knew by their Somali name, *barambara*. This specimen evidently wished to take part, incognito, in an ascent of Mount Kenya. For his daring he met death under my boot sole. "No useless weight," commented Enzo.

Finally there were the ice axes, the history of which I have related before. The mere thought of the huge shop I carried on my shoulders for so many days up the bed of the Nanyuki River still makes me feel weak in the knees.

With regard to the weight they had to carry Giuàn and Enzo were no better off than I. In addition to the items enumerated they had one woollen blanket each, certainly more voluminous than my tent and sleeping bag. Giuàn, as the doctor of the party, carried some first-aid supplies and a thermometer while Enzo had two loaves of bread, the panga or bush knife, the little axe and ten packets of cigarettes against which I railed furiously, but which were to play an important, perhaps decisive, role towards the end of this story.

In Enzo's words we were as heavily laden as pack mules.

Enzo was now free from fever, and felt battle-worthy and full of energy, much to our pleasure and much to the credit of Giuàn. Neither was he coughing any more, which might prove to be an important detail if we passed through an inhabited place.

At five o'clock we ate an egg each and half a loaf of bread divided between the three of us; then we prepared to move on.

Soon after half-past six I went off on a reconnaissance, mainly because I felt bursting with impatience. Crawling through the bushes I reached the "glade of the white cow", now untenanted. At the far end I noticed a track. I wondered if it was the same we had followed, and then left, the night before, and if it was the "gentleman's track". That being the essence of information I brought back, we discussed it with considerable verve but with little hope of getting a useful answer to the question.

The silence with which the forest seemed to watch the spectacular sunset sharpened, if possible, our eagerness to be off.

At 7.15 the last blush disappeared from the western sky and through the forest ran a shiver from a breeze. Strange new sounds became audible, but it was still not completely dark.

"What about the abrupt descent of darkness on the Equator? Poetic fancy of journalists!" cursed Enzo, *pianissimo*, between clenched teeth, and I was inclined to agree with him.

At 7.25 we could bear it no longer. It was not yet quite dark but we risked crossing the "glade of the white cow" and halted near the track behind a bush. This bore to the east passing not far from our hideout which explained how it was we had heard the two men so near to us. We advanced up the track in Indian file, so glad to be on the move again that our rucksacks felt less monstrously heavy than they had the night before.

Now, I thought, we should at last solve some of these puzzles: of the track; of the gentleman; of the locals who were talking today. Any risk will be better than another twelve hours of deathlike inactivity such as we endured today.

Little by little our eyes grew accustomed to the darkness and at last it was dark. By the light of the stars I could see that our track ran almost due south toward the peaks. The glades were rare, the track being bordered by seemingly sky-high trees. The forest seemed to become denser at every step. Slowly I became aware of a sense of awe, as though something immensely powerful but not evil, the true spirit of the forest, was hanging over us.

Presently we heard dogs barking. They were still a long distance away, but in the exact direction whither the track seemed to lead. I felt greatly relieved. We were approaching the obstacle whatever it might be. The moon was due to rise at 10.25 and we should then see what it was that lay between us and "our" mountain.

We felt exhilarated, I should say almost desirous of a contest, although we did not forget that very recently we had had to beat a strategic retreat because of a cow.

Sometimes our track forked, but by probing the earth with the point of the ice axe I always managed to follow the more used road, which bore the tracks of car wheels. We walked on the crown of the road itself now, no longer on the verge as this would have been an exaggerated precaution. If on the following day they discovered the marks left by our nailed boots no one, I thought, would consider it worth while looking for us up in the mountain forest.

The track became steeper and steeper and presently it seemed to run in a sort of trench. One yard to the left and one to the right of us were walls of tropical forest. We could not see an inch. In my left hand I had the torch, to be used only in a real emergency; in my right the ice axe with which I felt the ground like an insect with its antennae.

High above, the starlit sky seen between the branches appeared to be the size of a pocket-handkerchief. Marching was like diving at into an unknown sea at every step. The surface of the road was fairly smooth; rarely did I touch a stone. The sound of our steps was almost inaudible.

Our hearing became, or seemed to become, acute, so that we were soon aware of the thousand voices of the life which darkness had awakened and stirred inside the forest. Now and then I had the impression that I could hear the rustle of leaves trodden under the paws of some great animal, spying on us through the foliage. Or was it the beating of the blood in my temples? As a matter of fact we felt now clearly but inexplicably that we were not alone, that we were watched, surrounded. By what? I could not have said exactly, but I supposed by animals.

We did not actually hear more than slight rustles, snapping of twigs, the flutter of wings of night birds or bats, frightened calls of monkeys or birds disturbed in their sleep, strange hisses or whistles, perhaps of the wind in the tree tops. But we could not forget that we were in one of the richest countries of the world as regards big-game and in a district where lions and leopards were no rarity.

Whenever I had a feeling that something was near, perhaps crossing our track or even barring the road, I would thrust the ice axe forward into the dark but as I touched nothing, I concluded that my fears were born of imagination.

Still steeper became the road, and the trees higher. It seemed to me that we were listening, as a doctor listens to the heartbeats of a patient, to the very breath of the life of the forest.

In a small glade we halted where we had at least a small "security space" around us. It is extremely rare for a wild animal to make an unprovoked attack on humans but as it has been known to happen, it seemed better to be cautious.

Looking at the unbelievably clear stars of the zenith as from the depths of a pit, I thought I could recognise southward of Orion's belt and amid the three stars forming his sword, something like a slight Milky Way. Was it the famous Orion nebula, which ordinarily is only seen with the aid of good binoculars?

Enzo interrupted my astronomic studies. He felt a little nervous.

"Don't worry," I assured him, although not feeling at all confident myself, "this is the last night march we shall make. Tomorrow night we shall pitch the tent and light an enormous fire. We shall march only during the daytime."

"By day we shall meet rhinos."

"By night we might meet lions or leopards, but it is by no means certain that by day we *shall* meet rhinos."

I felt uneasy at the mere thought because if there was an animal that I feared, it was definitely the rhino. Stupid, heavy, with poor eyesight but very inquisitive, it can charge one with the speed of an express. Better not think of it!

"Listen to that bird!" I said. "Does it not sound like the ringing of a bicycle bell?"

"It is the Girardengo bird," Enzo said at once and we started off again.

The noises had by no means ceased. The sound of whispers, rattles, of snapping twigs and even of grunts seemed to come from the forest. With relief we heard dogs barking again, this time not quite in front but rather to our left. The track swung right, entered a broad glade and was joined by another track coming from our left.

At the road junction there was a signpost. I approached and peered at it, but the writing was rather faded and the darkness intense. As I was averse to using my torch, it was rather a puzzle to read it. My eyes ached with staring but at last I got it:

⇦ NANYUKI
SAWMILL – LORRIES ⇨

"The riddle is solved," I announced triumphantly to my friends. "The gentleman, the locals, the dogs, they all came from a sawmill!"

"A sawmill, a sawmill," they repeated.

"The track on our left is for lorries; the one we took is probably meant only for cars."

"A sawmill!" we repeated all together. Could we not have deduced it by ourselves? What else would be inside a forest? A sawmill, of course! Certainly it was very easy to guess, once we knew.

"It would be strange if the sawmill were not close to the river," was the first intelligent remark made, and it was Giuàn who made it. We noticed now for the first time that the persistent noise coming from the left was not the sound of the wind in the tree-tops but could be nothing less than that of the river, of "our" river.

Between the stream and ourselves was the last human abode. As we advanced we heard not only dogs again, but also human voices and drums or the beating of some semi-musical instrument. There were too many people not yet asleep. It was only 8.30 p.m., too early to try and pick our way through the sawmill, so we changed our mind and decided to wait until the people had gone to bed. Then with the assistance of the light of the moon we should find a way to the river.

As the moon was not due to rise for another hour, we climbed a grassy knoll on the right of the road and lay down. From our elevated resting place we enjoyed the sights. Beyond a valley, which seemed very deep, rose the huge pedestal of Mount Kenya, with the silhouette of the peak drawn sharp against the starlit sky, showing us a new profile of its topmost ridge.

Giuàn was cursing *sotto voce.*

"What's the matter?"

"I've lost my ice axe string."

"Never mind, I've got material for making a new one."

"We have been so careful, but now I've left a sign of our passage on the road."

"It's alright. Tonight we shall reach and follow up the stream and tomorrow we shall be where nobody can find us."

"Anyhow I don't think the Camp Commandant would bother to send a search party into such country."

"Of course not. What would three miserable P.O.W.'s fewer matter! Some trouble perhaps with the Higher Command in Nairobi; some red tape, possibly a rebuke to the Compound Officer, and that would be the end of it."

In the meanwhile, I slipped into my sleeping bag, and Giuàn wrapped himself in his blanket. Enzo was to watch. I advised him again not to show the light of the torch for any reason whatsoever as we were too near the sawmill, and I asked him to awaken Giuàn or me in any emergency.

I had scarcely fallen asleep when Enzo, evidently considering that an emergency was at hand, started shaking my shoulder as though he wanted to drag me from death to life. "Listen! Be quiet!" he whispered.

"Why should I be quiet? I didn't speak at all!"

"Listen, I say!"

"I am listening."

Brought by the night wind, blowing from the mountain, I heard the various noises of the life of the sawmill: clatterings of tins, songs, giggling and bursts of laughter from women, a confused din of would-be music; a medley of noises.

"I think the sawmill has a whole workers' quarter attached to it."

"No! It isn't that I wanted you to listen to."

"What then?"

Then I heard it too. A horrid, creaking noise rose not far from us, and it made me shiver. It was repeated more and more shrill, rising to a crescendo and breaking up abruptly in a gargling cry as though someone was being strangled. We listened aghast.

"It sounds as though they are killing a pig." whispered Enzo, and Giuàn, who was still not asleep, added:

"It comes from high in the trees. Could a night bird produce all that volume of noise?"

"It is the 'kill-the-pig', Enzo said, convinced; and by this name henceforth we knew "him" who made the customary music at many of our bivouacs in the forest. We did not then know that the musician was the tree hyrax, a relation of the elephant, although no bigger than a rabbit.

All the forest seemed astir, preparing an ambush for us. But sleep won. It is up to Enzo, was my last thought.

Two or three times Enzo had to shake me before I realised where I was. It was a hideous reality I had to face, as a damp cold penetrated my clothing and a heavy weariness was about to drag me again into the depths of sleep.

"What unpardonable stupidity to have made this escape and to have left my warm, snug bunk and blankets in order to come up here into this cold!"

This was my first reaction, born in a moment of cowardice. Immediately I became ashamed of it, repented and punished myself by accepting reality. I crawled out of the sleeping bag, which was

Fig. 7. The tree hyrax, a small nocturnal mammal with a distinctive territorial call.

almost damper inside than out.

The moon had risen, a red apocalyptical moon, bitten off on one side like an enormous, rotten mango. By its dim light we saw beyond the road a valley with dark blue shades, and above this a layer of floating violet mists. Not even the most imaginative of the romantic painters could have portrayed truly this almost gruesome scene, dominated by a Mount Kenya with its jagged outline.

The forest was silent, as though overwhelmed by the appearance of the moon. More clearly from the valley came the impetuous murmur of the river, resembling the delirious speech of one stricken with fever. The air was full of an indefinable scent, vaguely aromatic.

Adventure beckoned again. It was time to move.

"Did you hear any more noise from the sawmill?" I asked Enzo.

"None. I think they are all in bed."

"And from the forest?"

"A lot. A hell of a lot. Just around here there was a beast that started a horrible din."

"What sort of a beast?" asked Giuàn in a sleepy voice, hunting for his boots in the high grass in the darkness.

"How can I tell you? I didn't see it," answered Enzo rather acidly, as though he had noted in Giuàn's inquiry a shade of doubt, and carried on with the description: "It grunted; it was certainly one of the greater carnivores."

"Really?" asked Giuàn, this time definitely with a hint of sarcasm.

"And why should I tell you fairy tales?" asked Enzo, nearly losing his temper. "I should like to have seen you!"

Giuàn, lacing his boots, twitted him again: "I'm sure you've killed it, haven't you?"

Here I intervened: "How did you get it to go away?"

"When I lit my torch," he confessed candidly.

"Did you really?" I jumped up. "Didn't I tell you not to?" But then I remembered having read in the paper not long before of two leopards being hunted in the streets of Nakuru, a town with a white population larger than that of Mombasa. The article was entitled "Tally-ho", I remembered. Thinking it better to leave the subject of beasts and torches, I said: "I should have done a lot better had I left this disgusting sleeping bag at the camp and taken a blanket like yours."

At 11.00 p.m. we set off along the moonlit track towards the sawmill.

Soon we reached another junction, at which there was no signboard. As the river was on our left, we took the turning to the left. The track was bounded on one side by a fence, and behind this, maize fields sloped down to the valley. Further on there was a gate, which I opened.

A few steps from us, the corrugated iron roof of a hut shone in the moonlight. I closed the gate again and we continued along the track.

Here cypresses grew on either side and we noticed the scent of freshly cut timber. The soil was covered with sawdust and we walked as though on a carpet, without making the slightest sound.

The road veered to the right and ended abruptly in a square.

On our left stood piles and piles of timber, and on our right a long building – vaguely resembling a Swiss chalet – barred our route. The rays of the moon were reflected in the glass of the windows.

We stood in the shade of the cypresses, staring hopelessly.

Already I could imagine us, trying to pass between the house and the timber, being met by the sawmill owner:

"What the deuce do you want here?"

"To climb Mount Kenya."

"What? Amid the timber-piles?"

No, it would never do to be caught here. Perhaps someone had already seen us from the windows. Turning around, I saw between two cypresses what I hoped might be a path leading to the left of the stacks.

"Wait a moment!" I said to my companions and moved towards the valley. But I was wrong: it was only a gap where a cypress tree had been felled. The whole seemed a well-organised trap for over-laden, escaping prisoners of war. While I tried to avoid some holes in the ground, which were screened by dead branches, other branches entangled themselves in the superstructure of my ruck-sack, and a snag of the dead tree caught my trousers. I thought it better to retreat while I could, which I managed to do with some difficulty.

As soon as I had regained my starting point, we all three made off as fast as our loads allowed along the sawdust path until, breathless, we reached the shade of a big tree. We held a short council of war and decided to try to reach the stream via the maize fields.

Once again the rusty hinges of the gate creaked loudly. On tiptoe we approached the iron-roofed hut. The door was secured by a shiny padlock.

A path led down through the cultivated maize terraces, and the murmur of the water sounded louder.

At that moment I remembered that we were now faced by a new danger. Prisoners who had escaped and been recaptured had told me that the local people sometimes posted guards in the maize at night to drive off – by shouting or by rattling empty tins – deer, wild pigs and other animals which came to feed on the green maize.

Luckily the crop at that season was not green but a big waterbuck, frightened by our sudden appearance, galloped off and cleared the far fence with a mighty jump. We thought he was feeding on the ripe cobs. If there were any guards present, evidently they were not attending to their duty.

We descended the path and beyond the last terrace we came to forest again. I left my rucksack, slid down the slope, crawled through thorns and branches and switched on the torch; below my feet ran water, the stream, "our" stream!

I recovered my rucksack and, followed by my friends, managed to get down to the riverbed, after a long detour through thick undergrowth and finally through a swamp where we sank into mud above our ankles.

Sitting at last on the rounded stones of the riverbed we felt elated, happy and victorious. It was a quarter past midnight.

We emptied our waterbottles; we washed ourselves and even

cleaned our teeth. Above all we drank and drank. Then, as is the habit of good beasts of burden, we fed.

Nibbling half a loaf of bread divided into three with plenty of barley sugar, we tirelessly commented on the significance of our success.

"We have lost a whole day by taking precautions, but we should never have been able to reach the river last night."

"Look how much water the stream is carrying, and we're at the height of the dry season! I gather we were right in supposing that the Nanyuki rises in the glaciers."

"Now we have only to follow it as we planned and sooner or later we should arrive there ourselves."

"And to think that we shall have four pounds less to carry, now that we can afford to travel with empty waterbottles!"

"And the sawmill has been passed. In the five hours of darkness left we can leave it far behind and sleep a little too."

At half past twelve we set off again as we had no time to lose, and we were in high spirits. We did not foresee that at that very moment we were starting a full week of toil, jumping from stepping stone to stepping stone in the water or laboriously climbing the rocks that lined the banks of the stream.

Only too soon we realised what it meant to "follow" the river, and our mood of exultation suffered a beneficial cold shower. With the kind of rucksacks we had to carry it was not easy, in the fitful moonlight that filtered through the dense foliage, to keep our balance on the smooth, wet stones. Time and again, a splash and a muffled curse told of a false step. In spite of his smart gaiters Enzo especially, who possessed only nailed town shoes, was soon thoroughly soaked. He remarked gloomily that he had "lost his back-wheels", as they were frozen so stiff that he could no longer feel them.

Now and then the river widened, forming pools. In the gloom they looked bottomless, like pitch. We then had to scramble on the rocks along the banks or to plunge into untamed vegetation. Our progress was exasperatingly slow and tiresome.

In places cattle tracks led down to the stream from the direction of the sawmill, and at about two o'clock we decided to risk taking one of them. It soon led us to a path running parallel with the river and bordering on some fields. We quickly passed beyond the zone of cultivation, and presently reached a clearing in the forest some fifty yards from the stream.

Having left the sawmill and its dependent settlements behind, we decided that everyone had by now had enough.

We pitched the tent and prepared to rest until dawn. We insisted that Enzo should sleep for the remaining three and a half hours before dawn, as he was so wet that we feared his fever would return.

Giuàn took the first watch and I went to sleep.

Tuesday, January 26

How cold it was! A damp cold, freezing first the nose, then the knees and finally penetrating the whole body. And I had been the one who maintained that we were too near the abode of men to light a fire!

When Giuàn awakened me, passing me the wristwatch, I got up cheerfully. A pleasing responsibility is always accepted with a feeling of happiness; but now I cursed the cold.

I stamped my feet. With my hands deep in my pockets, my earflaps down, my collar up and a broad scarf around my waist, I still shivered.

I started walking around the tent, which, when pitched, was only about three feet high. It was so small that I could imagine it contracting and expanding with the breathing of my sleeping companions. With pride and longing I looked down at it and felt deeply pathetic.

Time drove on interminably. How cold it was! How could lions live in such a place?

While my thoughts struggled against sleep, indulging in nostalgic reminiscences of the quilts and cushions of home life, I was surprised to find myself singing, *sotto voce*: "How ever could lions live in a spot like this?" to the tune of an old waltz probably from "The Merry Widow" or something similar.

I patrolled, stamped, looking keenly around.

Something nagged at my memory . . . Yes, I had lost my torch.

I searched around the tent feeling in the wet grass, lifted our rucksacks which were by now dripping with moisture and retraced our route for a couple of hundred yards downstream but I was unable to find it.

I probed every clump of grass with the ice axe, but in vain. I began marching up and down again, as a good guard should.

"How ever could lions . . . Now stop it! Are you going mad? Are you tired because you have barely slept over the last forty-eight hours? You will have time enough to sleep in the cells after your return. You are cold? Did you think you would find bedrooms with central heating on Mount Kenya? Don't be silly and stick to your job."

I clutched the ice axe under my arm. The fact that I was speaking to myself already might not have been a good sign, but as an old farmer in Somalia once remarked to me, talking to oneself means nothing. The trouble starts only when one begins to reply.

The nightlife of the forest was in full swing. The moon was still high, and whispering voices and suddenly stopped screams were to be heard all around. All our friends were noisily present. "Girardengo", "kill-the-pig" and many more. The dead trees blasted by lightning had a ghostly appearance.

Giuàn snored and Enzo breathed regularly. Again I felt pathetic; they slept, trusting my watchfulness. It was up to me to ensure that they should sleep soundly.

It was five minutes to five by the watch. Still half an hour and more to go before I needed to wake them. The river grumbled. The "kill-the-pig" had stopped its nerve-racking noise. It seemed to have been killed definitely. The cold increased. Whence came all this dampness?

Still twenty minutes before I need waken my companions. As an antidote against a sudden longing for coffee, or better, brandy (it was so near at hand in my rucksack), I started reciting poetry: Leopardi, Carducci and Dante.

Was there not a faint flush of dawn in the east? A deathly silence reigned in the forest. Should I waken my friends? They were sleeping so soundly. Giuàn snored gently. Leave them a little longer!

What would I not have given for a cup of coffee!

At length it got light. At 5.40 a.m. I tried to wake Giuàn and Enzo singing "pa-pà-pa-pà-papà-papaaa", the *reveille* of the army. Nobody stirred. My companions did not seem to be military-minded. When I lifted one of the tent poles and allowed the tent to settle down on them they protested and rose.

While I rolled up the tent and they prepared to move, we nibbled some biscuits and toffee. The tent was as wet as though it had been immersed in water. The same applied to the rucksacks and their contents, but this did not put us out of our good humour.

Enzo was full of beans as always, although his town shoes were as hard as wood and his yellow gaiters as stiff as a stockfish.

It was fully light when we started. Needless to say my torch did not reappear. The steady rhythm of the march warmed us up quickly.

We noted a track leading down from the sawmill and later a bridge spanning the stream.

How right we were not to light a fire last night, I thought. We were still in the danger zone.

Following the stream as before, we approached the bridge in order to pass under it. Suddenly, between the tops of two tall trees and underlined by the dark timber of the bridge, there appeared a vision of Mount Kenya, as yet untouched by the sun, its thousand Gothic pinnacles violet-black against the pale opal sky, a glorious spectacle of rugged beauty.

For one moment I stood entranced and then, from the direction of the sawmill, we heard the sound of an engine starting up.

"They are coming," Enzo said.

Were we to be caught on the very threshold of the inhabited world? Never! Away we went, under the bridge and through to the other side, running, sliding on the wet stones with our sodden shoes. No longer did we feel the weight of our rucksacks.

The engine was in motion. It sounded like the panting of a diesel, accompanied by the rattling and clashing of iron. I guessed it was a tractor.

In no time it would be crossing the bridge.

"On, on, to the bend in the river!"

There lay freedom and safety.

Pausing for a moment on a larger stone for a breathing spell I noticed a logging track winding into the forest on the opposite bank from the sawmill. It bore recent tracks of plates, and as this was no place for Crusader or Sherman tanks, I guessed they had been made by a Diesel-caterpillar. Did the tracks lead to some department of the sawmill inside the forest? It didn't matter. Off we went again, sweating as though it had been midday at Berbera.

It was 6.45 a.m. by the time road and bridge were hidden behind the bend and before we could afford to slacken our efforts. The roaring of the engine and the rattling of the tracks of the tractor crossing the bridge were heard at that moment. The iron music was accompanied by the singing of workers – sawmill employees going to work. We had passed in the nick of time.

Although trembling knees and panting breath invited us to rest, we decided to carry on a little further. Only when the voices of the workers and the roar of the tractor were lost in the distance, and Enzo showed signs of impending collapse, did we drop our loads at another bend where the first rays of the sun coloured the running water with gay gold.

For a while we lay there recovering from the strain. Then Giuàn remarked: "If we had stopped to admire the peak . . . ", and I: "If I had awakened you only five minutes later . . . "

We stretched out our limbs in the sunshine, feeling like lizards in the first days of spring.

"Now that we are finally free . . ." Enzo said slowly; and Giuàn and I, divining what he had in mind because we felt the same craving, exclaimed together: "Let's make some coffee."

We lit a fire between two stones and, when the water boiled – thanks only to the puffing of Giuàn, as the wood was wet – I put into it three teaspoons of aromatic coffee, allowed it to boil up three times according to the rules of cookery, added sugar and served it hot in the mugs over which Enzo stretched a piece of gauze as a filter.

Solemnly we sipped the first hot drink of our escape, the "first coffee in freedom" for two years. Never in my life had I drunk better coffee.

No one could have persuaded us that we had not passed the zone in which we might have been seen by men and recaptured. Other dangers undoubtedly were in store for us, but not from mankind; only from nature. "More honest dangers", we qualified them.

So hungry for adventure and hazard were we, so convinced of our good luck that joyfully and happily we went on into the forest, towards the lonely equatorial peaks; into a world untainted by man's misery and bright with promise.

CHAPTER III

The Forest

In which we traverse miles and miles of trackless tropical forest, and we meet three of its biggest and not least dangerous inhabitants.

Can mere words describe the happiness of three prisoners of war who, after months and months of preparation and worry, have successfully avoided the initial dangers of being recaptured and are at last free?

All the landscape around us reflected our happiness. On that shining morning, everything seemed young and fresh as it used to during the school holidays of one's childhood, clear as after a shower of rain.

All that morning we marched along the banks of the stream, which maintained a regular course from east-south-east to west-north-west.

Golden-green sunrays filtered through the foliage and were broken into a thousand reflections on the stream, foaming among smooth, multicoloured stones. As I walked along, I thought over that fleeting vision of the peak we had had near the bridge. It seemed so near that it might have fallen upon us at any moment. Surely it could not be so very far to the glaciers!

We advanced, jumping from stone to stone where the banks were narrow or walking on the pebbles when the riverbed was dry on one side. Our gait was steadfast, calm; we felt that our main difficulties were over. Our eyes were free to appreciate the wonders disclosed by the forest at every step, amid colours so dazzling that nowhere in Europe could one have met with them, save only in dreams.

There were trees of great height, some with smooth, slender stems like masts and some with their trunks almost invisible, smothered under cloaks of creepers of every description, which in places ran from tree to tree forming dark green walls; stately trees with stems supported by clear-cut buttresses between which one could have parked a car; enormous epiphytic fig trees with whitish, fluted or tentacle-like stems enfolding and suffocating dark cedars and resembling statues of gigantic wrestlers, Laocoöns of the forest. Here were the ruins of a Gothic cathedral submerged by waves of green; there ropes, pipes and wires composed some huge machine. Poor modern man, amazed by the wonders of nature, we can only describe such things by comparing them with the monsters of our mechanical age!

The undergrowth was so thick at times that one could only hope to pass by carving out a trail with an axe and bush knife.

Along the river there were flowers, some shining like flames against the dark background, others hanging pendulous like bunches of grapes toward the water; the yellow swords of gladioli; bellflowers seeming to wait for some fairy to ring them; pale pink or ochre-striped orchids and thistles with monstrous purple heads.

Here and there were carcasses of trees which had been struck by lightning or which had died of old age, sometimes spanning the stream and showing their pitiful, useless roots or more often lying along the banks, already covered by newer and stronger creatures of the vegetal world, striving with ruthless inexorability, common not only to the life of the forest, to annihilate the defeated.

There were countless birds, from graceful sunbirds with slender beaks and bright colours, to harshly croaking lories showing in flight their blood-red wing feathers. Troops of monkeys jumped from branch to branch or tried to imitate Tarzan, swinging on creepers and uttering guttural cries. Butterflies of every size and colour dallied gracefully along the banks.

Where the river formed quiet pools, frightened black river ducks would fly off heavily at our approach, the wet plumage of their breasts shimmering like old gold.

At every bend of the stream, new marvels made us either shout for joy like schoolboys on a holiday trip or murmur confused words in a low voice, as though unwilling to violate such beauty by talking.

"Do you realise that all this splendour will cost us only twenty-eight days confinement to the cells on our return?"

"I would pay fifty-six days."

"I, a hundred and twelve."

"Highest bid. Sold."

Or: "I feel as if I were ten years younger."

"What? Only ten? Thirty!"

"Then we should have to carry you in our rucksacks. Imagine having to carry a baby as well, as though we hadn't paraphernalia enough!"

"By the way, what do you think about it? Are the rucksacks less heavy or are we getting accustomed to the load?"

"Look at those colobus monkeys!"

"Where are they?"

"They're waiting for you!"

"Yes! Now I can see them."

With shrill cries they seemed to fly from the topmost branches of one juniper to another. One had to twist one's neck to follow their antics. A branch that had just been vacated oscillated rhythmically while the colobus travelled through the air with its white cloak streaming bright as a sail in the sun.

Presently we noticed some clumps of bamboo on the banks. Was this the beginning of the bamboo-belt of which we had read in

Stockley's article? Or did this plant grow at a lower altitude here, owing to seeds being carried down the stream from above by flood waters?

Together with the bamboos, there appeared the first paths trodden by large animals. These tracks ran more or less parallel with the stream, cutting across some of the bends, sometimes coming right down to the streambed to provide drinking places, or so we imagined. What animals had made these tracks? No spoor was visible but the size and form of various droppings suggested buffalo as well as rhino and elephant.

"It's lucky that it is old stuff," remarked Guiàn, who was the only one of us with experience of big-game hunting.

After eleven o'clock, the sky suddenly became overcast and, as though by witchcraft, birds and butterflies disappeared, songs and hummings ceased. There was no breath of wind. A heavy silence hung over the forest. The murmur of the stream, hitherto so cheerful, seemed to have changed to a sullen grumble.

We too changed mood, losing the wish to joke and jest. I could not help toying with a thought I had so far successfully repressed: that we were perhaps the first white men to wander up this valley unarmed.

The colours, so vivid a moment before, had become dull; the water which had glittered in the sun was now like molten lead. The trees stood motionless and my eye was caught more and more by the shape of the ones that had died, stretching their barkless and leafless white branches above the heads of their living brothers, and seeming to call the world to witness their sorry plight.

This silence became exasperating. Something was about to happen. But what? I tried to analyse my strange feeling but could not find a plausible explanation for it. Perhaps it was about to rain – nothing more. In that case, I wished it would start. It would lessen our nervous tension. But not a drop fell.

We did not leave the streambed even for a single step, although the side paths trodden by beasts offered an easier and shorter way. Instinctively we kept near the water, where our field of vision was less restricted, but we did not feel comfortable. It was the same feeling as that of the night before, as though we were no longer alone, as though we were being watched. I tried to persuade myself that it was an excusable feeling in the night, the first night of our new life without arms and fire in a tropical forest, but utterly unjustifiable and silly during the day.

Later on, picking my way among the bigger stones in the streambed in order to avoid slipping frequently into the water, I noticed bloodstains on some of them. Or was it reddish moss? No, on closer examination it proved to be blood. Old blood it was, splashed in irregular blotches on the rough surface of the stones. Almost every stone I chose to step on had one. It was absurdly irritating. I tried to think of anything else, but my eyes automatically sought the next blot. I could not help imagining a sorely wounded beast, fleeing madly upstream for safety.

We felt tired, tired of the nervous strain especially, tired of fear, because fear it was. When I asked myself what, after all, we were fearing, I could not help answering that it was nothing at all, and that was the most irritating part of it.

Our breathing spells became more frequent. We started to sit back to back, each looking in a different direction with ice axes, axe and panga ready to hand.

I stared at every suspicious-looking leaf, creeper, branch or stone. They only increased my nervousness.

Finally, to add to our feeling of extreme disquiet, I noticed the print of a boot in the soft earth near the water, which showed no marks of hobnails and which pointed downstream. It was not very recent, the mud around the edges being hardened; but it was not too old.

The absurdity of our fears became more evident and even ridiculous. It was like a chapter from a murder novel: blood stained stones, a mysterious footprint. Did "he" wound the beast? Who was "he"? And what was the beast? We gathered round like Sherlock Holmes and Watson. Neither a rhino nor an elephant would have been able to jump from stone to stone in that manner, nor could these beasts have stepped on stones much less than a square yard in size. Why on earth had the beast followed the stream instead of choosing some forest path?

Then it started raining heavily and we felt relieved.

Upstream, the valley seemed to broaden. It was past one o'clock and we reckoned that we should allow ourselves plenty of time to collect firewood. We thought we should need a fire from one hour before nightfall until one hour after daybreak – a fire burning for fourteen hours, as on the Equator the night lasts almost exactly twelve hours.

Thus on reaching a clearing beside a big bend of the river, we decided to camp and call it a day. Needless to say, it stopped raining as soon as the tent was pitched. We spread out our wet clothes on the rocks to dry and started working.

With panga, axe and knife we cleared some forty square yards round the spot chosen for the fire in order to give the guard a wide field of vision. We had no need to go far to collect firewood as the flood caused by the last rainy season had left plenty on the banks. We needed a lot, and while collecting it Giuàn and I tried to get a rough idea of the surroundings of the place in which we should spend the night.

We noticed much spoor of big animals and droppings, which were disturbingly fresh. In a muddy spot by the riverbank we could clearly recognise the tweny-inch-wide footprints of big elephants, and in another place a high slope seemed to have offered an exciting toboggan run for a rhino.

"A nice spot, isn't it?"

"A regular zoo, it seems."

"One never knows. We might have struck something worse further on."

We had a swim in the chilly water of the stream and then Giuàn and I, regardless of the protests of Enzo, took the water we had put on the fire in preparation for dinner, and we shaved. Enzo had said from the start that he would grow a beard, or as he put it, "a Mount Kenya Imperial".

The meal followed: boiled rice with meat extract, corned beef with onions fried in olive oil, tea and toffee. Enzo, appealing to the repressed desires of Giuàn and myself, tried hard to persuade us to "celebrate freedom" with a drop, just a drop, of brandy. Gallantly we resisted and defeated him by two votes to one, thus preserving the coveted liquor for a worse night.

We lit a fire in a circle of stones to prevent it from spreading and settled down comfortably, leaning against our rucksacks. With quiet content we watched the smoke of our cigarettes, now and then lazily stirring the fire.

It was the longed-for perfect camping atmosphere.

Sunset came. On the highest masts of the forest, the yellow glow on the bark changed to red, then to violet. We watched the vultures seeking a roosting place for the night with slow and lazy wing strokes.

When darkness was complete, the entire world seemed to be centred on our fire. Spellbound, we watched the ever-changing play of red lights against the dark screen of the forest.

My first watch, from 11.00 p.m. to 1.00 a.m., passed uneventfully. The main task was to keep the flame high and at the same time to save as much wood as possible. When I was not nursing the fire I sat close to it, fascinated by the flames, which resembled a waterfall in reverse, and listened to the peculiar sounds of nightlife in the forest – the already well-known scream of the "kill-the-pig" and the voices of many other creatures of the night. Once, unforgettably, the trumpeting of an elephant echoed long and high in the valley.

When, for a while, the fire did not need my continued attention, I sketched the camp scene from close quarters.

During my second watch, from 4.00 a.m. to 6.00 a.m., sleep tried to overwhelm me several times as the soft, monotonous crashing of the burning wood and the murmuring gurgle of the stream made a soothing lullaby.

One hour before dawn, I was startled by a suspicious rustling of leaves upstream. I flourished the ice axe and standing with my back towards the fire carefully shone the beam of Giuàn's torch up and down the dense foliage, prepared at any moment to see the phosphor-gleaming eyes of some beast; but I saw nothing. To make quite sure, I made a complete tour of the camp clearing, with no more success. Either our visitor had gone or I had been wrong.

Fear plays funny tricks sometimes, I thought, and settled down again.

At last the dawn came, grey and sulky, though in the depths of the valley the gloom lasted longer. The water for coffee was simmering on the fire and I called my companions.

Enzo had a fever again, a few points above 99°F, but he was ready to carry on. Giuàn was packing his rucksack and I was trying, with a long stick, to lift the pot of boiling water off the fire, when we were rudely disturbed. A crashing of branches, as though a heavy body had landed, was followed immediately by an angry grunt, ending in a high-pitched snarl.

The kettle slipped, upsetting its contents into the fire. With the stick I furiously stirred the embers. A plume of sparks ascended. Enzo threw on a bundle of dry twigs and as soon as they were well alight we swung them round above our heads.

The beast, snorting and grunting, moved from our right side to our left, carefully refraining from showing itself outside the protecting foliage but not yet ready to leave us alone. Again it uttered a growl ending in a high whine. We felt distinctly uneasy. Giuàn threw a burning branch towards it. A fusillade of burning branches followed from my side. Enzo, jumping around with only one shoe on, collected our water bottles and the empty cooking pot and started clanging on them with an ice axe. (Clever chap, I remember thinking, surely he got this tip from the films – *Trader Horn* or the like.)

Together we screamed, shouted and whistled like mad. The beast answered by growling, hissing, snarling and grunting. Eventually it retired with a most resounding snarl.

We dropped our "weapons" and looked at each other. Was it the dim light of dawn that made our faces look so pale?

We retrieved our still burning missiles and after a quick breakfast, urgently needed, hunted for some sign which would enable us to identify our early caller. We found none, which only prolonged our debate.

I still believe it was a leopard as its peculiar grunting and its stubborn attempts to encircle us, while remaining carefully hidden, would not have been characteristic of any other animal. We shall never be sure, but we felt that it was as well that it had not introduced itself.

Fig. 8. African leopard: "we felt that it was as well that it had not introduced itself".

Marching on up the river, Enzo summed up our useless debate: "Whatever it might have been, do you know why it tried to get behind us? It wanted to find out if we were prisoners of war. Once it had seen the black patch on our grey shirts, it realised that we were 'below the salt' and made off to look for a better restaurant."

I do not think that in all the wide world there has yet been discovered a river which flows as the crow flies; but of all the streams I know, the Nanyuki is certainly the least addicted to what we should have considered a praiseworthy habit.

Doggedly we followed its convolutions, scrambling over rocks, sliding over wet stones, jumping and making very little progress at the cost of prodigious effort. Less than ever did we wish to leave the comparatively good field of vision of the streambed for the beast-trodden paths which often converged on the stream, giving out a most pungent animal smell as of a zoo.

It was not that we feared to meet our leopard again, for we knew that felines were of nocturnal habit. Above all it was the rhino that we feared. I had been told that on roads in the districts around Mount Kenya there were posters reading "BEWARE OF RHINO". For a driver in his car this is easy. He steps on the accelerator and, except in extraordinary circumstances, he gets away. If he is on safari, he probably has his rifle at hand. But what can wretched laden prisoners do? I wondered. Climb a tree? Alright. But when a suitable tree is not at hand? Well, the rhino does not always charge. But when it charges?

I was busy with considerations of the sort, when – or was it my excited imagination? – I saw a grey-black mass some two hundred yards away, rubbing itself against a small tree.

My companions who were expecting such a meeting no less than myself, stopped as I did.

"Rhino," whispered Giuàn.

"What shall we do?" asked Enzo.

"Avoid giving him our scent," I said staring at the animal. "The wind is in his favour."

The beast seemed still unaware of us as it carried on with its skin massage, without showing us its head. Anyhow the situation demanded instant action and we started off hotfoot; in retreat, of course.

We sat for a good twenty minutes on a rock, which emerged like an islet from the stream, and sucked barley sugar.

"Well," I said, when I saw that my companions were, like me, thoroughly bored, "we can't wait till evening, roosting here. Or did we escape from the British to become prisoners of a rhino?"

"Fig. 9. "Above all it was the rhino that we feared."

So we picked up courage, rucksacks and ice axes and went on again. The beast had gone. When we reached the tree, we saw that its white barkless wood was shedding tears of resin and around it, the muddy ground was trampled in such a way that no footprints were clear enough to enable us to identify the beast with certainty.

"Gosh," Enzo said. "It must have been pretty itchy!"

We did not inquire too deeply because we were not in the mood to do so and it was getting late. I confess frankly that we were afraid. Nothing can prevent one from being afraid, no military nor civil regulation. One can only be forbidden to *show* fear. We did our best and marched on.

The bamboo along the banks became higher, thicker and more continuous. The young culms along the numerous paths leading down the riverbed seemed to have been browsed down by elephants, we supposed.

Not only did the paths show that this part of the valley was a favourite haunt for these big beasts, but we also noticed huge clearings trodden in the forest by innumerable powerful feet. Every sign of vegetation here was obliterated, puddled into a mass of thick mud, and the trees around these openings showed signs of having been rubbed for some six feet above ground level. We wondered for what purpose the elephants had cleared those stretches of forest. Enzo's assumption that they spent their weekends playing soccer there was promptly rejected. For what sort of meetings, then? Playgrounds for the little ones or for duels among rivals? Or for the dances, "the sight that never man saw" but Kipling's little Toomai?

Now, after having learnt more about the private life of the elephant, I believe the clearings were made by them to get into the sun and to avoid the dripping of water from trees after rain. Not many years ago, when white men had not yet encroached so closely round Mount Kenya, the elephants used to leave the forest for the open plains during the rains. Now they are probably compelled to used *ersatz* open plains, on a smaller scale.

Anyhow, we felt a sense of awe in being lucky enough to get a glimpse of the domestic habits of the largest of living terrestrial mammals.

Again the valley narrowed, and the river no longer flowed in what one is accustomed to call a bed. One could call it a staircase, or better still a staircase after an earthquake or a blitz. The water did not run over pebbles or stones but between rocks, foaming and screaming over and among big boulders in veritable climbs to be accomplished only without rucksacks which the last man, Giuàn, had to push up to us.

On a rock we found a round hole, washed out by centuries and centuries of erosion by a big stone kept in motion by the streaming water. I had observed this phenomenon often on limestone in the

Eastern Alps, but had never seen it on a harder formation as is, for instance, the basalt-like stone of the lower Nanyuki valley.

Enzo, true "son of our times," rejected my semi-scientific explanations. "Look," he said, "now at last I realise why there are so many elephants in this valley. It is an elephant factory! They are made on assembly lines like motor-cars, and this hole is the mould for their feet."

At a place where the sun was shining on a smooth rock near the water, we stopped for a short lunch of biscuit and toffee, spreading out our soaked boots and socks beside us to dry in the meantime. It had already become our habit to keep watch in every direction, so I sat one side of the narrow stream near our drying footwear and my companions on the far side, some six or seven yards from me.

I was just dipping a piece of dry biscuit into the river to allow it to swell and give me a real mouthful when the bamboo thicket, some thirty yards behind my companions, parted.

Walking in our direction toward the stream was a magnificent, solitary bull elephant.

I say "magnificent" because my first impression was not of fear, either for my friends or for myself, but one of genuine, deep admiration. No other creature, I thought, could represent in such a perfect way the strength, the dignity, the gravity and majesty of creation.

At last I roused myself and shouted to my companions: "Look!"

They turned their heads towards the huge brute and leapt to their feet. Never in my life shall I forget the spectacle of my two bare-footed friends gazing in amazement at the equally amazed-looking elephant, scarcely twenty yards from them.

He was the first to take the initiative.

Renouncing his drink when only a few yards from the water he

Fig. 10. "Walking in our direction toward the stream was a magnificent, solitary bull elephant."

stopped and gave each one of us a short, almost contemptuous glance from his vivacious little eyes. Then he lifted his trunk almost vertically, together with his age-worn reddish brown tusks, and dropped it gently and slowly in a disdainful half circle. Immediately after that, he wheeled in a right-about-turn, surprisingly swift for such a huge body, and nonchalantly waggling his ridiculously short tail and flapping his umbrella-shaped ears, ascended the path by which he had approached. A moment later his shining black back, surrounded by a halo of midges, was hidden by the leaves which bowed to his passage and then closed as though to mark the end of the show.

For a long time we stood where we were, gazing spellbound at the closed curtain as if blinded by an unnatural vision.

Had we not met at close quarters the king of the forests of Mount Kenya?

"Was he not worth the twenty-eight days in the cells?"

"He was worth everything, all our past and future toils."

Trudging on along the river, we arrived at a spot where the water had smoothed the rocky walls of both sides in such a way that there were no footholds to be found. The place looked like a huge basin in which the stream flowed slowly and quietly without a wave. We had to circumvent this spot, passing through the forest above it.

It was more easily said than done. While ascending we tried to pull our way up by grasping the roots of small trees – the slope was too steep for big ones to grow – stems and creepers, but soon we experienced what it meant to shake the century-old balance of forest life. The roots we grasped transmitted the motion to their parent plants, which quivered and, through intercommunicating creepers, moved other plants, mainly bamboos. In this way dead bamboos, which if never touched would have rotted *in situ*, fell suddenly. In falling they tried to strike the head of one or other of us, a joke which they seemed to enjoy because it happened too frequently for our taste. Other plants, preferably thorny ones, or heaps of dead leaves and twigs and such-like rubbish of the forest would be dragged down with them. For a while, we just clung to our handholds, helpless and immobilised by our rucksacks, and everything came over us like an avalanche. When the forest seemed to have finished cleaning itself we dared to raise our noses and proceed, climbing the steep slope mainly from bamboo to bamboo. Sometimes we found a culm which would not collapse as soon as seized, or a living root which would withstand a pull and which was not a mere embellishment; and slowly we gained height.

The next problem with which we were confronted was how to traverse along the same contour, until we reached a spot where we could rejoin the river upstream from the rocky basin.

The bamboos were so closely spaced that we could scarcely get between them with our rucksacks. We did not actually touch the soil with our feet, but scrambled along on a sort of trashy carpet of forest debris, which had accumulated above the base of the bamboos. This carpet proved treacherous although it looked pleasant, and often we sank through it knee-deep. Without the help of my companions I should have remained there permanently. At other times the superstructure of my rucksack would get entangled in creepers, and as I advanced I would drag along big samples of vegetation. These, released with a pull, would spring back right into the face of Enzo, who followed. It was no pleasure for him, inasmuch as it was the first time in his life, he told us, he had had at his feet a sheer drop of some fifty feet. Luckily he did not feel giddy during this first rehearsal of mountaineering.

After we had endured a good half-hour of monkey-like scrambling, the valley got broader and, crawling like rats down the big stem of a large dead tree, we managed to descend to the river on the far side of the basin.

Further on we again noticed elephant paths leading to the stream, and they bore plenty of fresh footmarks.

At 1.30 p.m. we agreed that we should camp at the first suitable spot. For a long time we found none as the overwhelming vegetation on both banks concealed every feature of the ground, and the only openings were the animal paths. On these, for obvious reasons, we did not think it "hygienic" to camp. We then saw some caves in a rock provided with an elegant curtain of creepers, and roomy enough – so far as we could estimate by the size of the entrance – to give comfortable shelter to the three of us; but what if animals had had the same brilliant idea before us and had established themselves there?

It got later and later and by now we were thoroughly tired.

At Enzo's suggestion, I climbed a huge boulder, which, being flat-topped, looked as though it might offer a natural fortress with enough room for tent and fire. Once on top, I noticed with disappointment that the layer of earth with which it was covered was too shallow for tent pegs and poles.

Again we went on sliding, climbing, scrambling.

Presently Enzo pointed to a bank of pebbles, in a corner between two rocks: "What about camping there?"

"The tent poles would not stick in loose pebbles."

"Instead of pitching the tent, could we not build a sort of shed with bamboo poles and light a fire at the entrance?"

I considered the spot too wet, being at the very edge of the stream, and carried on alone for half a mile in search of a better place; but finding none, I returned and accepted the solution proposed by Enzo.

In the meantime Giuàn had climbed the slope above the selected bivouac place and was shouting to me.

"What news of the top floor of our house?" we called.

"Come on and you shall see."

I reached him – it was heavenly to climb without a rucksack – and saw a clearing trampled systematically by elephants amidst the bamboos. Spoor and droppings were very recent.

"An elephant apartment?"

"I suppose so. Do you think that the owners will come home tonight?"

"We shall see."

During the next three hours we cut poles for Enzo's shed and collected firewood. Enzo built a roof above the pebble bank and covered the bamboos with the tent and groundsheet. In the event of rain, we had a fairly good shelter.

Having lit the fire, we cooked our dinner. The menu was the same as that of the night before. After a long discussion we forced Enzo to renounce his turn as a watchman, as he was too tired.

Thursday, January 28

Giuàn shook me.

"What's the time?"

"Half past one."

We had divided the night into two halves and the luck of the toss had allotted the second half to me, which was the worse. Giuàn handed the wristwatch over to me and while I got out of the sleeping bag he passed me the "watch orders":

"Here are the dry logs, there the dry bamboos and these are wet ones which make a frightful smoke."

"Where is the torch?"

"There, hanging from the shed."

"Beasts?"

"None."

"Did the people of the upper flat not come home?"

"Not so far."

"I always thought pachyderms were good family men and model husbands. I see that this is no longer a tenable theory. They are evidently club-men."

"We shall write a scientific treatise. New evidence . . . "

"Not now. You had better go to sleep until daybreak."

"Good night."

"Good night."

The night seemed intolerably long. The dry bamboo culms were devoured in a flash by the fire, which had to be replenished almost immediately. The moist ones behaved equally badly. They became twisted, wept tears of dirty water, whistled and sent down the valley a pungent and heavy smoke.

Here, as in Alpine valleys, a warm breeze blows from the lowlands during the day and a cool breeze from the mountain sets in soon after nightfall; sooner perhaps than in the Alps.

Once it seemed to me that the river added to its habitually monotonous song a deeper, quicker note. Or was it the growl of some beast? Armed with torch and ice axe I leapt on to a large stone surrounded by water, whence I hoped to get a better view. I looked and listened in vain. I stood there for a long time, as the scene viewed from the river in the full night was very beautiful. So narrow were the banks that the branches of trees from opposite banks were interlaced and the water ran below through a dark tunnel. Not a star shone through this thick ceiling.

I sat down again near the fire and stocked it with new bamboos.

The watch was very long.

As we continued our march in the morning, the valley became still narrower and we saw no more footmarks of great beasts.

We caught one glimpse of a beautiful bushbuck, which stared at us, probably wondering what strange creatures these were creeping along the river in such inhospitable country. Then, rushing away up the slope, he disappeared into the bamboos.

We carried on, but it was no longer a march. We crawled, climbed, scrambled, slid and fell. This exercise on top of lack of sleep and insufficient food added to our awful weariness. And this was only the fifth day!

At one spot we were faced by a long pool formed by the stream between smooth rock walls. We decided not to enter the forest in order to go around the pool, as we had done the day before in a similar case, but to ford it. We were lucky. The water was not too deep, and it was so clear that after we had made a bundle of our lower garments and had stepped into it, we could see exactly where to put our feet. The water was cold, but it was a welcome change from our boring rock-scrambling.

On the far side we rested on a smooth horizontal rock and dried ourselves.

For the next few hours the valley was so narrow that we never saw the sky at all, but only a ceiling of branches and twigs and leaves. The prevailing colours here were utterly un-European – I might almost say unearthly. They reminded me more of submarine scenes. Nowhere but in the Aquarium of Naples had I seen these blue-green half-lights and indigo half-shades.

Fallen bamboos lying across the riverbed became more common. We had either to bestride them or to crawl under them, thus adding further trials to our extremely slow progress.

After eleven o'clock the scenery changed abruptly and we found that while the stream had previously been flowing roughly from east to west, it now ran from south to north. The vegetation changed too, and we passed the only tree ferns seen during the whole journey. The rock walls on either side became higher and higher and presently we found ourselves facing the junction of two streams.

We put down our rucksacks and began to discuss which branch we should follow. It was not an easy problem to solve, because after all we could only guess which would be the more convenient for our purpose, the main Nanyuki or its tributary. And firstly, of course, we had to decide which was the main stream and which was the tributary.

In order to settle this point I climbed a bamboo-covered knoll rising between the two streams. It had a flat top, which would have offered an ideal bivouac place, but it was too early to consider this. I found here beautiful dark red gladioli and bushes of the pink variety of helichrysum.

My observation of the two branches of the valley was not easy owing to the thick bamboo forest, but after a while I thought I had enough data on which to base my conclusions and scrambled down to rejoin my companions.

"The left branch of the valley looks broader and seemingly carries more water than the right one. At least it looks and sounds as though this is so. I infer therefore that the left branch is the main Nanyuki and the right one the tributary."

"Sorry to interrupt you," intervened Enzo, "I should like to ask you a question before you go any further with your guessing and reasoning."

Both Giuàn and I were a little startled at the seriousness, almost solemnity, of Enzo. He had asked to put us a question! We could not help smiling, so unusual was the tone of his voice.

Enzo frowned.

"There's nothing to smile at," he said, "I'm not joking at all. I should only like to ask you something in order to save you wasting your time."

"Get on with it. Ask your question."

"How have we marched until now? I mean to say, have we taken the left or right after reasoning or more or less at random, trusting to luck?"

Giuàn and I laughed heartily.

"Of course by reasoning, as much as possible," I answered.

"Well then, I apologise."

He lit a cigarette and sat down absent-mindedly, throwing pebbles into the water as if, after having heard my answer, the matter was no longer of any interest to him. He looked disappointed and I could not help thinking that he had hoped fervently to solve the question of taking the left or the right branch by the toss of a coin.

Giuàn and I rapidly made up our minds to take the tributary. We hoped that, unlike the main stream, it would lead us straight uphill out of the forest. Once there, if we found that the tributary did not come from the glaciers it would not be difficult to reach these, owing to the better visibility above the tree zone.

I still do not know whether we were right or wrong, because I still do not know what the main stream valley is like.

We soon felt that we were in fact on the tributary because the valley was steeper and more narrow, and we missed the ripple of the water. Our new stream flowed gently, with very little noise. The main direction of the valley was satisfactory, leading south-south-east.

At 3.30 p.m. we selected a place which seemed suitable for camping. It was near the stream, at the foot of a sheer wall of rock.

After collecting firewood, mainly bamboos of which we were compelled to gather plenty, I tried to sketch the camp, with the bamboos forming a roof above the rock wall, like a cathedral.

For dinner we ate a full pot of porridge and fried the last of the onions with corned beef. Having had tea with toffee as a dessert, Enzo remarked that the rock wall at our back was dripping moisture, and that only a drop of brandy would be a safeguard against rheumatism.

On being asked my opinion, I left the decision to the doctor as rheumatism was in his line of trade. Giuàn stated that the moisture on the walls was an irrefutable fact and that a drop of brandy could not hurt. So I uncorked the bottle.

When later on I settled down to my watch, the optimistic mood conveyed by the brandy had long since departed and gloomy thoughts overtook me as I sat alone by the fire.

We had actually "marched" only three and a quarter hours during the whole day. All the remainder of the time had been spent in resting or tackling passages where two had to wait for the one who was actually scrambling on the rocks.

Neither was there any sign whatsoever that we were near the gulley which we had seen from the P.O.W. camp with the binoculars, and which we guessed was about half way to the summit. Inevitably, therefore, our trip would last far more than the ten days for which we carried rations, perhaps more than the fourteen we had announced as a maximum to our friends in the P.O.W. camp and in our letter to the Compound Liaison Officer.

Would we be able to reduce still further our consumption of rations?

Probably by the time we reached the gully, the river would be nothing more than a series of waterfalls, and we should have to slash a trail through the forest. What this meant we had experienced the day before, while circumventing the basin. Inside the forest we should do probably less than three and a quarter hours of actual marching and by the time we tackled the actual mountaineering work, we should be not only at the end of the food, but also near the breaking point of our physical and nervous endurance! How would our nerves react to such a strain after two years of barbed wire and almost eight without rock climbing? The main peak of Mount Kenya, Batian, had been a hard nut to crack for a world-famous Alpine guide like Brocherel, who like ourselves did not know the easiest, or at any rate least difficult route!

Enzo's health caused much anxiety. He carried on with praiseworthy fortitude and spirit, but what would happen should he get worse? We should not be able to carry him on an emergency stretcher, scrambling from boulder to boulder. The only thing to do would be for one of us to stay with him and for the other to make his way back to ask for a relief party. The same would apply should one of us break a leg, and it was a miracle that this had not already happened.

And so on.

But all things considered, I saw no reason why we should give in and return defeated just yet. At the camp our absence would already have been noticed, and to risk being punished for a failure would be too much to bear. We had prepared for this trip for many months and had planned it so carefully, and after all we had had good luck. If we retreated now, before we were half-way there, we should bitterly repent it once we got back to the horrid life of the barracks.

"No," I concluded, noticing with a pang of worry that I had already reached the stage of answering myself, "let us carry on, carefully but stubbornly; and let us now add more bamboo to the fire."

I flung another bundle of bamboo into the flames, which rose high.

The gentle murmur of the stream seemed sometimes to waver, starting again with a few halting notes.

I thought that the river too had its moments of weakness.

Friday, January 29

The dampness of the moisture-laden rock forming our shelter had got us "in the bones" as Enzo said in the morning, but it was not he who seemed to have suffered. It was Giuàn, who immediately after getting up seemed to me to behave in an odd manner. So slowly did he move when packing his rucksack that it struck me that he was not feeling well.

143

Although I had seen our equipment spread out like this every morning, today for the first time I really appreciated how much of it there was. It seemed unbelievable that only three men had undertaken the task of carrying everything.

While Enzo was busy with the breakfast coffee I asked Giuàn: "What's the matter with you? You look a little crestfallen."

"I think I had a touch of fever last night."

"Do you feel able to carry on, or would you prefer a day of complete rest?"

"Not down here anyhow. But it's alright. I can carry on."

Later he inquired *sotto voce*: "Tell me, how many hours' actual marching did we do yesterday?"

"Three and a quarter."

"I thought it was something like that."

"Now tell me please," I asked him, trying to exchange secret for secret, "what temperature did you have last night?"

"One hundred and one degrees."

"Was it no more than that?"

"No more, I think. I suppose I was overexcited because I surprised myself talking English aloud to an imaginary chap who had come to fetch us. I tried to persuade him to let us go on."

We moved off later than we had done so far. Now and then I watched Giuàn and tried to regulate my gait by his. He is a doctor after all, I thought. He must know whether he's fit to carry on or not.

Great was our joy when, after about an hour's march, we reached the foot of a high waterfall formed by our stream. It was the first rocky step of the gulley! We were near the point that we supposed lay half-way between the camp and the peak. Giuàn seemed to cheer up. Together we had observed from the camp for hours at a time, and with the binoculars, the valleys radiating from

ABOVE: The ascent route with the "Molar Saddle" and the north-west ridge.

ABOVE: Burguret Camp, right on the edge of the forests of Mount Kenya.

LEFT: Mount Kenya, viewed from the prison barracks

LEFT: "We were disappointed to see that the peaks looked just as formidable from this new viewpoint…"

BELOW LEFT: The slopes of Mount Kenya.

BELOW: The north-west side of Mount Kenya with a sign marking the Equator in the foreground.

ABOVE: "All the landscape around us reflected our happiness. On that shining morning, everything seemed young and fresh"

ABOVE: Pencil sketch of the mountain, viewed from the camp through binoculars.

ABOVE: The "kill-the-pig", more commonly known as the tree hyrax.

RIGHT: Deep in the forest of Mount Kenya.

Towards the summit of Mount Kenya.

The Nanyuki tributary "amid a veritable botanical garden".

One of the camps on the mountain.

Morning mists on the north ridge.

"Can it be that the *Flying Dutchman*, released from her course of eternal restlessness, has found peace at last petrified on Mount Kenya?"

ABOVE: Cesare Glacier looms over Oblong tarn. Hausburg tarn is in the foreground.

RIGHT: Hausburg tarn and its valley.

ABOVE: Mount Kenya from the north-east. From the left: Gregory Glacier, Point Thomson, the Gendarme, Nelion and Batian.

ABOVE: Nelion, left, and Batian seen from the east.

RIGHT: Lake Michaelson and Georges Valley

"Even while I was sitting on a rock and sketching the scene of the flying colours at the climax of our trip, the mists arrived above us."

"A rat drifted noiselessly across the shadow of the iron window bars, neatly etched by the moonlight on the earth floor."

The view from Base Camp to the valley.

ABOVE: The Ripon Falls at the
northern end of Lake Victoria
in Uganda. Purportedly the
source of the Nile.

RIGHT: The summit of Mount
Kenya, drawn from the north.
The dashed line is the Shipton-
Tilman route; the straight line is
the Balletto-Benuzzi attempt.

BELOW: Lenana's club.

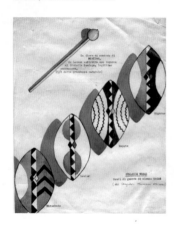

the peaks of Mount Kenya, and we had noticed that each one at a certain altitude became a gulley at the top of which the light green of the bamboo belt gave way to the dark green of giant heath. We hoped to be able to reach this heath the same day.

Thus we plunged into bamboo forest in higher spirits than usual. First we had to tackle moss-covered rocks, then the steep bamboo-covered slope. It was not easy to distinguish the sound bamboos from the rotten ones, and frequently we caught hold of the latter, which gave way.

Slowly we gained height and soon we could no longer hear the noise of the waterfall. When we rested, we missed the voice of the stream to which we had grown accustomed during the past three days and nights.

No leaf rustled, neither bird nor insect seemed to haunt this godforsaken valley; too seldom was to be heard the click of one bamboo against another. It resembled gruesomely the sound of rattling bones but it was, paradoxically, at least a sign of life.

As we sat during our frequent breathing spells there was complete silence, such as I have experienced in no other forest but only in the mile-deep caves excavated by water in the limestone of my native Venezia Giulia. Such was the absence of noise that one could hear only the beating of the blood in one's temples.

I felt so aloof from the world that I longed for the moment when we should strike the stream again.

When we thought we had made sufficient height, we stopped climbing and started crossing the forest along the general line of the contour. In this we were faced with the necessity of crossing little valleys, the bottom of each covered with layers and layers of forest debris – mainly a springy bamboo carpet covered with earth, dead leaves, and many plants among which were giant nettles. The latter introduced themselves readily, leaving blisters on my bare forearms the size and painfulness of which well accorded with the name of the plants that provoked them; for the Swahili call them *majani-ya-moto*, "fire leaves". At the time we did not know this, but the name has my full approval.

After much toil and heavy work with our big bush knife we again reached the stream, although by now this designation was scarcely justified as it consisted of a mere chain of pools and waterfalls. We rested a while and again entered the forest, this time, for a change, on the left side of the valley.

Up we scrambled, cutting our way and grasping bamboos, until we met huge, strange rocks, which reminded me unpleasantly of the concrete rocks built in zoos for the larger felines.

When visiting a zoo, I always used to commiserate with the animals not only on account of their being prisoners but also because of their surroundings, as I thought these were usually too artificial to remind them of their natural resorts. Above all, I thought, the concrete rocks would appear to the beasts to be nothing less than a colossal blunder. Now I have changed my outlook on the matter. Not that I no longer commiserate with beasts in zoos; on the contrary, I do so more than ever, having lived in a cage of barbed wire myself for more than four years. But after having seen the rocks on Mount Kenya in this part of the valley, I am almost ready to apologise to the zoo builders for having thought their concrete rocks unnatural. I say "almost" on purpose because we did not relish the idea of ascertaining whether, in the many caves among these strange rocks, there were indeed wild animals living in freedom.

Accordingly we quickened our pace and sped down towards the stream using a well-trodden but extremely steep path which we thought must have been built by former or actual inhabitants of the rocks.

146

We entered the forest on the far side of the rocks and carried on, grasping bamboos, cutting undergrowth and gaining height again. After two more hours passed in this wearisome work we met the stream in a broader part of the valley. We could now advance more or less up the streambed, greatly to the relief of Giuàn who seemed very tired.

On a rock we saw droppings, which Giuàn stated to be those of a leopard.

Eventually, high above the bamboos and surmounting a wall of rock, a fringe of dark trees appeared on the horizon. We looked again and again with the binoculars; it could be nothing but the heather. There was no hope of reaching it today. Giuàn had done too much already.

We camped in a glade near a stream, after three and a half hours of actual marching. It was a strange scene. The heather bushes, the first we had come across, looked like poor little Christmas trees to be sold for a few pence, northern children lost in the equatorial African bamboo forest.

Giuàn lay down on a rock in the sun and was covered by Enzo with two blankets; he swallowed two aspirins and we left him sweating while we started working.

First we had to clear a camping place big enough for tent and fire, then to pitch the tent and to collect firewood. While cutting and gathering logs and bamboos we soon felt the want of Giuàn's strong arms.

At a small pool formed by the stream, I washed some socks and handkerchiefs, interrupting my work in order to dive into the pool at Enzo's request. He had dropped his bush knife and there it lay shining on the pebble-covered bottom in the crystal clear water. I fished it out, and while Enzo lit the fire to cook our dinner I shaved off a three-days' beard.

As Enzo told me later, merely to watch me performing domestic duties like washing linen and shaving "in the wilderness as though we were at home" reassured him greatly as to the happy end of our adventure. I remarked that at home I used neither to wash my own linen nor shave at a pool; but was agreeably interested to note once more how little and seemingly silly events reacted on one's spirits.

By evening Giuàn's temperature had dropped to normal. The happy outcome of his illness gave us a good excuse to add to our porridge a heaped spoonful of meat essence and to drop a little of the treasured brandy into our tea.

As Giuàn insisted in taking his share of guard duties, Enzo and I allowed him the first watch, from 8.00 p.m. to 10.00 p.m. and divided the rest of the night between ourselves.

Saturday, January 30

Giuàn was without fever and we made an early and hopeful start.

Our stream, as regards the quantity of water it carried, had already become no more than a rivulet but the going became still worse. A number of waterfalls again compelled us to climb through the forest which appeared to be even richer in "traps" than on the previous day. To the springy carpets of rotten bamboos and to the nettles were now added deep and soft cushions of moss, into which one sank knee-deep, as though trekking through high snow.

Towards midday we traversed once more along the contour and reached our stream amid a veritable botanical garden. White helichrysum bushes and cushions of moss and tiny flowers seemed to have been arranged so as to show contrasts of colour to the best advantage. And what colours! Every shade of yellow, from ivory to ochre, every shade of green from mould to emerald, was to be seen. The "garden" even overhung the borders of the stream, touching it, so that not a sound of running water could be heard.

I happened to look back down the valley and what I saw was a very pleasing vision indeed. Beyond several theatre-wings of diminishing hills, clad with dark green forest, the yellow, barren plains of Nanyuki stretched out in a seemingly limitless vista.

The refracted glare over the plains shimmered like silver.

We reckoned that we had now surmounted the worst difficulties of the gully, and were at the edge of the open alps and the heather. More than half the distance from the camp to the peaks seemed to have been covered.

Near a shiny white everlasting bush, we stopped in the shade of a rock wall, oddly sculptured by the stream, and celebrated our success with a lunch composed mainly of the last of the hard-boiled eggs. Their smell and taste after having been squashed for more than a week inside the rucksacks reminded me of reports by Far Eastern travellers about Chinese egg delicacies, but we ate them courageously and completely. Not a single crumb was lost.

As we went on up the valley we soon realised that we were by no means on the open alps and out of the gulley. The latter got even more narrow and on either side the rock walls rose smooth and high. There was no possibility of going through the adjoining forest; we could only retreat to our lunching place or perhaps even further back. So we carried on scrambling up the huge boulders of the stream, hoping for the best.

The stream led us presently into a natural tunnel, about eighty feet long. We passed through this wading knee-deep in the roaring torrent, and when we emerged on the far side we found ourselves at the bottom of a big cauldron where the stream formed a pool. The outlet of this was the tunnel we had just passed through and the inlet a waterfall. We looked all round at the barren rocks. No way seemed to lead out of this pretty kettle of fish.

We did not like the idea of retreating for hours with the hope, but with no certainty, of finding a trail through the forest. We therefore examined the rocks closely on both sides of the waterfall to explore the possibility of ascending them by an actual rock climb. We found a "route" in the end.

A mossy couloir on the left of the waterfall led to a ledge, which became more and more narrow as it approached the waterfall itself, and ended at the foot of a vertical crack. This crack terminated on the platform whence the waterfall started, but as it was only a few inches broad, we could not guess if there were sufficient handholds for climbing it or not. Only by trying and testing it out could we solve the problem.

We climbed to the very end of the ledge, hauling our ice axes and rucksacks up with a rope. Then I had a close look at the crack. It overhung for the first eight or ten feet. Giuàn wedged himself into the bottom and gave me a shoulder.

"Be quick, please," he said, "because I don't feel very steady."

The crack offered a few shallow holds for my left hand and left foot. On the right side, I had to use the rocks smoothed by the waterfall, when it carried more water after the rains.

Blessing my parents for having given me 6 feet of height, I overcame the pitch. On the upper platform a big boulder proved an ideal anchor for a rope-ring. I made one and passed the main rope into it. A few minutes later Enzo, followed by our paraphernalia, and lastly Giuàn, joined me after the first actual mountaineering exploit of our trip.

The other rocks were tackled without ropes and half an hour later we stepped out of the gulley on the heath of the open alps.

*

So abrupt was the change in the landscape that the eye instinctively sought for a glimpse of the familiar bamboo; but now, had we offered a million pounds for one, we could not have found it.

A primeval silence hung over the rolling plateau. The stream veered silently between moss-shrouded boulders. Gentle slopes were covered with dark green giant heather, festooned with the long grey lichen appropriately called "old man's beard". The undergrowth was scarcely knee-high and was composed mainly of helichrysum bushes with white papery flowers. The air was cool and unbelievably clear, although the colours were less bright and less improbable than in the forest below. Everything seemed more sedate in this new world, almost solemn as though there was a spell in the air.

Our amazement and pleasure gave way to mixed feelings when one of us, quoting Stockley's article, observed that "rhino like lying up in the Giant Heather".

Walking upstream, we soon found rhino spoor with the three peculiar rounded toe prints, distantly reminiscent of clubs on playing cards.

Enzo, looking at them and sighing for the bridge table in his barrack, exclaimed, half gloomy and half smiling:

"One club!"

"No trumps. We really have none."

"Three clubs!" insisted Enzo, headlong as always.

"And what if a rhino doubles you with its horns?"

No rhino materialised however and as the sky was clouding up rapidly and mist already enveloped the upper slopes, we had hastily to seek a suitable camping place.

The riverside offered none. We left Enzo to watch the rucksacks and climbed a rhino path, shouting at the abandoned bridge player:

"One, two, three, four, five, six, seven EIGHT clubs!"

Eventually Giuàn and I reached the summit of a knoll. On three sides there was a rather sheer drop and on the fourth we decided to light the fire.

We were about to descend to call Enzo and to fetch our kit when a gentle breeze rose from the mountain and, passing through the thousand needle-like leaves of the heath, played on them a tenuous, soft, weird music. It started *piano* like a tune on a flute and it increased, *mezzoforte, forte,* till it resembled a magic harp concert.

We looked at each other and listened fascinated. The *arpeggio* rose and fell, and as it rose, it was accompanied by a deeper music which started like the fluttering of wings and strengthened to the sound of a double-bass, caused by branches of heath trees rubbing one against the other.

I have never listened to anything so eerie, so unearthly. We both felt very humble. Were we worthy of hearing this wondrous music?

Mist enveloped us as we brought our loads to the campsite and as soon as I had unfastened the tent from the superstructure of my rucksack, it started raining as it rains only on the Equator and a cold wind set in, cold as it blows only at 11,000 feet.

We were not ready for such an attack. The tent was not yet pitched nor the surrounding ditches dug. We sat compressed into as small a space as possible and tried in vain to keep ourselves dry, together with the rucksacks and a few dead branches with which we intended to start a fire as soon as the wrath of the elements allowed us to do so.

It soon became evident that our strenuous struggle to cover everything by holding the tent over us was born of wishful thinking. With the best will in the world, the poor tent could not accede to our demands. It had been designed to shelter two men lying down and was only eight feet long, four feet broad and four feet high.

There we sat while the wind blew and the rain came down like a waterfall. The flounces of the tent were continually lifted by gusts of wind and time seemed to stand still. The storm lasted two full hours.

Conversation languished as we became more and more wet. There was nothing to discuss, apart from some silly wish beginning: "Let's hope . . ."

From the start, we had agreed to impose a ban on any topic dealing with war or politics, as we heard enough of these subjects in the camp where, moreover, it had been my weekly duty to review news and to keep the maps illustrating the various theatres of war up to date. As regards camp life in general we had enforced a law that enjoined us to speak about it only in the past tense. For instance, if one of us wished to mention something that had occurred during the past two years, he had to start the sentence: "When *I was* a prisoner . . ." or "When *I was* at Camp 354." This had given us a lot of fun, because transgressions of the law were frequent and were followed by long, pseudo-serious comments. One said, for example: "In our camp . . ." and the others were quick to mock him: "Do *we* own a camp? Why have you not mentioned it before?" And so on.

Now nobody was in the right mood for a joke.

When at last the weather cleared, we were completely soaked and had not a single dry rag to put on. Happily we were compensated for this by the wonderful view, which allowed us to forget our impending pneumonia and rheumatism for a few moments. As the mists started to lift, the setting sun illuminated a group of rocks towering above the heathlands. We christened them immediately

"The Castles" as castles they really resembled; castles after a legendary battle, their jagged ramparts bloodstained and their misty, tattered flags still hanging from the topmost towers.

Leaving these fantasies of our imagination we turned to the more immediate necessities of life. Enzo was entrusted with the building of quarters for the night in which we three and all our belongings would be sheltered in the event of more rain blowing up. Nor could the possibility of a snowstorm be excluded as, from the camp, we had observed that snow sometimes reached the belt of heather, although at this altitude it did not lie on the ground for more than a few hours.

While Enzo was hauling ropes and fastening groundsheets and blankets on to quivering heath stems or damp mossy rocks, Giuàn and I, armed with axe and panga, set out to collect firewood.

After the storm, which had raged for a good part of the afternoon, we could not find one single dry branch, but at least the exertion of cutting and cleaving wood warmed us a little. It was not easy to light the fire, but with the united strength of our lungs we started a poor flickering flame on which we put the water to boil for our dinner.

Meanwhile the sky had cleared completely and, as on a map, we saw at our feet the plains of Nanyuki stretching out westward to the distant hills of Laikipia, and far away to the north-west the course of the northern Ewaso Ng'iro which was fringed by a dark belt of vegetation.

"Look there! Isn't that the railway line?"

"Must be. And there's the wood by the church of Nanyuki. And further on . . . Yes, it's our camp!"

"Wrong! It is not *our* camp that you see. It is the camp where we *were* prisoners."

"I apologise," I answered studying the scene with the aid of the binoculars: "I can see the big black barracks of Compound E!" I added. "Would you mind pulling that branch towards you, so that I can see better? . . . Thank you. It *is* Compound E!"

"I can hardly believe that we were ever there!"

"Neither can I. How far away it looks!"

Yes, it was aeons away. Had we really experienced all this or was it a dream? Queues for having a shower bath, queues for filling a water bottle, queues for washing one's linen, roll-calls in the morning, roll calls in the evening, quarrels between prisoners over a drop of cooking oil, secret wars for a piece of soap to be bandied among the thirty-two inhabitants of a barrack, the endless chattering and gossiping of idle people, all the hours, days, months, years spent in doing just nothing but trying to keep oneself sane and as clean as possible; and all that amid the most sickening pettiness and meanness of human nature, as is inevitable in the confined, artificial life of people of all ages and conditions, on the wrong side of the wire. How remote that life seemed – and was!

As we could see the camp, our friends in the camp ought to be able to see our bivouac, if only we could give them a signal. According to arrangements previously made, they would look out every evening between seven and nine o'clock to try to spot any fire lit by us.

"A fire! A huge fire after dinner!" we decided.

We dragged in as many dead heather trees as we could find, and after dinner – during which we finished, as an antidote to the wet, the rest of our brandy – we lit a fire on our hilltop, which we reckoned would be seen not only by our friends in the camp, but also by the Commander-in-Chief himself.

The wood burnt rapidly and the effect of the brandy was more ephemeral still, so that when we crawled into Enzo's proud building, we felt even colder than we had after the rainstorm.

This night will remain in my memory as the worst of our whole trip, owing to the intense cold that did not allow me to close an eye, and owing to the still greater weariness that prevented me from getting up to rekindle the fire until a few hours before dawn.

At this uncertain hour, I summoned all my determination. Scrambling out of Enzo's draughty shelter I tumbled towards the fireplace. There I found the fire already lit; with Giuàn stocking it from time to time.

"What are you doing? You were still sick yesterday! Didn't we agree that we should have no guard tonight?"

"I agreed at first but later I thought it better to watch. I have read that sometimes lions *are* found at over 11,000 feet."

"You go and have a good rest. I'll watch the fire alone." I confess I felt moved, and we watched and tended the fire together.

Sunday, January 31

At last the dawn broke, misty and extremely chilly.

By half-past six we were already on our way following the brook, as it could no longer be called a stream. To follow it now was child's play in comparison with the toil of previous days, but we ourselves were tired, especially after our bad night.

It was Sunday, exactly a week after our escape, and we were not yet even in sight of our goal, but as the mists cleared and a glorious sun came out, the whole landscape seemed to have put on its best Sunday clothes.

The heather-crowned slopes were sprinkled with flowers: dark blue bell-flowers, light blue myosotis, yellow buttercups and white everlastings, which became more stunted as we gained altitude.

Butterflies and sunbirds flew joyously along the banks of the brook. The air, shiny and clear as in the high Alps, was full of the subtle scent of heather resin.

Lords of the scenery, the "Castles" raised their reddish towers against the deep blue sky. Resembling the Dolomite peaks of Cadore, they looked homely to me.

With the greatest interest, we examined the first lobelia plants, some spreading long white plumes in the breeze, others showing bright little violet flowers inside their hive-like conical structures, which attracted insects of all species and sizes.

The strange plants, the bright colours, the clean scent and the thin air gave us the impression of living in dreamland. At any moment we feared that we might wake up and find ourselves back behind the wire. Fortunately we saw no sign of rhino or buffalo but I was sometimes startled by the sight of rhino-shaped grey basalt boulders along our brook.

Here the grass did not form a lawn-like carpet as in the Alps but grew in coarse, knee-high tussocky clumps separated by foot-deep ditches excavated by rainwater. As the ditches were hidden by the grass itself, one risked spraining one's ankle at every step and the going – heavily laden as we were – was even more tiring than that along the streambed in the forest. We cordially agreed with Stockley's statement that marching on the tussock-grass of Mount Kenya is sheer "toil and misery".

Presently, on reaching what appeared to be the head of the valley, we found that our tributary did not spring from the glaciers but from rivulets fanning down from an amphitheatre of grassy slopes. Where the orchestra would have been located in a Greek amphitheatre, there was a boulder as high as a two-storeyed house with some fine heather trees growing on the top – a remarkable sight.

We decided to climb over the left shoulder of the top of the valley in order to rejoin the main Nanyuki stream that, we supposed, ran on the far side of this ridge. We advanced therefore in that direction, aiming towards a high rocky outcrop, which rose like the fingers of a giant against the sky. It resembled in miniature the famous Five Fingers of the Dolomites, and we called it "The Fingers".

We had refilled our water bottles as we did not know when we should find water again, and our rucksacks seemed heavier than ever.

Whether it was the four pounds extra weight I was carrying, the thin air, the sleepless night I had had, the "toil and misery" grass or a combination of all these I do not know, but I found that I could not take more than ten steps without having to stop for a long breathing spell.

"No," I told myself, "this isn't the way in which your father taught you mountaineering. 'Slow, short, steady steps without resting,' he said." I tried this but could not manage it. I rested for another spell, shouting to my companions to wait for me at the "Fingers".

I was rather depressed and hurt in my pride, as I began to suspect that I was suffering from mountain sickness. I felt so weak and dizzy. It had never happened in my life, as I had been brought up not only to love and revere the mountains, but also to be accustomed to walking on them. I should have repudiated with scorn any hint that I could ever feel mountain-sick. But – alas, after years spent in Africa, two of them inside a barbed wire fence, I found that things could be very different.

Whatever the cause of my plight, I promised myself solemnly that if or when I returned to my beloved Alps, never again should I swear at the seemingly endless paths leading from the valley bottom to the huts, as I used to do when on mountaineering holidays.

There at least there were paths, not this endless, heartbreaking labour on the tussock grass.

For a while I lay there, asking myself whether I should be able to reach, before collapsing, the first giant groundsel I could see high above me on the slope. I tried to move off again, comforting myself with the thought that both Enzo and Giuàn had had their black days and that this was mine. I cannot remember whether I made more than twenty steps before I collapsed. I had just time to take off my rucksack before I fell asleep.

For a long time, I slept on the sunny slope below the stone fingers. A spike of my crampons stuck into me under my shoulder blade, and this, I fancy, is why I dreamt that I was in a crowd where a rude youngster prodded me in the back with his umbrella, which he carried under his arm. The sleep did me good. When I awoke, the shades of the heather bushes had grown long, the air was chilly and I felt restored.

After less than an hour's march I rejoined my companions who, owing to my prolonged absence, were preparing a camping place under an overhanging rock at the foot of the "Fingers". Enzo was cutting grass for our "beds" and Giuàn was collecting firewood higher above on the slope.

"Do you think there would still be snakes here?" asked Enzo.

"I should say not."

"What height do you reckon we have reached?"

"About 13,000 feet, I guess. This type of giant groundsel does not grow below 12,000, so far as I remember from Stockley's article, and here they extend far below the slope I have just climbed by instalments."

When at last the tent was pitched, I too started collecting firewood, and soon had an odd experience: I found that lobelia stems as thick as a man's thigh and almost six feet long, broke as if made of cardboard; ten foot-tall giant groundsels would be pushed over easily. Once again we experienced that "Alice in Wonderland" feeling. Had I become so strong owing to my refreshing nap? Or were the laws of gravity altered up here? I had the same feeling as, when a boy, I had first lifted a big stone under water.

When we tried to light the fire, things became still more topsy-turvy. We wondered what the lobelias and giant groundsels were made of. Although perfectly dry they would not burn at all. Even the dry grass curled and blackened but did not blaze up. We united our efforts: "One-two-three-blow." We wasted half a box of matches, but all in vain. We could not start a fire, nor did any scientific explanation we could put forward prove satisfactory. If there was not enough oxygen to keep a fire burning, how could there be enough to allow us to breathe? But breathe we did, and well.

In the end we lit our alcohol burner and made a brew of tea with which we ate corned beef, biscuits and chocolate.

At this altitude we did not think it necessary to keep a watch and it would certainly have meant asking too much of any of us to sit without a fire outside the tent. Thus we all three slipped into the tent. As it was only four foot wide, we had to lie on our sides like sardines in a tin. If one of us had turned on his back in his sleep, the tent would have burst open or its pegs would have given way; but since it was the only way in which we could sleep, it had to be.

On either side of me lay Enzo and Giuàn, each wrapped in his blanket. I lay in the centre ("like the best part of a sandwich" as Enzo said) in my sleeping bag. As we had put all our available clothing on, there was little comfort in the arrangement, but at least it was warm and we were tired enough to enjoy a long and refreshing sleep.

After twelve hours of sound sleep, we got up betimes, feeling fresh and energetic. It was cold, well below freezing point, and the water in our bottles was hard frozen. While my companions prepared coffee on the boiler, I tried to sketch the landscape, but I could hardly hold a pencil, so stiff were my fingers. A thrilling and unusual experience on the Equator!

After a while we turned the corner of the "Fingers" and reached a broad saddle. At the bottom of the valley beyond glittered a brook, the main Nanyuki again.

"Now wait and you will see," said Giuàn who had explored these surroundings the day before when collecting our useless, misnamed firewood.

"See what?"

"Batian. It is so marvellous that you will just sit down and stare."

He was right and we did.

As soon as we had passed the last of the heath, by which time we were already in the Nanyuki valley, Batian appeared. I had not expected it to be so near, so beautiful, so tantalising. There it was at last, our ultimate goal, its appalling north face armoured with ice, its jagged pinnacles not yet touched by the rising sun, dreamlike, overwhelming as it had appeared to me on that well-remembered May morning in the camp, when first I fell in love with it.

We were eager to rejoin our old friend, the Nanyuki, which really seemed to have its source in the northern glaciers. We hastened across the slope and entered a small but dense forest of giant groundsels. As I have read since, true giant groundsel forests are a rarity on Mount Kenya. We were therefore lucky to have come across this one.

The stems of these weird plants were so close together that they hid sky and mountain. I was again reminded of submarine scenes in an aquarium as the leaf clusters of this plant, often likened to cauliflowers or to huge artichokes, resemble certain types of marine flora. Individual trees, many of them more than fifteen feet in height, grew so close together that those that died remained standing, rotting but propped up against their living companions. It was not easy to pass through the grove.

Beyond the giant groundsel forest, we met swampy marshland camouflaged by bright green moss, which at a distance looked like a lawn. The moss was dotted with buttercups and often we trod on a strange plant which I saw here for the first time. Its leaves formed a cup sunk in the moss and at the bottom of the cup there was a yellow flower. I have since identified it in Engler's textbook on African flora as *Arctotis Rueppelii*.

For the second time we emptied our water bottles at the Nanyuki and with pleasure drank its ice-cold water, before following its course upstream once more.

Along the "baby Nanyuki", as we called it, we were delighted to see cushions of dwarf helichrysum which may be compared with the edelweiss on the Alps; on Mount Kenya, so far as I have observed, it grows at a higher altitude than most, if not all other flowering plants.

Undoubtedly when compared with edelweiss, helichrysum comes off second best as it has stiff, papery petals compared with the smooth velvet of edelweiss, but I like to think of helichrysum as the Cinderella of Alpine flowers. There is a wealth of literature in Italian, German, French and Ladin (a Romansh dialect) dealing with edelweiss. Among the better known of the many legends concerning its origin is that which relates how it was brought to the Dolomites by no less a person than the Princess of the Moon.

Now, I thought, why is helichrysum not equally well known? Obviously because of mere lack of advertisement, a vital necessity in these modern times. Surely it would be only right and fair to coin a legend for helichrysum; its wonderful name, derived from the Greek, is in itself a vindication of the science of botanical nomenclature: *helios* = sun, *chrysos* = gold.

"*Once upon a time there lived a princess; not of course the Princess of the Moon, because she was busy in the Alps, but her sister the Princess of the Sun. She had fair, golden hair and sparkling eyes flecked with gold . . .*" But no, I thought, this is not my business. Better leave it to someone in the trade.

We marched on following the Nanyuki, now fringed with long icicles although it was nearly midday. I hoped that we should be able to reach this same day a col at the foot of the pinnacles of the north ridge of Batian, and from this col choose the best place for our base camp. There, according to plan, Enzo should remain and from thence Giuàn and I should make the attempt on the main peak, or failing that on Lenana. I had hoped that our base camp would be equidistant between the two peaks; but all my hopes were shattered in a moment by the most grievous blow our party suffered during the whole trip.

I had just caught a glimpse of footprints and droppings, which could not have been left by an animal smaller than a buffalo, when I heard my companions shouting behind me. As I swung around I was prepared to see them being charged by an angry bull buffalo, but the quarry they pursued, after having dropped their rucksacks, could not have been a buffalo, because Enzo shouted: "It looks like a snipe!" and no buffalo could ever be confused with a snipe, not even in the wonderland of Mount Kenya.

"It's never been a snipe in its life," I shouted back as I saw what I thought to be the object of their attention flying towards me. It was a sunbird with long tail, curved beak, and shimmering plumage on its breast. I believe now it was *Nectarinia Johnstonii.*

I turned and for a moment walked on, my eyes following two tiny dark blue butterflies and my thoughts wandered again to the Alps, where I had once seen two red admirals on the ice-clad, 13,000 feet summit of Order. Then I heard shouting again. This time it was Giuàn's voice, and he sounded worried.

I looked back and what I saw made me drop my rucksack and run.

Enzo lay on the ground. Giuàn, having turned the limp body over, put his ear to his companion's chest and then started opening his shirt. When I, breathless, reached our unconscious friend, Giuàn was holding his pulse and had a look that I did not like at all.

"Is Enzo's heart bad?" I asked.

"Yes," answered Giuàn in a harsh voice. "Make some coffee, please. Quick."

I flew to my rucksack, fetched a cooking pot of water, lit the alcohol burner and waited.

At about 14,000 feet, water has a lower boiling point than at sea level and should boil quicker, I thought; but minutes passed and nothing seemed to happen. Often I glanced at Giuàn, still busy with the motionless Enzo, and I became more and more worried by his hard and business-like face. I did not dare to ask for details, for woe betide the man who interrupts a doctor performing his duty.

At last the water boiled and Giuàn poured some drops of hot strong coffee between Enzo's pale lips. To our intense relief Enzo stirred, swallowed the next few drops of coffee and at last looked around and started smiling weakly.

I could not help rebuking him: "That will teach you to chase sunbirds at 14,000 feet!"

He shook his head slowly and answered in a whisper, but as stubborn as ever: "It was a snipe!"

Today still he firmly believes that the sunbird I saw was quite a different bird from that which he was chasing; and I have since read that in the marshy valleys of Mount Kenya the Ethiopian snipe occurs. After all, he might have been right and I wrong!

Whatever it was, both Giuàn and I were extremely relieved to hear his voice again and we shared the rest of the coffee. We needed it badly.

While Enzo received further attention from Giuàn, I had a look around for a camping place as I realised well enough that for today at least we should not be able to march any further.

Across the valley were two equidistant V-shaped lines of erratic boulders, the apex of the V being the brook. They would have gladdened the heart of any geologist although one needed no further proof of the glacial origin of the high Nanyuki valley, as it was clearly U-shaped; but the lines of boulders were as neatly drawn as though a playful giant had amused himself by arranging stones in ranks like soldiers.

I selected the right side of the valley, which would get the morning sun and soon found an overhanging boulder facing the valley. This would shelter us from the night wind blowing from the glaciers and would get the benefit of the day breeze, coming up from the warm plains. I carried the rucksacks and implements over while Giuàn brought the patient into shelter at a slow walk.

While I pitched the tent with Giuàn he said, *sotto voce*: "Enzo must not be allowed to climb a single foot higher."

"Alright," I answered, but I knew that in order to avoid endangering Enzo's health or even his life, we should now have to give up any hope of establishing a reasonably placed base camp, thus reducing further our slim chances of a successful climb.

So it happened that our tent, fastened between two giant groundsels and sheltered by an erratic boulder, became our base; too low to give us a good start for an ascent of Batian, too far from Lenana, to reach which we should have to walk 180 degrees round the base of Batian itself.

We spent the afternoon reinforcing the sides of the tent with grass sods and stones. Enzo, eager to show that he was still of some use to the party, was allowed by his doctor to cut grass with the panga for the tent floor.

At half-past four we cooked a combined lunch and dinner consisting of porridge, corned-beef, biscuits and tea. We also devoured our second and last tin of jam in order to celebrate Enzo's promotion to "Base Camp Commandant". As disciplined ex-prisoners we felt that we could not live any longer without a Camp Commandant, and as Giuàn and I were going to climb only Enzo was available for this task. His "banner" was my towel, to be hoisted on the rock that sheltered the tent. It would be used for signalling to Giuàn and me when we were on our mountaineering trips, and to serve to us as a guide during our return from these expeditions.

After the meal Enzo was ordered to bed, but Giuàn thought it would be quite safe to leave him and to take a walk in the vicinity of the camp. Walking in rope-soled boots without a load was a sheer delight. We soon reached the end of the erratic boulders and sat down comfortably on one of the last of them.

Before us, in a magnificent semicircle, Mount Kenya had spread out its treasures. Here, above the shining, glittering glaciers, were Point Peter and Dutton Peak. High above all towered the king, Batian, and down on the other side Point John and Midget Peak. We knew the names of none but Batian, but perhaps this fact added to their fascination.

For a long time, we sat and gazed. The shadows thrown by the rocks and by the weird-looking lobelias and giant groundsels grew longer and longer. The fairy architecture of pinnacles, ridges, points, buttresses, jagged peaks and ledges, bejewelled with sprinkled ice, blushed at last with rose while the vast north glaciers froze into shades of violet.

Two insignificant, humble, escaped prisoners of war, numbers 41304 and 762, sat there gazing spellbound at the glowing colours cast by the setting sun on the mount of their dreams, now resplendent as though celebrating the glory of creation.

CHAPTER IV

The Mountain

*In which the party is driven off the north-west ridge
of Batian Peak (17,040 feet.) amidst a blizzard,
but hoists the flag on Point Lenana (16,300 feet.).*

Tuesday, February 2

As Enzo's condition was satisfactory, Giuàn and I set out on a half-day's reconnaissance. We wanted to find out how best to attack Batian, to have a look at Lenana which we had never seen, and incidentally to practise a little rock climbing as a prelude to the more serious attempts we intended to make later.

We left the base camp early, after a good breakfast of Ovaltine mixed with powdered milk, cocoa and sugar. With such an unwonted "foundation" in our stomachs, and above all without rucksacks, we felt as elated and as energetic as though we had been transferred to a smaller planet and were no longer subject to the normal laws of gravity.

The cold was intense and the rocks on the left side of the upper Hausburg Valley, towards which we were making, shimmered with ice.

We crossed the Nanyuki and presently reached the scree below the rocks. The frozen stone ravine offered a compact foothold and the crackling of ice under our nailed soles was music to our ears. Later we were still more delighted to feel "real rock" under our fingers on a "real mountain". At this hour, far to our left under cover of the morning mists which blanketed the Nanyuki plains, our fellow-prisoners were now being paraded in serried ranks for the morning roll-call.

*

Fig. 11. Mount Kenya, seen from Hausburg Valley

One and a half hours after leaving our tent, without having met with the slightest difficulty so far as mountaineering was concerned, we gained the crest of the ridge and were confronted by a magnificent sight.

Hausburg Valley which we had just left lay below us, dotted with giant groundsels which from above resembled broad-headed nails. On the line of erratic boulders we could distinguish my blue-bordered white towel, the proud banner of the Base Camp Commandant. More to the north, an emerald green tarn showed the reflection of a few rocks on one side. Its polished surface was as calm and as unruffled as stained glass.

Beyond the tarn rolling grassland, broken here and there with giant groundsels, descended in a gentle slope to the forest, which looked like a dark green stormy sea. Beyond this again arms of

Fig. 12. "Facing us, rose an amazing mass of rock, completely isolated from the central peaks of Mount Kenya."

forest reached out into the bright yellow plain of Nanyuki, stretching flat and barren to the uttermost limits of vision.

Opposite Hausburg Valley was Mackinder Valley and on the far side of this, and facing us, rose an amazing mass of rock, completely isolated from the central peaks of Mount Kenya. It showed a sheer drop of about a thousand feet on our side and it was crowned by age-worn pinnacles of the strangest shape.

We were immediately struck by the likeness of this peak to the wreck of an ancient vessel. It needed but little imagination to visualise the storm-crushed forecastle and poop, the remnants of protruding ribs, the stumps of masts and bowsprit. Even a porthole was open, in the form of a natural window in the rock wall. In

173

bygone years I had imagined the wreck of the *Flying Dutchman* as just such a weather-beaten and eerie-looking craft.

"Can it be that the *Flying Dutchman*, released from her course of eternal restlessness, has found peace at last petrified on Mount Kenya?" I asked.

"It might well be," said Giuàn. "She has not been seen on the open seas for several centuries."

"One could spin a yarn and add it to the old legend: wouldn't *The Flying Dutchman compelled to seek harbour on Mount Kenya* be a good title for a new version?"

Thus we jested and gazed bewildered. To the very end, seeing this mountain from different angles, we continued to find in it further likeness to an old stranded wreck. We became accustomed to calling it *The Flying Dutchman* as we did not know, of course, that it had been named Sendeyo by Sir Halford Mackinder forty-three years before.

We had seen the top of Sendeyo from Nanyuki and had wondered if it could be Lenana. Now we knew definitely that this was not so as Sendeyo did not, even from this side, resemble Lenana as it appeared in the pencil sketch I carried with me.

Where was Lenana then? In order to find an answer to this question we scrambled along the rocky ridge towards Point Peter.

On the way we sought for and found "training grounds". For this purpose we made detours that were not necessary and chose not the easiest route as ordinary tourists would do, but the most difficult. At length, having reached a spot from which we could look right up Mackinder Valley, we saw a mountain that could have been none other than Lenana.

The sight pleased us. As a "first reserve" it looked imposing: a violet-black rock perched on a bright white ice dome. Very odd looking was a pinnacle near the top resembling a baroque column

174

Fig. 13. "Lenana: a violet-black rock perched on a bright white ice dome."

or a corkscrew or a hundred other things. When referring to it among ourselves we called it "Lenana's handle."

If Lenana seemed rather worryingly far from our base camp, it did at least look as though it would be child's play in comparison with the north face of Batian.

Having satisfied ourselves that we had identified Lenana, we decided that it was time to study the approaches to our main goal, Batian. In order to do this we crossed from the north to the south side of the ridge. In doing so our attention was immediately diverted from the forbidding ice overhangs of the peak to a sight that was the more awe-inspiring for being so unexpected.

What from Nanyuki had appeared to be two glaciers revealed itself as one only, shaped like a horseshoe round a huge rocky outcrop, which reminded me of an eagle as portrayed in heraldry.

175

At the foot of one of the branches of the glacier there were two little tarns, one a delicate azure, the other green-gold, the colours pure as jewels. So unexpected was this sight amid the savage scenery of Batian, that I could not help thinking, it is too beautiful, do I deserve to experience it? and unconsciously my thoughts wandered to the simple character of the Humpback of Breuil who, as Guido Rey relates, having climbed the Matterhorn with the first party from the south, knelt down and thanked God for having created such a marvellous universe.

It did not occur to me to exclaim: "Those two tarns are worth so many days in the cells," because spiritual wealth such as we were storing in our memories could have no price at all. Having enjoyed the wonders of the forest by moonlight, by day and by the fire of our bivouacs, having listened to the music of the heath and having seen the ice-bound northern ramparts of Batian at sunrise and sunset, were we really worthy of this further display of beauty?

For long we stood on our rock and gazed down.

The air was crystal clear, the solemn silence broken only now and then by the distant roar of an ice-avalanche. Our solitude was perfect.

If ever since our escape from barbed wire we had utterly forgotten that there existed in this world hatred, war and captivity, we did so at this moment.

At last we descended to more practical matters. Following with our eyes the course of the rivulet which formed the outlet of the lower tarn we noted with delight that this was the source of the Nanyuki and that we had therefore been right, when as prisoners in Nanyuki Camp – and now we could not help remembering that we had once been prisoners – we had deduced that the river would lead us to the glaciers.

Our problem demanded consideration.

From where we were the north face of Batian looked formidable. We knew that the peak had been climbed, but wondered from which side the ascent had been made. Would it look more feasible from other aspects? Was there any standard route to the summit, and if so where was it? In order to answer these questions we should have to make a detour all round the base of the peak, but we did not know if this could be accomplished in one day and we had promised Enzo to be back soon after noon. Moreover we had very little food left and Enzo's condition would not allow us to move the base camp nearer to the peak even if we had been able to locate a more promising route. We had not the faintest idea, of course, that there was a hut on the far side of Batian, a thousand feet higher than our base camp and at the very start of the standard route. For all these reasons, we resolved to attempt the ascent from the north.

Having reached this decision, it remained to be seen whether a plan could be worked out in detail.

Two ridges buttress the mass of Batian on the north side, running left and right from the appalling Northey Glacier, the north-eastern side of which is very long and unbelievably jagged and the north-western, which is shorter, steeper and smoother on the whole but with a few very doubtful pitches.

We agreed that if there was any possibility of scaling Batian from our side, this could only be done by bestriding, or traversing the north-west ridge. As you will discover in a later chapter, this ridge has been climbed only once, under summer conditions by climbers of worldwide fame, Shipton and Tilman.

This being settled we were faced by a further poser – how best to get on to the north-west ridge which has at its base a rock tower with a roughly conical top, called by Shipton the Petit Gendarme.

*

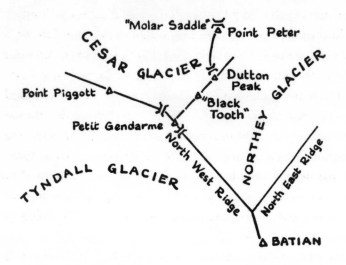

Faced by the same problem, Shipton and Tilman abandoned the idea of an approach from the northern side and decided to make for the gap in the ridge behind the Petit Gendarme, attacking from the south. Their decision proved wise as they were successful. Had we known that these two English aces had declared that any attempt to approach the ridge from the north was hopeless, we should have made other plans; as things were, we proposed to try a route where Shipton and Tilman saw no hope. We decided in the end to traverse Dutton Peak and a black tooth behind it, reaching Petit Gendarme from a gap between "Black Tooth" and Petit Gendarme itself. It looked difficult but not impossible.

To get a closer view, we decided to try out the first stage of the proposed route there and then, a plan that would have the advantage of giving us a practice climb.

We descended from the rocks to a large saddle just north of Point Peter, marked by a rock shaped like a molar tooth. As this saddle has no official name on Dutton's map and as it is mentioned many times in this story I shall call it, as we did, "Molar Saddle".

After eating a piece of chocolate we got round Point Peter on a scree and found an easy couloir, covered with hard snow. After half an hour of gentle climbing we reached a gap some fifty or sixty feet below the summit of Dutton Peak from which we looked down to César Glacier. Had we known that we were so near the top of a named peak, and one not often climbed, we should have attempted to scale it; but as we did not know this and as our attention was wholly absorbed in studying our approach to Petit Gendarme we were quite content to sit in the gap, dangling our feet above César Glacier and eating another piece of chocolate in lieu of lunch.

We guessed that a traverse on the north face of Dutton Peak would bring us to the "Black Tooth" and to the very foot of Petit Gendarme. From thence with our "eyes of faith" as Mummery used to say, we thought we could see a possibility of carrying on, although the difficulties seemed to increase towards the higher rocks.

As it was getting late we left our lofty observatory and scrambled down until we reached the foot of Point Peter. With regret we decided not to make an attempt on it. Enzo would get anxious if we stayed out longer and Guiàn was getting worried about him.

On the scree below the rocks of Point Peter were the last lobelias, mostly dry and dead. We broke and bent some of them to mark the route when we should return to make our actual attempt on Batian.

At 2.00 p.m. we were back at the "Molar" pass whence we slid down a long scree to the upper tarn.

The colours of both tarns had changed as we were now looking at them from a different angle, but the impression of complete peace and beauty was the same as from above.

After having drunk at the cool waters of the upper tarn we walked along its shore towards the lower one.

"Dreamland," murmured Giuàn, struck, as I was, by the sheer perfection of the landscape. Between the tarns and round about the lower one was a veritable flower garden made up of numerous tropical alpine species, many of them in bloom: groundsels with violet-gold inflorescences, giant groundsels, some of them with a crest of young mauve leaves, lobelias shaped like fingers, mosses of all sorts and colours, cushions of ivory-white dwarf helichrysum, scabiosae, anemones and many others which I do not know by name. An occasional blue-grey granite rock or a tuft of the long tussocky grass scattered among what appeared to be well-ordered flowerbeds, added effectively to the harmony of the setting. Between the upper and the lower tarns the newborn Nanyuki would be murmuring, and beneath its crystal clear water one could count the stones on the bottom.

I could not help recalling what I had read about the masterpieces of the wise gardeners of ancient China, said to have been experts at making miniature wonder gardens. Again, a poor modern city dweller, I had been reminded of human craft and artificiality by an example of Nature's own supreme taste as shown in the selection and blending of colour and forms.

This sheer loveliness of plant life had a background, which at first sight contrasted strangely, so cold and harsh did it look, for between reddish rocks on the left and grey-blue walls on the right hung the snout of César Glacier. The savage seracs forming a huge frozen waterfall ended in tongues and curls and embroideries of green shaded ice protruding from the main mass; but on looking again from the fairy garden in the foreground to the ice and rock world behind, I soon found that this apparent discord merged in the placid mirror of the tarns which reflected both glacier and flowers, blending colours, smoothing contrasts as a chord links and welds seemingly contrasting musical notes.

When we arrived back at the camp we found that Enzo had been busy. He had doubled the ropes supporting the tent roof, dug a ditch all round the tent and had made a cup for me of the empty jam tin, as I had mislaid my own mug. He had also carried out several minor works in *his* base camp to show that, though ill, he was in no way a passenger and was still an active member of the party.

The camp looked more comfortable, but unhappily we could do nothing about our greatest problem, that of food. Our rations being almost at an end we divided the last tin but one of corned beef for our dinner, put the last drops of olive oil on it and ate it with a few buttered biscuits. Following the advice of Giuàn we had reserved our butter to be eaten at the higher altitudes. He had been right as now we really craved it more than any other food.

It is true that the quantity we ate left very much to be desired, but we comforted ourselves with the thought that our eyes had feasted on unforgettable scenes to compensate us for what our mouths had lacked. The day was ending in a crescendo of beauty.

Beyond the real mountain of rock and ice appeared a phantom shape, a fairy mountain of those huge rounded heaps which the scientists call "cumuli" but which the Venetian painters of the seventeenth century used to call "heroic clouds". At first they were so dazzling white that the eye could not withstand the glare, but later, as the sun set behind a bank of mist overlying the Laikipia plateau, they slowly changed colour, forming at last a crimson halo round the blood-red crags of Batian, while the rosy glaciers over-hanging the invisible tarns faded slowly in sympathy.

Wednesday, February 3

This day, according to plan, was wholly devoted to rest and to final preparations for our attempt on Batian.

We got up late having slept soundly for twelve hours on our grass palliasse in the narrow tent. The night had been so cold that the water in our bottles was still frozen solid at 9.00 a.m., though the bottles had been well covered and had been placed inside our rucksacks.

This ice was the best answer to a question I had put to myself: was it or was it not foolish to sleep without keeping a watch? As a rule dangerous beasts like lions and leopards do not frequent very high altitudes, but there are exceptions. As keeping watch without a fire was not possible I decided that it would be perfectly safe to trust to luck in so far as mountaineering felines were concerned.

In order to get boiling water for breakfast coffee and for shaving we experimented again and again with dry lobelia and giant groundsel wood, but we could not get it to burn. The reason why we could not is still a mystery to us, as all parties on Mount Kenya whose records I have read managed to get giant groundsel to burn. It might be that local porters are experts at making a fire from anything and every party that climbed before us was served by local porters.

Thus we ate two tiny biscuits with plenty of butter and meat extract, and shaved with cold water. But still we did not give up hope. If giant groundsels and lobelias did not like the idea of being burnt by us we should have to try other fuel, as Enzo reckoned that the alcohol left for the boiler would be just enough for breakfast on "Batian-day". Therefore we burnt dry grass heaped between two boulders under our closed cooking pot. The grass curled, black-ened and smoked furiously without showing a flame, but it did

182

develop heat. After more than an hour the water in the cooking pot started boiling, and for lunch we were able to have good tea with our last tin of corned beef.

Unexpectedly ambitious hopes of being able to cook "game" arose with our discovery of the rats. Actually the discovery had been made by Enzo, but had not been credited by us.

This is what happened: as I was returning from washing and shaving at the ice-fringed brook, I found Enzo busy fastening our rucksacks halfway up the stems of giant groundsels near the tent. I commended him:

"It gives an impression of order and tidiness wholly worthy of a base camp commanded by you."

"There's nothing to laugh at," he answered. "There is a reason apart from order and tidiness and I bet you could not guess what it is."

I tried first "moisture," then "danger of a sudden snowfall, subsequent thaw and deluge". Finally I guessed "animals" scoring from a shot in the dark. "Marmots" was my next guess and at last "rats". Enzo answered with a mysterious "Might be."

"What do you mean by 'might be'? Either they are rats or they are something else, perhaps shrews or ground-squirrels."

"I don't know what they are. They seem to be rats."

"Rats?" I repeated, wondering what rats could live at this altitude. Enzo, misunderstanding my doubts and knowing that as a rule neither I nor Giuàn took his remarks at face value, retorted:

"I don't see why you have to make such a fuss about it. Whatever the animals are, they live under the boulders."

Triumphantly Giuàn intervened: "How did you see them if they live under boulders?"

"When they come out, like they did yesterday when you were both away. They have dark brown fur and a white stripe running from the neck to the base of the tail. The fur is very thick indeed."

"Fur-bearing animals then!" I said, still wondering if it was one of the yarns Enzo sometimes liked to spin, or if I could believe him.

"Exactly. I was wondering how many of them I should want to make a cape for my wife."

Giuàn and I ended the interview with a hearty laugh and decided that Enzo was joking.

But after lunch when we were all three sitting quietly near the tent basking in the weak sun, Enzo sewing the flag, Giuàn fastening a new cord to his ice axe and I oiling my boots, Enzo suddenly pointed to the next boulder. It was a gesture of pride which reminded me of that made by a conjurer when he produces the white rabbit out of his silk hat, points at it and remarks with theatrical modesty: "Voilà!"

There it was, and Enzo who had been proved right smiled in a self-conscious manner. His description proved exact. The animal's tail was rat-like, not furry like a squirrel's. It sat on its hind legs, its forefeet close to its breast, and looked at us in the half-suspicious and half-concerned manner with which an old solicitor's clerk looks over his glasses at an intruder in his office.

It did not stay long and at the first movement it dashed off.

Anyhow rats formed the main topic of our conversation in the afternoon and we left it to Enzo's well-proved ingenuity to discover the proper bait and to make a trap to catch some, not in order to make a cape for Enzo's wife – of which Giuàn's and my wife would have been rightly envious – but merely to provide us with something to eat as we were at the end of our rations. True, neither my companions nor I had any particular craving for rat meat ordinarily, and as a matter of fact we had never tasted it; but we felt at that moment that we could have eaten not only one but several, bones, skin and all.

Our day of rest and preparation passed in a flash. Washing, darning, mending, checking over ropes and crampons, putting spare hob-nails into the soles of our boots which had lost a lot of them owing to the continuous wading, oiling boots and other odds and ends took a lot of time.

Enzo had at last sewn together the three sections of our flag, which we had carried separately. In order to prevent it from being seized in case we were caught during our escape, the flag had been divided between us as follows: Enzo had carried the red section using it as a bag for our biscuits, Giuàn the green sewn into the lining of his cap as a business-like protection against ultraviolet rays, and I had concealed the white with the royal arms inside my shirt.

I wrote on a sheet of drawing paper a message with our names (but without our prisoner of war numbers as this would have been against our rules) and put it into the – alas! – empty brandy bottle and sealed it with candle wax, while Enzo tackled the matter of the flagpole, to be carried inside my rucksack.

The five-foot pole that Enzo had carried fastened to the tent poles or had used as a walking stick was cut in half. On top of the lower half he fixed a mortise made of an empty corned-beef tin, into which the tenon of the upper pole could be slipped when we planted the flag. On the upper part of this pole Enzo sewed the flag and at the very top he fastened four wire rings through each of which we could pass a string to support the whole affair.

It looked business-like and not at all "improvised", and we were proud of it.

Both parts of the flagpole, complete with flag, fitted well into my rucksack leaving only a few inches protruding.

At dinner we tightened our belts, and immediately afterwards we went to sleep while it was still light.

I do not know how I managed to wake at the agreed hour and rouse my companions.

It was 2.00 a.m. when I got out of the tent and the sky was amazingly starry.

Tent and boots were frozen hard and we had to wait a long time before Enzo was able to melt the lump of ice in our cooking pot over the weak flame of the boiler, and to announce "Breakfast's ready!"

It was at length *the* breakfast for *the* day. With slow delight we swallowed the almost solid brew of cocoa, Ovaltine, powdered milk and plenty of sugar, followed by two biscuits for each of us, with butter and meat extract.

Enzo shook hands with us, perhaps slightly moved. We told him not to worry if we did not return at dusk because we should possibly have to bivouac on the mountain.

We anointed our hands and face with the anti-sunburn cream prepared for this purpose by Giuàn, put on our mitts and set off shortly before three o'clock feeling in good form and in high spirits, joyfully aware that the day had in store the climax of our trip, whatever it might be.

The swamps were frozen hard. The ice crackled under the nails of our boots but it held. The giant groundsels seen in the beam of the torchlight had a ghostly appearance.

With slow and steady steps we followed the Nanyuki upstream and passed between the two pitch-black tarns. High rose the overwhelming bulk of Batian, black and threatening, the cauldron of the north glaciers only slightly less dark in colour.

On the upper shore of the top tarn we rested. The water was so still that we could see the stars of the zenith reflected motionless in it. We lay down and solemnly, as if performing a strange ritual, we drank in small, slow draughts the ice-cold, black and starry water.

It was ten past four by the time we started the wearisome ascent of the scree, which the day before we had descended in one cheerful slide. Steadily our nailed boots rasped the loose stones with a grinding noise and the cone of light from our torch slowly gained height.

The "Molar" was at first silhouetted against the stars as if it were a feature of a far horizon, but gradually its size increased until it stood out as a bulwark against the sky, which still bore no sign of the dawn.

As soon as we reached the saddle we were met by an icy gale. The *Flying Dutchman* reared its storm-battered breakwater into the night. It appeared even more fantastical than when seen in the light of day, separated from us not by a valley but by centuries. Two bright stars seemed to us to be riding lights on her invisible masts, eternal lights for her motionless voyage through time.

Although it was only twenty minutes to six, we were quite ready to rest and nibble a biscuit, but the wind blew so cold that our fingers became stiff as soon as they were out of the mitts. Accordingly we went on, ascending the scree east of Point Peter, where the broken lobelias showed us the way.

As we reached the rocks that marked the beginning of the actual climb, the dawn broke rapidly beyond the jagged outline of the north-east ridge. We ate a tiny biscuit each and as soon as it was light enough we started.

We progressed rapidly, aiming at the gap below Dutton Peak, which we had reached in our reconnaissance two days before.

The morning was fine. Not a single cloud appeared to mar the sky, which was of that deep blue-violet shade it assumes only when it is seen from over 16,000 feet. It occurred to me that if I looked westwards over the Aberdares from the edge of the ridge dropping down to César Glacier, at this hour and in this glorious weather I might be able to recognise Lake Baringo or even Mount Elgon.

Giuàn agreed to my proposal and we moved off our main route on the crest of the ridge between Point Peter and Dutton Peak. We saw neither the lake nor Mount Elgon owing to a thick bank of mist covering everything below the 8,000-foot level, but our efforts were rewarded by a view which I shall always remember as one of the most amazing of the whole trip.

On the undulating silvery grey sea of mist was cast the dome-shaped shadow of Mount Kenya, surmounted by the tooth-shaped form of Batian, all in a dull violet-brown hue. The peculiarity of this natural shadow-play was that from the very summit of Batian's image there rose a second cone of shade pointing to the west, together with an exactly similar, complementary cone of light pointing to the east. It was a phenomenon of reflection I am still not able to explain.

We stared, forgetting for a moment that we were due to climb Batian. It was as though a giant with magic scissors had cut a wedge from the shade of the mountain and, pivoting this on its apex, had turned it 180 degrees filling the empty space with silvery wool.

We turned, and after following the crest of the ridge for a while, reached the gap below Dutton Peak where we immediately roped on.

A mountaineer when writing his memoirs usually refers to the rope, to which he often owes his life, as "trusty". I fear that I must deny our rope the customary adjective. From the very beginning it looked so untrustworthy that we thought it better to link ourselves together with a double length. We hoped that two "untrustworthys" added together would make, against all rules of arithmetic, one "trusty". I cannot blame our poor sisal ropes for being unreliable, because it was our fault for bringing them. They had been manufactured for the purpose of fastening bedding nets to bunks and were satisfactory when used thus.

Guiàn led, and by 8.00 a.m. we were climbing steadily.

It was great fun traversing the north face of Dutton Peak more or less on the contour with the white, cracked surface of César Glacier at our feet far below. At last, after months of preparation, we were climbing Batian, the goal of our dreams. It was almost too good to be true.

The rock, although exposed, was sound, and the holds even when small were safe. The rocks of Batian (nepheline syenite, as discovered by Gregory) seemed to offer the same degree of reliability as the granite of the Mont Blanc Group and Giuàn, whose last climb in the Alps had been a severe ascent of the Grandes Jorasses, was delighted to find many similarities so far as the rock was concerned.

On our route across the face we were forced to cross a few couloirs filled with very hard ice. There our camp-made ice axes proved their worth gloriously.

We left the contour so as to reach a small, lower terrace offering a foothold for both of us. Here I left the first of our red-painted paper arrows, brought to show us the way back in case we were surprised by mists.

So far everything had gone well. We both felt in good fettle and in high spirits, and only the sisal ropes worried us. They seemed to have been made deliberately in such a manner that they clung to every minute irregularity of the rocks, owing to their coarse, hairy texture. They continually got entangled and alternately Giuàn and I, according to who was managing the belay at the moment, cursed them soundly.

From the terrace we had to regain our height, and it was only possible to do this by scaling an oblique crack leading to a ledge some thirty feet above. Giuàn managed it in good style with a "pressure grips" technique and soon shouted that on the ledge he had found a good belay and that I could follow him.

I started, but halfway up the crack my arm muscles weakened and I felt that I would have to yield. As I expected my left hand gave way and for a moment I dangled above César Glacier, supported only by the grip of my right hand on a tiny hold. As I felt I could stand the strain no longer, I shouted to Giuàn: "Give me rope," and let myself glide – or better fall – towards the terrace, which was some twelve feet below me and slightly to my left. I managed to push myself – I had almost written "my body", but at this stage of my story it would have had too gruesome an implication – towards the left and I actually landed on the terrace.

The anti-climax of the incident came soon. My knees started trembling pitifully and I had to sit down.

Giuàn had no clear idea as to what had happened, because as he was facing the rock, he had not seen me. Apart from this, the rope had become entangled for the hundredth time on some small projection on the rocks.

"Have you got enough rope?" he asked from above. "Are you coming?"

"Coming," I answered, partly because I had no breath left to give him a longer explanation, which would have been unavoidable had I said "No" or "Not yet"; and partly, I have to confess, because I felt ashamed. Why this was so I do not know. Who can fathom completely his own feelings? There was, I imagine, some "loss of face" for having failed in a pitch which my companion had overcome brilliantly, if not easily; but there was also, I know, more than a prick of conscience for having dared to attempt more than my training should have allowed me to undertake. A good mountaineer may take justifiable risks, but is never foolhardy.

Anyhow, I started again breathing deeply and regularly and summoning all my energy.

"Pull the rope," I said to Giuàn.

While resting on the terrace I had noticed high above the left (upper) lip of the crack a little fingerhold. Thanks to my height – blessed again be my parents! – I managed to catch hold of it with my left hand, thus avoiding the necessity of continuing to work by pressure in the crack. In a few minutes I was sitting on the ledge near Giuàn.

"You're looking rather pale," said my friend and doctor, and I explained what had happened.

After a good rest we went on.

Following the contour we reached a black rock-rib, which we had noticed on our reconnaissance climb. It would lead us to the "Black Tooth" between Dutton Peak and Petit Gendarme. Behind the rib there was a narrow gully, which we ascended vertically. A few pitches were covered in ice but offered no other difficulty. I myself was not in the same mood as I had been when we set out. Something had gone wrong with my conscience and I was mentally no longer at ease. I felt as though I had wronged someone and was guilty of a crime.

At ten o'clock we were on the ridge dividing Northey from the César-Josef Glaciers and very soon afterwards we reached the rocks on the ridge we had called among ourselves "Black Tooth". We found no cairn and wondered if by chance we were the first to have reached this sequestered and unimportant feature of Mount Kenya's north face. Now I think that it must have been climbed by other people during reconnaissances on this side of the peak.

We sat there for a quarter of an hour studying the next move like chess players, not knowing that though they were far more skilful at the game, Shipton and Tilman had classed as "hopeless" every attempt on the summit from this point even during "summer conditions" on the rocks.

We were mesmerised by the formidable, glistening white ice cliffs of Northey Glacier. No, definitely here was no bread for our teeth. It looked as if they could be overcome only with first-class crampons, ice axes, pitons and ropes, after first-class training and first-class food; a mere dream for escaped prisoners!

We studied again the north-west ridge itself, the route we had planned originally. It was an awe-inspiring view and technically very difficult, sprinkled with ice and snow as it was, under the existing winter conditions. The first five hundred feet or so from the gap behind Petit Gendarme did not seem too bad, but higher up it looked rather grim although we were too far below to be able to see details clearly even with the binoculars. Still, whatever route we decided to try, we had to reach the gap behind Petit Gendarme.

To do so we first descended from our observatory in the direction of Northey Glacier and, without meeting any difficulty, we reached by a detour the gap between "Black Tooth" and Petit Gendarme. Had we had better and longer ropes, it would have been quicker to have made a rappel straight down from "Black Tooth."

At 11.00 a.m. we were at last attacking the rocks at the foot of Petit Gendarme; in other words the very body of Batian.

The first rope lengths were rather easy, although the rocks were rotten and offered no sound belay. Soon we met much damp snow, covered now and then with a thin, frozen crust. At every belay I left an arrow.

First we kept trying to swing to the left in the direction of the gap, our immediate aim, but the rocks became smoother and soon they offered no holds at all. Thus we climbed vertically, hoping to find higher up a traverse to the left.

More and more snow plastered the slabs. Had it been frozen to any depth it would have offered us in exchange for the relatively light labour of step-cutting a good and quick way up; but it was not and Giuàn had to clean it off and as I was as a rule directly below him little snow avalanches hit me regularly. If I looked up to give him another foot of rope from my belay the snow would fall on my face, and if I bent my head it landed on my neck and went under my clothes and down my spine. I comforted myself by trying to imagine that it was an agreeable change from our camp showers, but I could not find it agreeable for all that.

A sad disappointment was the discovery that the rocks under the snow plaster appeared to be smooth slabs as devoid of holds as those we had already decided not to try towards the gap. Presently I could give no more belay to Giuàn. We were already risking too much, or as the Italian proverb has it "pulling the Devil by his tail". Had Giuàn fallen he would have dragged me with him and viceversa.

Nevertheless, we continued to advance by inches, hoping to strike a possible line of traverse towards the gap or an ascent line towards the arète between the gap and the top of Petit Gendarme. It was a distinctly tough struggle. In some places, I was able to leave an arrow, fixing it with a piece of crusty snow. After all, we had to consider our return journey.

I wondered if we had reached 16,000 feet, which would have been an achievement in itself for any Alpine climber, as the highest peak of the Alps, Mont Blanc itself, is only 16,020 feet.

Giuàn was faced with a peculiarly awkward pitch and the minutes dragged on into a quarter of an hour without any appreciable gain. My fingers were already numbed with cold. I managed to move the ropes, which were our very theoretical safeguard, only with great difficulty.

At 12.30 p.m., to my horror, I noticed rags of mists coming from the south. In no time they enveloped the upper part of north-west ridge, while other tongues, blown by an increasingly strong wind, passed through the gap we had so far failed to reach and condensed on our side of the mountain. Soon they enveloped Northey and César Glaciers, Dutton Peak, "Black Tooth", everything.

The temperature dropped. An icy storm brought more and more misty clouds. I started shivering. Giuàn's ghostly grey figure alternately disappeared and reappeared on the rocks above my head.

He seemed unable to advance. He too was probably considering the situation from this new point of view.

"Hello!" I shouted to him.

"Hello!" came his answer, half drowned by the whistling of the wind.

"How are you going on?"

"Not at all."

I didn't answer.

"I see no way," he carried on after a while, "of going an inch further, nor perhaps of getting back." I still do not know – and neither does he – how he had managed to climb as far as he had.

I cannot remember the exact words we shouted to each other in the roar of the storm, but it was a very short conversation that, as a novelist would say, "held life and death in the balance".

We decided to retreat, if possible.

While Giuàn, bit by bit, made his sorrowful and awkward way down, the temperature seemed to me to rise again, and it started snowing and hailing together. Not only would any attempt to climb further have been unpardonable lunacy, but the prospects of a safe retreat began to appear rather problematic.

For the following forty minutes – and it took Giuàn that long to reach the spot where I still clung to the rock – the storm was dead against us. Slowly my numbed fingers, cut and bruised during the past week by bamboo and rock, retrieved the rope that separated me from my friend. Fortunately the wind was so strong that the falling snow did not immediately cover the rocks. Had it done so, the red arrows I had left would have been hidden and we should have been hopelessly lost.

When Giuàn joined me at last on my precarious perch his eyebrows, moustaches and blanket suit were frozen with ice and his lips were almost white. According to my reading, people in similar circumstances shake hands. We had neither the inclination nor the time to do so at that moment.

The wind dropped a little but the snow fell more steadily and more thickly. Snowflakes whirled round us, snow heaped on every irregularity of the rocks and plastered the wool of our caps, jackets and trousers with an icy crust.

Thus we started the descent, doubly difficult as we were retracing our steps not only because of the blizzard but also owing to the fact that we had been "technically" defeated by the rocks.

Clinging to my small holds, I peered down into the fury of the elements, trying to locate a red arrow in all this white hell. At last I saw one, a welcome sign of life in this dead world. Slowly and with great effort we reached it. "Shall we have the strength to attempt Lenana tomorrow in order to hoist our flag there at last?" I asked myself. "Shall we be able to descend from Batian today?" was the question I was afraid to ask myself.

Our fingers were frozen from continuously cleaning the snow from our holds. The sisal ropes were as hard as iron rods and their icy fibres stung our hands like needles.

The few rope-lengths down the slabs of Petit Gendarme amidst the whirling blizzard seemed miles long, and even now as I am writing this I can scarcely believe that all these things happened to me. Sometimes I am inclined to think that I only dreamt it.

When at last we reached the gap between Petit Gendarme and "Black Tooth" we felt exhausted in every muscle and nerve. We sat down awhile, relaxing and compelling ourselves to swallow a piece of toffee and the handful of sultanas which my mother had sent me in her Christmas parcel and which I had kept for "Batian-day". Only I know how often I had resisted the temptation to eat them before this.

At 2.50 p.m. we unroped and started crossing the easy rocks round "Black Tooth". Fortunately we managed to find the red arrow marking the point where we should start the descent of Dutton Peak north face. We roped on again and started our traverse back. It was 3.30 p.m. Only three and a half hours of daylight remained.

Descending the more difficult rocks – and descending in mountaineering is as a rule more difficult than climbing – we realised at every step how weary we were. Every hold had first to be cleared of snow with hand or foot and tested thoroughly for its stability. Several times we had to cut ice off the rocks or to cut steps in an ice couloir.

It had almost stopped snowing but the mists were so thick that we could see no further than twenty or thirty feet ahead. The whole face of the mountain which we had crossed the morning before seemed totally new to us.

When I was lucky enough to find an arrow we made for it and remained there until I had discovered the next one. It was a nerve-racking job. Frequently having mistaken some reddish-looking spot on the rocks for an arrow, we went astray and had to retrace our steps. I cannot remember how many times I concluded that we were irretrievably lost on that hostile, snow-covered face. I remember only that when at last I saw the terrace where I had made the "landing" in the morning, the episode seemed to me to have happened weeks, not hours before.

We roped down to the terrace on a rappel, avoiding the ominous crack, and there we rested a little.

Looking at the crack Giuàn remarked: "I can't understand how I managed it this morning."

"You're telling me!" I answered.

The mists cleared.

The sight of the gap below Dutton Peak was as welcome to us as is the flash of a lighthouse to the crew of a boat endangered in stormy waters. Even so we were more than an hour in reaching it.

Once there we un-roped. We had got out of a tight corner.

Before leaving the scene of our unsuccessful struggle for good, we glanced back. Batian's north-west ridge looked grand, sprinkled with ice and partially enveloped in clouds. Perhaps it looked even more superb for being inviolate.

We consoled ourselves by thinking that at least we *had* stretched out our hands towards that magnificent goal, and though we deeply regretted having been defeated, we felt sure that in our condition we could not have done more.

In one of those abrupt changes of weather, which occur so often on high mountains, the mists were now lifting *en masse* towards the setting sun. César and Joseph Glaciers glistened at our feet, all their crevasses covered by new snow.

Point Peter, also newly whitened by snow, scintillated in the flashes of sunlight like a giant sugar loaf. It would prove a good climb, I thought, for those who love mountains are incurable dreamers – even before they have recovered from one defeat they begin unconsciously to plan a new attempt. I chased away such

197

thoughts. Every crumb of our energy – and it seemed that only very little was left – must be stored for Lenana.

I wondered then, perhaps for the first time that day, how Enzo had fared; whether it had snowed at the base camp too and whether he had been worried at seeing the fury of the blizzard on the peak.

Making a bundle of our frozen ropes we started to descend the easy rocks. We had neither the time nor the energy to roll them up in an efficient manner. We slid and jumped downhill until we reached the more or less level going of the scree where the last lobelias grew. As soon as the last of the rocks lay behind us we felt ready to collapse.

So long as we continued climbing on all fours, our muscles and nerves had carried out their functions almost automatically; but we had been engaged in actual rock-climbing for almost twelve hours, not under the easiest conditions, and now we felt the anticlimax and exhaustion was near.

We ate a bit of toffee but I could hardly swallow mine. I craved for liquid food like soup or milk.

While resting, we discussed my proposal for bivouacking near the "Molar" and attempting Lenana on the morrow, as I assumed that we should never be able to make the long march thither from our distant and low base camp. Giuàn turned down this foolhardy idea on the grounds that after the day's strain we should literally freeze at night and that we must look after Enzo. I had to give in, but my hope of climbing Lenana was vanishing.

However, the next forty minutes' march around the base of Point Peter to the "Molar Saddle" showed me how right Guiàn had been to turn down my proposal. Every step was sheer misery. My ears were humming and a nervous hiccup shook me at every few steps. Giuàn was not much better. Feeling his pulse he said that he had a bit of temperature.

In a hollow of the "Molar" I hid the ropes and crampons. If we were to use them for Lenana we should pass here and pick them up. Then we tried to slide down the scree towards the tarns, but our lassitude did not allow us to keep our balance. It was getting dark and late.

Hoping to find a shorter way from the scree directly to the lower tarn, I got into a ravine of big rocks where we had to climb on all-fours once again. Giuàn who from the beginning had been against trying to take this short cut grumbled angrily behind me at this extra exercise in semi-darkness, but we were too weak to argue.

It was almost completely dark when at last we reached, after our useless detour, not the lower but the upper tarn.

A few clouds scurried westwards and the last shimmer of daylight cast a gruesome, dim light over the tarn, revealing a broad ice belt round its margin and a few large ice plates floating in the centre, reminding me of the description of some horrid skin disease. Among the flower gardens, which erstwhile had fascinated us with their true expression of beauty, we stumbled sullen and worn out, without enthusiasm, without strength. In the fading light, the giant groundsels seemed monsters trying to grasp us with their tentacles.

I shivered and hiccupped. Before me I saw non-existent dancing lights.

Now and then Giuàn behind me murmured: "Oh dear!" I wondered again how we should be able to make a fresh start for Lenana tomorrow. It seemed impossible. We must have a whole day of rest. Our strength could not be restored with food, for almost none was left.

As we descended, following the outlet of the lower tarn, the Nanyuki, the mists closed in more and more. It was already inky dark, but by the light of our torch I could see the rags of mist performing their *danse macabre*. Soon the fog became thicker and thicker and the mist in front of my torch was a whitish wall. We could not see more than a yard or two. It was frightfully cold. Every leaf of groundsel, every grass culm, every stone was dripping moisture.

"How long have we to go before reaching the tent?" asked Giuàn.

"Not much longer," I answered, adding to myself: "If we ever find it at all."

Presently I heard a strange sound, like the chiming of bells. Yes, I positively could hear bells.

"Giuàn!"

A grumble answered me.

"Do you hear?"

"Hear what?"

"Bells."

"Bells?"

"Bells."

"You are mad."

Was I going mad? And yet I had heard them distinctly, like the cowbells of the herds in the open Alps in summer, or the bells of the little churches with steeply roofed towers emerging from clusters of houses in the highest villages of the valleys. The chiming seemed to invite me to sit and rest but I rebelled against its soft suggestions. Stopping to rest would have meant perhaps . . . well, after all I think now that it was only the deep-rooted instinct of self-preservation that dragged us along this night.

Later a thought flashed through my half-numbed brain: could we by any chance have passed the erratic boulders where our tent was?

A glance at my watch showed me that we could not have done

so, but in order not to lose the way we kept closer to the brook, and where it passed through swamps we walked right in the water, wherever it seemed to be running fastest.

We were cold, exhausted and wet, and it was still not the end of our day. Lucky are mountaineers who, after an unsuccessful climb in the Alps, can at least find a hut in which to dry their clothing and a fire at which to warm themselves.

Our feet splashed in the water of the brook or squelched in the marshy grass. We fell and rose again. Luckily the torch never failed. How we managed to carry on, I scarcely remember. All I know is that I must have been delirious as I "saw" and "heard" people. I knew exactly who they were: characters from the last books I had read before escaping. There was Thomas Buddenbrook of Thomas Mann's novel, his pale face with its small pointed beard and a small Russian cigarette between his lips; and there were two characters from Charles Morgan, Piers Lord Sparkenbroke after an attack of angina pectoris, just back from the threshold of his Platonic world, and Mary; though characters of different authors, they talked together of distant and supreme topics, of Death and Love and Time.

There at last was the row of erratic boulders. We called Enzo. We screamed with all the power of our lungs. No answer came.

It occurred to me that there were two rows of boulders and that the tent was behind a rock in the second row. We carried on.

Things danced before my eyes. Now and then Giuàn sobbed. Every step was an exertion which it seemed impossible to repeat. We marched and marched and the second line of boulders did not appear.

My heart was sinking into my boots; I realised that the row we had seen was the *second* row, and that we had passed the first un-noticed, owing to the fog.

I turned back. Giuàn followed automatically, without even asking why I was retracing my steps.

Those last minutes were the worst. I only remember that it was long, almost unbearably long before I reached the boulders again.

"Were they the first or the second line?"

I did not know but I began to realise how a man goes mad.

"Enzo," we screamed again.

No answer came.

Dripping groundsels stood around us. None of the boulders had a familiar shape. Which row was it? And where was the other one? On the left or on the right?

I started following the row, casting at every boulder a beam of light and looking for footprints. Everything seemed strange and new.

Then I saw – yes, I saw, it was not a mirage – the tent. It was almost invisible, low and small, seemingly crouched under the big boulder; and yet for us it meant everything.

"Enzo!" we shouted with renewed energy.

There was a grumbling answer from inside the long low bag which started tossing and at last ejected a crawling Thing wrapped in a blanket: Enzo. He was perfectly right in having gone to sleep as we had told him that we were probably going to bivouac on the mountain.

"Is there a drop of alcohol left for making tea?"

"Only enough to boil one pot of water."

"Please make tea."

He lit the boiler while Giuàn staggered towards the tent, crawled in on all-fours, turned over and fell asleep.

I tried to take off my puttees, sodden with water inside and covered with a crust of frozen mud outside. Puttees, hands, legs, all together trembled and shook. It was the last hard job of the day.

"What time is it?" asked Enzo.

"Ten to nine," I answered. We had been out for almost eighteen hours.

Enzo did not question me any more.

He had seen the flagpoles still protruding from my rucksack. He knew we were beaten. He knew that in our condition we could not attempt Lenana on the morrow. He saw clearly that his agony would continue for more than another forty-eight hours. He had not eaten a bite the whole day. He had been mountain-sick and terribly hungry. He knew that after Lenana we should have to march back practically without food. His condition could not improve and he had only to wait, and to wait is one of the most horrible things on earth, as every prisoner knows; but he did not grumble.

I had not known him before our escape. On our trip I had found him funny, crazy in a way, quick-tempered, full of the spirit of adventure. I had found him amusing. Now I appreciated him fully. He was worth his salt.

Friday, February 5

By silent agreement the day was devoted to rest.

Our boots were so soaked that we could not put them on and our clothes were still damp, though we had not taken them off during the night. We felt exhausted and frightfully hungry.

When I washed and shaved at the ice-fringed brook, I saw in the mirror a strange worn-out face that almost frightened me. If we were attacked by buffaloes, I thought, we should not even be able to climb the boulders as we had planned.

After having had the last of our porridge and two biscuits each (size 1 in. x 2 in.) with butter and meat extract, the whole ration allotted for the day, we took careful stock of the remaining food: three little bags of salt, coffee and tea; the bottom of the bag (a part of a pyjama-leg sewed at one end) of our "climbing food": consisting of a few pieces of chocolate, toffee and a dozen sultanas; four teaspoons of sugar; some four ounces of barley sugar; half a pound of rice; ten biscuits; a heaped knife-top of meat extract; some five or six ounces of butter.

On paper it looks plenty, but we could have devoured the whole lot in one meal. Instead, it had to last us for at least four days.

At 10.00 a.m. I made a sketch of the base camp with Batian in the background. While I was drawing a new storm started raging on the peak. Enzo who had seen "our" blizzard the day before remarked that that had been more severe; but whether this was so, or whether he said it to flatter us, I do not know.

Before dark we were already lying in the tent, waiting for sleep to put an end to hunger and cold.

Saturday, February 6

It was 1.00 a.m. when we got up after only a few hours of sleep. On the last flickering flame of the boiler Enzo melted the lump of ice that had formed in the cooking pot. When the water was getting warm the flame died out. The alcohol was finished.

In the warm water Enzo washed the inner side of the bags which had contained Ovaltine, powdered milk and cocoa, added the four tea-spoons of sugar, a few leaves of tea and served almost cold.

It proved a delightful mixture. In addition we had one biscuit each and the last of the meat extract.

At 1.50 a.m. Giuàn and I started. The torch cast a dim failing light, perfect symbol of the strength of our party.

The night seemed to me colder than the one preceding our attempt on Batian, and if the same rules as regards weather were applicable to Kenya as in the Alps, this presaged a fine day.

Though we had started one and a quarter hours earlier than on "Batian day", we only reached the lower tarn at 3.00 a.m. We lost our way several times among the boulders, and after having made a longer detour between the two tarns owing to the weak light shed by our torch, we arrived at the upper tarn only forty minutes earlier than on the previous day.

We were amazed when we saw the whole surface of the tarn covered with ice. In the light of the stars it was a wonderful sight. More wonderful, although not entirely necessary as we were not at all thirsty, was the new experience that followed. With the point of our ice axes we opened a hole in the ice and, lying on the smooth surface, we sucked a drink of water through the hole.

The ascent of the steep slope below "Molar Saddle" was particularly hard. To avoid repeating the error made as we came down from Batian when we found ourselves in a ravine on the left side of the valley, I erred in the opposite direction, as happens not only while mountaineering. We struck so far to the right that we finished on the front moraine of Joseph Glacier.

As soon as we became aware of my new mistake, we climbed down a steep gorge and up the far side to the scree. This new waste of time upset us thoroughly. We wanted to reach the top of Lenana at 10.00 a.m., as on the day before the storm on the peaks had started at this hour and we feared that it might repeat itself.

Scarcely had we started up the scree when the torch decided to call it a day and the fading light died out completely. In pitch-black darkness we scrambled on, often sliding down several yards in the attempt to make one step up.

It was a long tiring job, and we were very relieved to reach the "Molar" at last. From the cache I produced the crampons and ropes and slowly we started descending the side of Mackinder Valley. The stars shone brightly, giving us some light, but as neither of us had been here before we had to conduct this night march on *terra incognita* with care.

There was a nip in the air that pierced the very bones. We were over 15,000 feet up and it was the hour before dawn, the coldest of the night.

The sky was clear; the Southern Cross hung glorious over Point Piggott and Magellan's Cloud was setting on the western horizon, but not even from this altitude could we see the Polar Star.

We reached two little pools on the moraine of Northey Glacier. Beyond them, the ground proved rocky and we thought it better to sit down and to await daylight.

By and by the gloomy forecastle of the *Flying Dutchman* grew paler and paler and round the pools we could distinguish the lobelias, looking in the first dim light of day like funerary torches or stones in an Arab cemetery.

At last the sky between Sendeyo and Lenana blushed rosy. There was no breath of wind. An abysmal silence reigned.

Always, and more especially on mountains, have I watched daybreak with deep awe. It is an age-old miracle which repeats itself again and again, every day the same and every day different. It is the hour of Genesis.

Then, on the high bowsprit of the *Flying Dutchman* there rose a flag the colour of flames, while her petrified bulwarks showed faintly rose. A breeze passed over the rocks and rippled the surface of the pools slightly.

It was day and we could start marching again.

The morning was glorious and as we walked straight towards

sthe rising sun, the whole of Mackinder Valley was bathed in golden light.

The curled pinnacle near the summit of Lenana twinkling on the horizon above the violet-shaded Gregory glacier looked cheerful and inviting.

We passed close to the foot of the formidable north-east ridge, making our way between boulders of all sizes and shapes. I particularly remember one of them of the exact size and shape of a grand piano.

On our left, the valley grew narrower and at its head we saw the unbroken blue-green mirror of a tarn. The brook formed by its outlet roared down the valley, recalling to my memory the noises, as of another world, made by trains that run through some Alpine valleys.

Frequently we looked at the western face of Sendeyo (our *Flying Dutchman)* not yet touched by the sun and appearing gloomy and terrible, and wondered if ever a bold climber had scaled those fascinating rocks from this side.

We did our best to keep along one contour at the base of the north-eastern face of Batian, but soon we realised that we should have to lose some height as one of the pillars supporting the gigantic walls had its base below our altitude. While descending slightly we could not help being attracted by the features of this north-east wall. It was still virgin ground as no party had managed to reach Batian's summit from this side. Only on July 31, 1944 did Arthur H. Firmin, Nairobi, and Peter Hicks, Eldoret, in a brilliant climb, make the first ascent of the north-east face.

Dutton compared this sight to gigantic organ pipes. I, not having read Dutton's book at this time, recalled a forlorn valley-top under the sheer 14,000-foot drop of the west face of Jof Fuart in the western Julian Alps, where from time immemorial the herdsmen had called a place like this *lis altaris*: "the altars." Not by mere chance is the mountain climber induced to think of organ pipes or of altars as he looks up those towering rocks; it is a religious feeling which fills his heart.

As we reached the edge of the buttress that had forced us to lose height, we found ourselves facing another little marvel, recalling homely mountain customs. At almost a man's height the rock showed a niche, rounded as though carved by man's tools. At the foot of the niche and round it, the rock was covered by heli-chrysums clinging in a compact cushion and enjoying the sun. One could hardly believe that the flowers had grown there spontaneously; they seemed to have been put there, in homage to an invisible Madonna in a wayside shrine, by some wanderer who saw in the majesty of the mountain a sign of the Creator's might.

Gaining height again, we set foot on the moraine of a small glacier bearing the name of the discoverer of Mount Kenya, Krapf. Later we crossed the scree that comes down from Point Thomson and soon found a large, almost horizontal ledge of rocks, partially split by ravines and resembling an ancient road. It led straight to a flat saddle, which I think is Flake Col, although on Dutton's map it bears no name at all.

We did not make for the col but scrambled up easy, partially ice-covered rocks, aiming toward the ridge of Lenana itself. Only our desire to be on the summit of Lenana by ten o'clock lent us speed. We felt very weak and every step was a real effort.

At 8.00 a.m., six hours after leaving the base camp, we were on the top of the ridge. We sat down, basking in the sun and finishing the contents of our "climbing bag", crumbs of chocolate, toffee and sultanas.

We were generously compensated for the lack of food by the magnificent view. At our feet lay Nithy Valley between two gentle slopes dotted with rocks and groundsels and showing several shimmering pools.

Further down we noticed the Hall tarns glittering with water and the clear-cut drop above the dark green Lake Michaelson; further on a seemingly boiling sea of clouds cloaked the plains, but two dark ridges protruded looking like whales among the waves. I believe they were Mount Ithungani and Mount Fangani. Almost at the uttermost limit of vision on the north-eastern horizon rose a black table-topped mountain such as may be seen commonly in Ethiopia. We wondered if it was Marsabit, the paradise of big-game hunters.

The eastern face of Batian presented a totally different but an equally beautiful sight. It was an unbelievably bright yellow ochre in colour. Any painter portraying it would be blamed for exaggeration, but perhaps no painter in the world could reproduce *this* yellow.

After a short pause for resting and sketching, we followed the crest towards the summit. The rock has a reddish colour totally different from Batian, and its "behaviour" in so far as this affects the climber is quite different as well. On Batian's north side we had found on the whole solid, reliable rock, sometimes even too smooth. Lenana had craggy rotten rock. As soon as the climber grasps it, whole vertical slabs tend to break away with a slight pull.

Since reading Gregory's *The Great Rift Valley and Geology of East Africa* I have learnt that the differing "behaviour" of the rocks on the two peaks corresponds to a different geological origin. Batian, like Nelion, Piggott, Dutton and Peter is derived from the plug of rocks of plutonic origin (nepheline syenite), which choked the crater of the decaying volcano. Lenana, like Sendeyo (as noticed so far as I know for the first time by E. E. Shipton) is of volcanic origin and its rock is a type of lava, discovered by Gregory himself and by him named kenyte.

Once we had reached Lenana's "handle" we tried to circumvent it from the glacier side, but we were so weary that we found the rocks too difficult and had to make a little detour to the east. Here we should have found, according to Dutton's map, Kolbe Glacier; but owing to the general retreat of all glaciers on Kenya, as well as on Kilimanjaro and Ruwenzori, we did not see even a remnant of it.

By this route we reached the shoulder above the "handle".

Giuàn showed me some stones he had collected. They bore strange oblong crystal plates ("rhomb-porphids") looking like stamps. While he was trying to increase his new stamp collection he noticed a pair of sunglasses with the once white glare refractor yellowish and weather-stained. The owner of these glasses was not popular with us. Instead of blessing him for losing something which might have been of use to us – as a rule everything is of some use to a P.O.W. and the exceptions to this rule have still to be found – we blamed him for having lost only his glasses. Could he not have mislaid, for instance, a tin of sardines or some meat or cheese? We should have devoured it on the spot, as in the "refrigerator" at 16,000 feet it would have kept for several years.

After advancing a few yards along the broad shoulder we saw the cairn marking the top not far from us.

I waited a while for Giuàn who was still busy collecting "stamps" – or hoping that the owner of the glasses or someone else might have dropped something edible – and together, filled by an odd feeling almost of solemnity, we reached the point whence one could ascend no further.

We shed our rucksacks and ice axes and sat down, looking around. It was 10.05 a.m.

A great peace hung over the broad expanse. Under the dark velvety sky the wonderful scenery of the country at our feet had a strange radiance.

This was the climax of eight months' preparation and of two weeks of toil. It was worth both.

If a touch of bitterness marred our bliss it was the thought that we stood on Lenana and not on Batian. And there he towered, separated from us by a broad ice saddle, above the pedestal of his yellow buttresses. The climb from this side certainly would not be the same as our vain attempt.

Roughly three hundred feet below the peak of Lenana and to the south, we noticed an iron hut, a sure indication that this was on the standard route used by those who wished to climb Batian. It stood near a frozen pond.

The actual climb from the south-east seemed far shorter than that on the north side, as the beginning of the vertical ascent was there at a lower level than it was on the south-east.

"The standard route is probably a difficult climb," we remarked studying the face, "but at least the climber who tries it has probably been assisted by porters, has eaten enough and has slept in the hut, some two thousand higher than our base camp. He has usually read accounts of previous climbs even if he is not led by an experienced guide. When he is on the rocks he is reassured by the knowledge that others have already managed it, men maybe with greater technical skill and knowledge, but always men of flesh and blood like himself."

Yes, we were delighted to be on Lenana, but at the same time sorry not to be on Batian.

After resting a while, we scrambled around the rocks trying to find at least a remnant of the cross, gift of the Pope, placed on Lenana on January 30, 1934 by the Fathers of the Consolata Mission of Nyeri, as we had read in P. Cagnolo's book. We found none and were at a loss to explain how a big cross, a photograph of which we had seen in the book, could have disappeared in ten years. We did

*Fig. 14. All that remains of the glacier descending from Lenana,
seen from the hut.*

not know then that the cross still exists and is well preserved, and
that it had not been left on the very summit of Lenana, but on the
south ridge nearly 150 feet below.

Like Giuàn, who in looking for "stamps" had found the glasses,
I looking for the cross found another trophy, a wooden tent pole
top once painted red and bearing the letters J.H.H. – F.L.V. and
the date II.IX.37. I still keep it as a souvenir, and in many a transfer
from one prisoner of war camp to another in East Africa it has
caused astonishment to the officers searching my kit. At first glance
nobody can make out what the blessed thing is as it bears some
resemblance to a hand grenade.

It was getting late and distant mist banks were approaching
rapidly. Mist to the south had prevented us from seeing Kiliman-

jaro, which has been observed from here several times by more fortunate parties. The mist was tossing and tumbling like surf but now and then when the curtains parted we had a quick vision of quiet tarns in remote valleys or of jagged rocky peaks.

Presently it was almost on us. Fragments of cloud would reach the rocks at our feet only to burst and dissolve like a pricked soap bubble.

It was time to hoist the flag.

We stuck the lower pole into the stones of the cairn, and fitted the upper part onto which the flag had already been fastened, into its tin mortise; then we tied the four strings onto four rocks, roughly north, south, east and west. It looked solid and steady, not at all "improvised" as the paper had it when describing the discovery of the flag by a party of climbers from Nairobi only a week later. Neither was it "flying upside down (signal of distress?)" as imagined by the author of the article in same paper.

We asked ourselves how long the flag would remain there, as after all we had hoisted it in order that it should be found. We certainly did not suspect that at the very end of the winter climbing season, only a few days later, Lenana would be visited once again by a party that would discover it with the aid of binoculars from the camp at Thompson Lake.

Even while I was sitting on a rock and sketching the scene of the flying colours at the climax of our trip, the mists arrived above us. The breeze at first blew gently only stirring the colours slightly, but soon increasing in strength, it spread out until they were flickering, tossing, flying.

If anyone wonders what it meant to us to see the flag of our country flying free in the sky after not having seen it so for two long years, and having seen for some time previous to this only white flags, masses of them, I can only say that it was a grand sight indeed.

Fig. 15. Nelion, photographed from Lenana.

We left the note with our message and names in the sealed brandy bottle, picked up the rucksacks and ice axes and plunged into a raging battle of floating and swirling mists.

We had intended to enjoy a prolonged rest at the pools where we had awaited the dawn because from there we should have a last view of Northey Glacier and the north-west ridge, but as the mists were by now covering Batian also, we had to travel at high speed. Quickly descending the rocks of Lenana to a pond, which I imagine is the one called Harris Tarn on Dutton's map, we shot down a long scree to the bottom of Mackinder Valley.

There we had a breather, which we needed badly, then slowly we started the descent of the ravine towards our immediate goal. Behind us Lenana had long since disappeared in a grey cloak and the beauties of Batian's north-east face were already obliterated.

Fig. 16. From left, Nelion, Thomson's Flake and Point Thomson, seen from the base of Lenana.

By the time we reached the pools, only the snout of Northey Glacier protruded from the cover of the clouds. It looked like a white dragon enveloped by smoke from its own throat. The northwest ridge was quite invisible. As it was only half-past twelve we decided to enjoy a good rest at any rate.

We had just settled down at a spot selected to give a view which included the lobelia-fringed shore of one pool with the seracs of Northey Glacier in the background, when the mists suddenly closed down further and it started snowing.

It was not a snowstorm like that which finally encompassed our defeat on Batian. It started gently and gently it carried on, without a breath of wind. It was such a quiet and kind snowfall that we thought it could not last long. Thus we decided to take shelter and to wait for it to cease. Shelter was soon found under the overhanging brow of a big boulder, but as far as the rest of the programme was concerned – well, that was another matter.

Patience is a virtue that becomes a well-trained P.O.W. more than any other, and we did not feel the lack of it. Thus we made the best of a bad job, put on every rag of clothing we had with us, and just started to wait. We did not like the idea of moving on and of reaching the base camp so soaked once more that we should have to pass another night with wet clothes on.

We ate every crumb we could find in the bottom of our "climbing food" bag, we divided one biscuit between us and spent half an hour in eating it, while in the meantime I explored the inside of the Bovril bottle as industriously as any ant with the point of my knife. The reward of my microscopically accurate work was worth the toil as we each got a thin film of meat extract on our half biscuit, in itself only the size of a postage stamp.

The storm showed no sign of slackening. Snow accumulated slowly, steadily, stubbornly, on the frozen edges of the pools, on the boulders, on every stone, even on top of every lobelia.

Mist rose everywhere as if emanating from the soil. Of the wild scenery of Northey Glacier, nothing was visible. By and by we heard the grumbling roar of falling seracs, ending with the whistle of minor fragments of ice thrown far into the air, but the silence that followed seemed the more awe-inspiring. Of the great work of destruction which weather and time carry on ceaselessly on the ice-fields of the mountain we could see nothing, but the sound was enough.

Hours passed by.

We were frozen but did not feel at all unhappy. For a while we even sang some of our alpine songs to pass the time.

The white hoods on top of the lobelias increased in size. The plants looked stranger than ever and recalled to our memories,

216

unconsciously busy with food topics, visions of cream-covered chocolate cones. We felt like Charlie Chaplin in *The Gold Rush*.

We hoped that before dusk the weather would clear and allow us to reach our base camp. From Nanyuki we had noticed that in the dry season the mists usually cleared towards the hour of sunset but after the heaviest storms and during the rains.

At last it stopped snowing but the mists did not seem to have the faintest intention of lifting. We set off anyhow and warmed up on the ascent towards "Molar" saddle.

Once there we stopped. As we had decided to get rid of every ounce of useless weight, we made a bundle of all the ropes but one to be used in the passage of the gulley, added the crampons and even the remaining paper arrows and put everything in the hole of the "Molar" situated at the side of Mackinder Valley. I scribbled a few lines on a piece of paper and put it into the Bovril bottle: "Mountaineering tools made in Prisoner of War Camp used during an outing on Mount Kenya. Good luck to any who may find and use them." So far as I know, they are still there, covered by the stones I put on them, for when Alpini Lieutenant Colonel G. Sora of Spitzbergen fame climbed Nelion in January 1945, he had no time to dig for them, and nobody else knows anything about them. I do not think that treasure hunting is much practised on Mount Kenya, and only a treasure hunter or a dentist would think of excavating in the "Molar".

In the meantime, the mists had cleared above Mackinder Valley, and as though from a stormy sea, the *Flying Dutchman* bade us farewell. She looked even finer than when we had first seen her.

Overleaf: Fig.17. The peaks of Mount Kenya. From left, Lenana, Point Thomson, Thomson's Flake, Nelion, Batian and Point Piggott.

The ghostly rags of whitish mists against the dark background of stormy sky suited her to perfection. Billowing clouds hung round her like slowly lifting cannon smoke after a fight in buccaneering days, while the lazily drifting clouds above her castles looked like trailing and battle-torn sails under the tattered Jolly Roger.

I looked back at this strange mountain with a pang of regret. The word "end" already hung above our adventure.

We ran down the scree towards our tarns and met the mists ascending, like cotton wool clouds in a children's theatre, from Hausburg Valley.

Flashes of sunlight made the frozen surface of the tarns sparkle when we reached them. It was like a last smiling farewell: "Good-bye, little prisoners! Don't forget us!" Had they not faithfully reflected our mood every time we had passed?

Before leaving them forever, we collected some flowers, which we meant to bring back when we returned to our own home, whenever that might be. The sun lit up the ice-sprinkled surface of the tarns as I saw them for the last time and thus they are engraved in my memory.

We loved them for they had given us the memory of an inexhaustible store of beauty, on which we could draw during the years of imprisonment that would follow our adventure. I shall never see them again, but I shall never forget them.

The Nanyuki tumbled foaming along as we followed its course on our way back towards the inevitable barbed wire. We were strangely moved, sad and happy at the same time.

Presently we approached the rows of erratic boulders, and there was the would-be white towel flying from a giant groundsel, and soon between two rocks we saw the pale and exhausted face of Enzo with his grey beard. He had been watching.

Giuàn and I agreed to pull his leg for as long as possible. We did our best to assume the most doleful expressions, pretending that not even on this occasion had we been able to hoist the flag.

But it cut no ice. As it was still early – not more than 6.00 p.m. – he had guessed that Lenana at least had yielded to our weak efforts. Enzo was no fool.

Giuàn and I had to summon all our strength, and there was little enough of it, in order not to spoil the game.

On the grassy stretch beside the boulders Enzo met us and immediately tried to get behind me to make sure that the flagpoles were no longer protruding from my rucksack. As he turned I turned too, always facing him.

At last Giuàn and I made several steps to the rear and presented arms with our ice axes to the "Base Camp Commander".

"Sir," I addressed him, and he saluted in military fashion, "please strike your dirty banner, as from 10.30 a.m. today far better colours, our colours, have been flying from the top of Point Lenana."

We had tried to joke, but the joke did not last. Enzo was no longer able to conceal his feelings. He bit his lips, clenched his teeth, and, if I am not wrong, two good hearty tears ran down his sunken cheeks as, with one leap, he embraced us both.

With less emotion but with the same cheerfulness, we celebrated the achievements of the day by skipping our dinner.

CHAPTER V

The River

*In which the party passes from escapist mountaineering
to other sports, namely girdle-tightening and meal-jumping.
In which also a strange meeting with two locals is related.*

Sunday, February 7

A faint hint of dawn lit the sky over the "Molar" saddle but we were already up and ready to march.

The morning was grey and chilly and Batian proved himself a rude host as he was still under his soft blankets of clouds apparently disdaining to speed the parting guests. The landscape was whitened with a veneer of hoarfrost.

My companions were already on the move as I turned to take a last look at the site of our base camp. Of the camp itself only a few traces remained, such as empty tins, bags, string and the scrapped alcohol boiler. A clear-cut, dark rectangle surrounded by frosted grass marked the spot where the tent had stood. The scene reminded me of a snow-covered cemetery, with a grave newly filled in the foreground. French serial novelists of the last century loved the theme: "It was a livid morning. In the cemetery the grave had just been covered with earth . . . "

I felt in no mood for joking. It really was as though we had buried something there. In every departure, even in the most longed-for, there is a trace of sadness. After all, this place had been our springboard for the mountain, the goal of our dreams and hopes. But it was no occasion for pathetic farewells. There was no time to waste as we had an ambitious programme to accomplish.

It had taken us nine days to reach our base camp. We believed that we could make the return journey in three days if we could do three stages each day. Thus today we should omit bivouac 8 ("The Fingers") and 7 ("The Heather") and camp at bivouac 6 (where Giuàn had recovered from his fever). It was more easily said than done, but it had to be so as the penalty was too grim: real starvation.

An alternative scheme had been rejected unanimously, i.e., to occupy the hut we had discovered the day before, to eat the food that we might find there and to attempt Batian again, following the standard route. This idea had first been proposed by Enzo, when we told him about the hut, but after his initial enthusiasm had evaporated, he himself had turned it down as, after examination, no fewer than five reasons were adduced against it:

1. It would not be safe for Enzo to ascend 2,000 feet higher;

2. It was by no means sure that we should find in the hut either food or reports by previous climbers which would enable us to follow exactly the standard route;

3. We did not know whether the hut would be locked up and to open it by means of violence would be little less than burglary. If we had found stores we could not have paid for them as all we had between us was only ten shillings in cash. We could of course have paid the balance through the Pay Office by a long and complicated process but it would have looked little better than glorified theft;

4. Before attempting the standard route to Batian Peak we should have to recover the flag from Lenana in order to hoist it on Batian; but if we were in the end defeated by this climb we should have to replace the flag on Lenana, which would have been too much of a good thing;

5. We had "hoisted the flag of our despised country despite British barbed wire" as we had stated in the message left in the bottle. It would be contradictory and definitely unsporting to use a British hut now.

Thus we marched downstream trying, paradoxically enough, to get inside barbed wire as soon as possible. Indeed, as from the heathery slopes near the "Fingers" we saw the camp through the binoculars it was no longer a vision of horror but one of food. It seemed to call to us with impartial heartiness: "Come on! Come quick! You will have plenty of beans and cabbage but at least you will not starve."

We left the "Fingers" on our right and descended through heather-fringed gullies, eroded by rain, till we reached the head of the valley of the tributary.

By 9.00 a.m. we were already in the "toil and misery" grass, near the huge rock with the heather trees on its top. We rested on the bank of the tributary and ate our last crumbs of barley sugar, the first "food" we had had since that which we had scraped from the bottle of Bovril during the snowstorm on the previous day.

We searched ourselves again for something to eat although we knew that this was only wishful thinking, but our whole stock of food proved to be no more than a few ounces of butter, carried by Giuàn in a glass container; less than half a pound of rice, carried by me; three biscuits, each carried by its owner, who was free to eat it when he liked; three small bags, with salt, coffee and tea, carried by myself.

The main topic of conversation during that day was of boiled rice and butter that we should cook in the evening.

Several times I thought of Shackleton's South Pole diary. The explorers spoke for hours of the meals they would have when they returned home, and that at a time when they were compelled to ration their food to an extreme degree. Many years before, while reading the book, I wondered why the explorers had added this refinement of torture to their horrible hunger, almost I thought to the point of sadism. Now that I was enduring a similar experience – of course, to a far lesser degree – I could understand their behaviour. At least I believe that it was not sadism at all that compelled us to speak of food the whole day, in spite of our ravenous hunger. I thought, and still think, that speaking of food is the natural outlet to the craving for a meal; one just cannot help it. After all, why should one not do so when it is a mathematical certainty that one's companions are thinking of just the same subject? It is only human and honest to exchange personal views on a matter that is the *idée fixe* of all at the moment.

As we followed the tributary down, I began to feel very sleepy. I wondered if it was the air, which seemed to get thicker and more difficult to breathe at every step, or if it was due to my weariness. The rucksack seemed even heavier than on the way up although we had eaten or scrapped a good deal of its previous contents; thus I was inclined to believe that it was only my weakness that was worrying me.

We lost a good half-hour while collecting a few roots of the giant heather. We had read in Stockley's article that the roots of *Erica Erborea* were one of the best materials for making pipes, and thus we did not fail to take advantage of the opportunity. Needless to say we never got even the shadow of a pipe out of our wood as it split badly owing to the heat during the time we spent in the cells on our return.

At noon we passed under the brows of the hill where we had camped amid the heather after the rainstorm, and half an hour later we were tackling the rocky step at the side of the waterfall in the gully. The rope-ring was found in good condition and we quickly lowered down ourselves and our belongings. At the foot of the pitch I was inclined to scrap the rope but in the end I kept it. It might, I thought, prove useful for an emergency stretcher if something should happen to one of us before the end of our trip.

Once again we passed through the natural tunnel and saw the "botanical garden" where we said goodbye to the helichrysum and mosses. On the smooth and wet rocks we slid and fell more frequently than we had done on the way up, but reminded ourselves philosophically that at least we slid and fell in the direction we wished to go, and not backwards as we had done when ascending.

At 3.00 p.m. we reached the camp where Giuàn had recovered. Before pitching the tent we rested a good while to summon up our last reserves of strength.

By pitching the tent on the exact spot it had occupied on the way up, we saved ourselves trouble and time as we did not have to clear and level the camping place. The disadvantage to this, however, was that all the firewood within a reasonable distance had been collected on the way up, and we had to forage further afield. It was a hard job. It needed our united strength – or better, weakness – to bring in a log that one of us could easily have shouldered a week before, and it took longer. Every minute we wasted meant a minute longer to wait for the boiled rice and butter. Only this thought gave us confidence and good will.

At length the fire was burning near a good supply of fuel, the tent was pitched and the great moment drew near. The water boiled and I shook into the cooking pot the two handfuls of rice which dispersed like a pinch of sand in the sea.

"Give me the butter, please; in a moment the rice will be ready." I said to Giuàn.

"Here . . ." Giuàn said, putting his hand into the exterior pocket of his rucksack. I wondered why he did not end his sentence. Spellbound, Enzo and I looked at him.

He was getting pale and embarrassed. He searched and searched, then he turned his rucksack upside down and spread out its contents. No trace of the butter was to be seen.

"I suppose," he stammered, "I have lost it."

"You're pulling our legs!" Enzo exclaimed, getting excited.

"This isn't the time for a joke, nor is the subject a joking matter!" I added seeing my hopes of an almost substantial meal vanish.

"I'm not joking," Giuàn assured us, deeply concerned. "The

butter-glass was in one of the outer pockets of my rucksack. I've lost it, perhaps when we roped down near the waterfall."

Enzo and I looked at each other, speechless. Well, we should have to eat the rice without butter.

"At least don't forget the salt," Enzo warned me.

"Right you are."

I opened my rucksack and searched for it; boots, coffee and teabags, the rope, dirty socks, the compass, little odds and ends were produced under the watchful eyes of my companions. A shiver ran down my spine.

There was no salt.

I had taken out everything and the rucksack lay empty and collapsed before us.

"I suppose I left the salt-bag where we took stock of our food this morning, at the head of the valley," I explained in a trembling voice.

"This is *too* much!" shouted Enzo desperately.

Giuàn smiled. He had his revenge at least.

Thus, spoonful after spoonful, we ate the hot tasteless water in which a few over-boiled grains of rice swam sadly.

After this we had tea without sugar. Enzo's attempt to sweeten it by boiling in it the bag that had contained our barley sugar was completely unsuccessful. And the menu for the two following days was to be the same – sugarless tea or, according to choice, sugarless coffee. It sounded really hopeless.

We lit a great fire. The warmth was snug and pleasant, as it was the first fire we had had for a whole week and our bodies needed "calories" at least from outside.

During my watches I had to struggle against sleep. The few logs we had managed to drag to the camp had soon burnt to ashes and the bamboos were devoured still more quickly by the fire.

I could scarcely hold in my sore fingers the pencil with which I strove to register the main features of the past few days in my diary. The trip was by no means ended, as we had to march for at least two more days and one night, and had still to pass two main danger-spots, the "valley of the pachyderms" and the approach to the camp. Yet I felt the end of our adventure was near and I was strangely sorry.

The deep roar of the stream; the flickering light of the stars; the thin sickle of the young moon seen between the branches of the trees; everything seemed to say to me: "It is the last time." Even the crackling noise of the "kill-the-pig" seemed pathetic, like the cry of a baby lost in the woods.

I wondered if it was time to sum up the results of our trip. No, I answered myself, this not the end, whatever I may feel about it now. But I was already sure that the memory of these days, so vividly lived, would not leave us unaffected. So much beauty could not have been experienced in vain.

I felt weary beyond every belief, yet I was sure that everything we had endured, even the pain and hunger of this very moment, would be sweet in memory.

Monday, February 8

In our breakfast tea Enzo had again boiled the bag that had contained our barley sugar. It had not sweetened the bitter drink at all. Moreover we could not help passing a few sad remarks concerning last night's fiasco – an affair difficult to forget.

Thus we were inclined to be gloomy and cantankerous when we set out.

On the previous day our march through the bamboos had been

a nightmare, so today we did our best to follow the stream whenever it was possible. In due course, however, this policy forced me to enter a sort of grotto, from which I retreated at full speed when I found straw spread in it as though for a litter, and such an ugly smell of wild beasts that I was sure I had entered the den of an animal. Possibly I had paid a call on a leopard, unintentionally breaking the local laws of etiquette, which tend to frown upon premature advances by newcomers to the district.

Now no alternative was left but to enter the forest. Giant nettles, deceptive carpets of leaves, thorns of every description did their best to hold us up. Our fingers, cut and bruised, could scarcely grasp the bamboo culms. Fortunately we were descending in any case, so we could not grumble when we slid and fell. We had also made it a rule that when one of us was making a bigger jump than usual he had to utter Tarzan's war-cry. Now it seems silly; but at the time this helped considerably in keeping up our spirits.

When nearing the stream we came to a steep slope where the bamboos grew exceptionally sparsely. There we slid on the soil covered by leaves and twigs. The first man was lucky enough because if he lost his balance and had to slide down in a sitting position he found himself on a running cushion of leaves and twigs; but the second, and to a greater degree the third found not only hard soil but protruding stones and roots which tried their best to tear his trousers.

Soon after 9.00 a.m. we rejoined the stream at the foot of the gully and were glad to recognise several landmarks that told us that we were near our camping place number five (where Giuàn had suffered as a result of sleeping under the damp rock-face). We passed the spot and then rested for a while on a rock where the sunlight filtered through the ceiling of branches and twigs. After cleaning ourselves, for the passage through the forest had covered our clothes and rucksacks with rubbish of every kind, we basked a while, motionless in the sun.

Soon we became aware that we were not the first to have chosen this spot as a resting place. A swarm of beautiful butterflies approached. They were as big as the palm of one's hand, velvety black with blue stripes, and they had tails like a swallow. I believe they were *Papilio Nireus* but I do not know if they were a migrating swarm or if they had come together by chance on this sunny rock in the streambed.

By 10.30 we reached the junction of the tributary and the main Nanyuki. I was delighted with the speed of our march and began to hope that we should reach camping place number three, or "Leopard Camp", this day. These hopes were dashed not long afterwards on account of an encounter that lost us a lot of time.

Swimming in the calm waters of a little pool on the Nanyuki we saw a black river duck, followed by two ducklings. As we drew near, the mother flew off heavily, quacking a warning but leaving the young to their fate.

Our mouths watered at the thought of roast duckling – even without salt – but the birds were, alas, far too clever to be caught, and not at all at their wits' end. On one bank of the pool an eddy had heaped a broad mass of driftwood, branches and leaves, under which they dived. We started a systematic search but only lost precious time. The ducklings were nowhere to be found and we had to give in.

As we waded through the next pool the water seemed far warmer than it had been on the way up. The air too was getting so hot that we regretted having put on our heavy blanket suits again. We rested for a long while after this wading.

It was bliss to lie back and look up at the sky, framed between rustling twigs, as we were certain that this vision of peace and liberty would only too soon be remembered with regret. I felt already in true P.O.W. mode.

Our hopes of reaching camping place three had long since vanished but I wondered whether, on the morrow, we should be able to tackle the long trek from camping place four to the sawmill and so back to the P.O.W. camp on the following night.

It was 1.30 by the time we reached camping place four (Enzo's shelter) and it was too late to carry on as we needed lots of time for collecting firewood. Fortunately the bamboo shelter was still well preserved and needed no further attention, so we could devote the whole afternoon to collecting fuel. We found a few good logs, but we no longer had the strength to carry them to the fireplace; thus we relied entirely on bamboos.

Our so-called meal was a cup of bitter tea. I still had my biscuit, which I wished to produce as a surprise for my two companions on the morrow.

Keeping watch in our exhausted state was a trial. Again, as on the night after the attempt on Batian, I was "visited" by characters from books read shortly before escaping. The last watch from four till dawn was particularly tiring. I kept awake by smoking and was soon in a state of such mental lucidity that my thoughts worked and worked almost in exaltation.

I scarcely needed to move because I had piled all the bamboo fuel within reach.

I was well aware that this would be the last night I should sit near the fire in freedom, the last time I should listen to the music of the stream, now roaring, now murmuring in its unsteady rhythm. The word "last" was the undertone of all my thoughts.

And what about the "budget" of our trip?

Solely from a mountaineering point of view it had been unsuccessful, or at best an "honourable failure", for Lenana had proved to be only a "tourists' mountain" and Batian had slammed the door in our face. But after all, I thought, ours was not solely a mountaineering trip with a patriotic gesture thrown in. Above all our outing had been a reaction against the sluggish life in a P.O.W. camp, an act of will amidst all that inertia. Had the trip been a success from this point of view?

Only the future could give me an answer to this question, but I firmly believed that the adventure would unquestionably have a lasting influence on our lives as prisoners, and perhaps later, as free men.

At last the light of the day was stronger than the flames of my fire. The dawn of our last day of freedom had arrived. It was time to call my companions, to drink bitter coffee and to rejoin once more the men of the valleys, the everyday world of the camp.

Every step would bring us nearer to food, but nearer also to captivity.

Tuesday, February 9

We started late, at 8.30 a.m., in order to avoid any beasts which might linger near the river after their morning drink. In point of fact we met none.

Our progress was even slower than on previous days. Most of the time one of us was either falling – almost invariably into the water – or just picking himself up after a fall, which was a slow and difficult business.

Black shadows dancing before my eyes and a persistent humming in my ears deprived me a good deal of my balance on the wet, smooth, round stones. I marched automatically and I have therefore only a very dim recollection of what I saw.

We passed the caves with the curtains of creepers, the rocky basin with the passage through the forest, the place where we had seen the elephant (where there were now new footprints), the "elephant dancing places", the spot where the rhino – if it was a rhino – had been seen rubbing itself against the tree and other familiar spots. The well-worn game paths again smelt of zoo and we kept carefully to the riverbed, sliding, falling, getting wet, drying off and getting wet again.

After crawling under a fallen bamboo Enzo released the springy culm without warning Giuàn, who was close behind him. The bamboo struck off Giuàn's sunglasses, which broke into a thousand pieces on the stones.

At any other time, the matter would have caused either much laughter or an endless argument, but now nothing happened. We were too apathetic to care and after the exchange of a few "compliments" we just carried on as though nothing had happened.

The only creatures we saw were whistling and screaming parrots. We deeply regretted not having brought a catapult.

We chewed wild olives, bitter as bile, and were even tempted to eat the bean-like fruits of a shrub, but feared that they might be poisonous. And yet had we but known it, there was plenty of food, which we ignored. As I read later in H. W. Tilman's *Ascent of Nanda Devi* young bamboo shoots are excellent and proved to be real manna to the author's party in want of food.

Near the camping place where we had had a morning call from the unidentified beast I fell, bruising my right knee badly. It gave me a real shock although Giuàn said, after examining it carefully, that it was nothing. As I had to rest and to massage my knee for a while I thought that the moment had arrived when I might produce the biscuit.

I cannot describe the amazed looks of my companions as I put my treasure on a stone and asked Enzo to divide it exactly into three portions. They gave me the impression they believed themselves to be dreaming.

Each part was no bigger than a normal fingernail. I put mine into a cup of water for a minute or two and it swelled up until it was as large as a thumbnail.

It tasted heavenly. It was the first solid food we had eaten since our dismal dinner of rice two days before.

At last, after we had meticulously examined the stone on which Enzo had performed the operation on the biscuit and had satisfied ourselves that we had overlooked no crumb that could be seen without the aid of a microscope, we set off again.

I myself, limping painfully, soon became weary of continuous falls and took an elephant track which appeared to cut across a bend of the river. My companions protested against this foolhardy move, pointing out that it was not worth while looking for trouble right at the end of a trip during which we had, until now, exercised the greatest care. Thus I retraced my steps and once more followed the river.

While resting on a stone after one of my countless "landings" it seemed to me that I heard the humming of a distant engine. At first I did not want to announce my discovery to my companions as I feared it was born of my imagination, like the chiming of the bells on "Batian-night"; but I noticed that Enzo also was listening attentively without saying anything, having perhaps the same suspicion as I had.

"Engine?" I asked.

"Aeroplane," he answered.

We listened for a while but the noise of the engine neither increased nor decreased. It could not be an aeroplane.

We walked on and the noise of the engine became louder as we advanced and this gave us something on which to speculate. We located it eventually on the opposite bank of the river to the sawmill – the same rattling noise of a diesel, which we had heard on that memorable morning near the bridge.

We guessed that the tractor engine had been adapted by the sawmill owner to provide power for sawing timber in the forest, but we were surprised to find ourselves so near to civilisation. We had reckoned on reaching the bridge at about 5.00 p.m.. and it was now only 3.00 p.m. This was the first sign of human life we had encountered after fourteen days of solitude, except for a brief sight of the hut on the southern side of Mount Kenya.

We decided to make for the bridge at once and to stop near it for a wash and shave. After dark we intended to take the sawmill road and to make for the camp, arriving, with luck, that same night.

We had reached a bend of the river where the noise of the diesel engine was very close on our right, when I saw – yes, I saw, it was not imagination – a man standing by the fringe of the forest some two hundred yards from us.

He appeared to be waiting for us.

I wondered what this meeting would mean to us. The African would see at first glance that we were escaped prisoners of war, as we were on safari without porters and in a very poor state.

Our contacts with the people of Kenya had been – before our escape – very few, but we had tried to learn as much as we could about their customs and languages as we had anticipated that this would be of some use to us during our escape.

I shall not mention various unpleasant contacts with some of our local sentries in which I do not know if I should blame more their foolish irresponsibility or their wildness, but I might record a few typical examples of the way in which we learnt our Swahili.

The following very instructive scene I have witnessed more than once at P.O.W. camps in Kenya.

SENTRY, *making signs to the* PRISONER *to approach the barbed wires,* "Kuja! (Come on)".

PRISONER, *startled as he does not know what might happen, answers with a non-committal* "Hm."

SENTRY, *repeating unmistakable signs that he wants* PRISONER *to approach,* "Kuja!"

PRISONER, *becoming curious, approaches.*

SENTRY: "Taliani mzuri. (Italians good)," *or if* PRISONER *shows signs of not understanding even this rudimentary Swahili,* SENTRY *raises his hands to show how "great" Italians are.*

PRISONER, *still suspicious, keeps silent.*

SENTRY: "Angleza mbaya! (English bad)," *or if* PRISONER *still shows no signs of understanding, spits disdainfully or makes other signs of contempt.*

PRISONER, *becoming amused, laughs.*

SENTRY, *having scored a point, gets down to the meat of the matter:* "Nipa cigarra! (Give me a cigarette)."

PRISONER, *greatly amused, nine times out of ten, throws him a cigarette end.*

SENTRY *picks up the cigarette end, examines it carefully and then, changing his tone:* "Sasa kwenda! (Now buzz off!)"

At other times the prisoner himself offers a cigarette to the sentry who nine times out of ten is ready to start a short talk in broken Swahili, sometimes leaning his rifle against the wires.

These, normally, are the first "practical" Swahili lessons of the prisoner.

Our conversations, however, were not confined to those held with sentries.

Once Giuàn watched a few Askaris cutting the grass just outside the barbed wire. They sang, as the locals often did when working. Listening for a while Giuàn noticed that they were singing the well-known Catholic hymn "*Tantum ergo*". In the conversation that followed Giuàn asked one of them if he was a Catholic. The African answered with pride that he was "not only a Catholic but also a Protestant". Apparently he had attended missions of both persuasions.

While we were prisoners we had little chance of practising our Swahili, even on our one-mile walk. Sentries posted along the track chased off any local people who showed signs of wanting to accost us. Nevertheless, occasionally a man who hoped to sell us eggs ventured to appear from the grass when the sentry's back was turned, and trade and practice in Swahili followed.

Once I heard a prisoner discussing the price of a dozen eggs in the dialect – very closely related to Spanish – of his Sardinian town. I stopped, wondering how the African could understand him and was amazed to hear the local man answering in Portuguese, which language is also very similar to Spanish. The two men understood each other perfectly. The explanation was that the African had worked for years in Portuguese East Africa.

Once only Giuàn and I were lucky enough to find an old shepherd who, ignoring the fact that it was forbidden for him to use the track during the prisoners' exercise hour, was kind enough to grant us an interview on the subject of Mount Kenya. Not that we got a lot out of him because he knew practically nothing, but we heard and spoke a little broken Swahili. He shook his head when Giuàn asked him – as he thought – if one would meet animals.

"So there are no *simba* (lion), *chui* (leopard), *kifaru* (rhino) or *tembo* (elephant)?" Giuàn said at last.

"Oh yes, there are plenty of all," he answered.

"Then why did you say that there were no animals?" asked Giuàn, but the old man broke off the interview rather abruptly.

Only later we realised that instead of saying *nyama* (animals) Giuàn had used the word *nyana*, which means tomatoes.

As we advanced further in our studies we practised reading a Swahili paper, *Baraza*, which, like many other things, entered the camp mysteriously. Apart from its educational value we found the correspondence columns very amusing. I remember particularly one letter asking the editor to let the writer know the Pope's salary.

Anyhow when we met the Kenyan on the Nanyuki river, we felt reasonably sure about our Swahili but feared that we were about to be recaptured on the last day of our outing.

We had been told that the British authorities had offered a reward of ten shillings to be paid to Africans for every escaped prisoner of war brought to the nearest police station by their captors. Ten shillings is not a great deal of money and I personally believe myself to be worth at least tuppence farthing more, but for the local people in East Africa in 1943 it was a lot. Thus I strongly suspected our Kenyan of being busy reckoning what three times ten amounted to, and perhaps of drawing up plans to recruit sawmill labour to assist in catching us. Moreover I credited him – assuming the locals of East Africa to be similar to those of Abyssinia in this respect – with scheming out in detail how to spend the money in feasting and drinking.

When we reached the place where he stood I answered his greetings and passed on, as did my companions.

Our appearance, however, evidently struck him as being so unusual that he felt compelled to satisfy his curiosity by asking us a few questions:

"Where are you coming from?"

"From the mountain," we replied.

"Where are you going?"

"To Nanyuki."

"What would you give me if I carried one of your rucksacks?"

"Nothing," we said. Had we not carried them, heavy as they were, from the first moment of our escape?

"Why do you not follow the sawmill path, which is far better, instead of walking down the streambed?"

"Because we prefer it," we answered.

Now it was our turn to question him, though we continued to walk on while asking where he came from.

"From the sawmill," he said.

At this moment another Kenyan appeared from the forest.

While the first man was dressed in shorts and shirt and a European style hat with a little feather stuck in the ribbon, his friend was covered only by a rough piece of cloth, ochre in colour. He wore a necklace of red glass beads and was armed with a long spear. He suited the surroundings and the atmosphere of an "escape in an African forest" far better than his companion, and we stopped to look at him.

The man in town clothes took advantage of this to ask if we were thirsty. I think our eyes gleamed at the thought that, as he had inquired about our thirst he *might* even realise that we were hungry. Without waiting for a reply he sent his wild companion off and told us to wait. We waited full of hope. The prospect of getting food had altered the whole situation.

The wild fellow soon came back, his spear in his right hand and a pot in his left. As I had been leading, he thought that I was the Number One of the party and after they had exchanged a few remarks in a language unknown to us, the bearer of the pot put it under my nose. I was sorry to see that there was nothing solid in it to eat, only a liquid of nondescript colour and with an agreeable smell of fermented honey. I drank a little; it was sweet and fairly alcoholic.

After Enzo and Giuàn had drunk their share we asked Enzo to pay the men with a few cigarettes, and moved on.

Immediately I felt a pleasant swimming sensation in my head and my pangs of hunger eased off deliciously. I was drunk; but I was sober enough to be a little shaken by what I saw when I glanced over my shoulder. Our benefactors were following us closely, bombarding Giuàn with questions, which he did not deign to answer as he was probably in the same vague and happy state of mind as myself.

At last Giuàn asked me to stop, saying: "I'm so fed up with these people I can't stand their chatter any more."

"You're getting fussy, I think," remarked Enzo.

Ignoring Enzo's interruption Giuàn carried on:

"They are insisting that we should leave the riverbed and go toward the sawmill. They offer to show us a good path. I propose therefore that we pretend to follow their advice in order to get rid of them. As soon as they leave us alone we can make for the river once more."

I objected, expressing my deep-rooted doubts as to whether our two new friends would ever leave us alone. "If I were they . . ." I started, but Enzo interrupted me:

". . . you would have a full belly."

"If I were one of them," I started again, "I should try to get us to the sawmill and should then inform the police, and in due course draw the reward of thirty shillings. I think it would be rather foolish to play their game."

As Enzo agreed to Giuàn's proposal, however, I had to give in, grumbling, outvoted by two to one.

The town-dressed Kenyan took the lead, and jumping like a

bushbuck amidst the tangled undergrowth showed us, a few minutes later, a path leading uphill toward the noise of the engine, now very loud.

Contrary to all my expectations, the two Africans then said goodbye politely and withdrew into the thick of the forest.

After they had disappeared, to the great satisfaction of Giuàn and Enzo, whose theory had proved right, we left the path and entered the forest once more. It was not easy going, but after walking for a quarter of an hour on a course at right angles to the mill we again approached the river.

On the way Enzo thought it would be a good thing to get rid of his bush knife (panga) as we were by now too near to the inhabited world to want it. He threw it into the thick bush, glad to be without another half-kilo of weight to carry, and we scrambled down to the riverbed thoroughly tired, as the struggle through the forest had used up what we thought to be our last energy.

We walked slowly along the riverbank, thinking that we must be very near the bridge, as we had already left the noise of the engine behind us. I looked around to find a suitable place where we could clean ourselves up, and where we could rest while waiting for the dusk, which would enable us to follow the sawmill road towards Nanyuki.

Great was my disappointment when I saw we were once more being shadowed by the two Africans who were only a few yards behind Giuàn. The one in town dress proudly wore Enzo's panga in his belt.

We felt beaten; we felt desperately prisoner-like, and almost sure that we had been betrayed and were about to be caught. We dropped our rucksacks and sat down on the stones in silence.

Evidently they had been watching us without being seen. At the time I was struck with sincere admiration for their ability to follow us so closely that they had been able to pick up Enzo's panga. Now, however, I realise I had little reason to admire them. They were in their natural surroundings, and obstacles that seemed to us to be almost impossible to surmount were, to them, normal features of their everyday life. Had they been able to cross a street in a big town during a rush-hour without being killed by the traffic, then and then only should I have been entitled to be amazed.

However, there they were.

I thought that at any moment one of them would go off to call the sawmill people to aid in capturing us in order to claim the famous thirty shillings reward, while the other would be left to watch us in case we moved on.

"May I ask you what you want of us?" asked Giuàn at last.

The man with a spear was resting with one leg twisted around his spear-shaft. The town-dressed one was standing near him. It was he who answered:

"To go with you to Bwana Tumbo. We showed you the way but you seemed not to want to follow it."

"What does Bwana Tumbo mean?" asked Enzo who understood Swahili only in bits and pieces.

"Mr Fat-Tummy. Evidently the Englishman of the sawmill is better fed than we are."

Hearing us commenting on the nickname of the saw-miller and thinking perhaps we were afraid of him, the African said:

"Bwana Tumbo is a good man."

We never doubted it. As a rule fat people are good-natured. We felt sure that Bwana Tumbo would not do us any harm and perhaps he might even ask us to dinner; but we much preferred to re-enter the camp unseen and by our own devices, as we had left it, instead of being brought in "officially" on the lorry of Bwana Tumbo which was what would probably happen if we were to meet him.

We felt fatalistic.

Let the worst happen if it must, we thought, and started our washing and cleaning up without further delay. We performed the operations with particular care as we wished to appeared as civilised and respectable as possible in the event of our having to dine *par force* with Bwana Tumbo. It was, I confess, an attractive thought after all.

Once again our friend said: "Will you come with us to Bwana Tumbo?"

"Later," I answered, "don't you see that we are getting *maridadi* (smart) in order to call on him?"

They conversed a lot more between themselves. I was surprised that they did not take the obvious course – one to call the Bwana or sawmill labour, while the other remained to keep an eye on us – but at last I understood their object. As soon as we had finished our tidying up they became more daring and asked for soap and razor-blades. We graciously presented them with these coveted items and Enzo generously added a few cigarettes. Both Africans were very pleased and thanked us again and again.

A troop of baboons passed on the far riverbank. A few old males were ahead, females with little ones clinging to their backs followed and the "convoy" was closed by other males on rearguard duty. Was the whole tribe moving to new feeding grounds, or beating a strategic retreat? Or might this even be an evacuation of civilians? There are still mysteries in forest life.

The town-dressed man told us that baboons could be very dangerous and that they had once killed even a *mazungo* (white man) with stones.

Finally the other asked: "Will you come now?"

We answered: "You carry on and we shall follow later."

We could hardly believe our own eyes when both said "goodbye" and went away.

They had hardly disappeared around a bend of the river in the direction of the sound of the engine, before we were ready to seize the opportunity and to run off.

After all they might have intended to come back with the sawmill people to get those "thirty pieces of silver" in spite of the presents they had had.

How we found the strength to do so I do not know, but suddenly we were going down-stream like Marathon runners. We reached the bridge and passed under it, wondering why it was we could never pass it at our leisure but always in a tearing hurry, and a few minutes later we had put the best part of half a mile between ourselves and the place where they had left us.

In a small wood, still in sight of the sawmill road, we stopped. We could do no more.

Some twenty minutes passed before we were able to breathe regularly and then Giuàn took off his clothes. He had fallen head-long into the river after slipping on a wet stone and was soaked to the bone. How thin he was. When I remarked on this he answered:

"Giovanni Rossi will be glad."

"How does Giovanni Rossi come into it?" I asked rather puzzled.

Giuàn explained: "An hour before escaping, when I was having my last shower bath, Rossi looked at me critically and said: 'Giuàn, you are getting fat. You must take more exercise.'"

"And what did you say to him?"

"'Don't worry, I shall start today.'"

It was only twenty to six and we should have an hour and half to wait before it would be dark enough to take the sawmill road. The prospect of such a long rest did not please us at all. Our nerves were too worn out to permit us to enjoy a quiet siesta and we should have preferred to carry on immediately.

While Giuàn dried himself, Enzo cut a walking stick for use during our night march to the camp, and I prowled around the wood. After a while I found a good lookout from which I could give my companions the news of the road without being seen, as I was covered by a screen of leaves.

I had not long to wait. The noise of the engine came nearer and nearer and soon the clashing of plates was heard. The tractor was coming home after work.

At last it entered into the field of my vision and I proceeded to give my companions a running commentary of the scene in the same way as wireless commentators describe a football match for the benefit of their listeners:

"There's the tractor going slowly uphill, driven by a white man."

"Is it Bwana Tumbo?" asked Enzo.

Giuàn immediately answered:

"Go and ask him."

I went on: "He is sitting and I can't see his 'tumbo.' Close to him sits a man. . . "

"Our friend perhaps?" asked Enzo.

"I can't say whether it is he or not. They are too far away. A few Africans walk at the side of the tractor . . . several Africans . . . lots of Africans . . . The tractor drags a few long logs, probably supported by pairs of low wheels, but I can't see them. Other Africans are sitting on the logs. The tractor is going towards the sawmill. It has disappeared."

"Anything else?"

"Nothing . . . no, wait . . . other Africans, many Africans are following, thirty or forty, all carrying tools on their shoulders: axes, shovels, cross-cut saws. They are singing as you can hear."

Even as the platoon of people coming home from work paraded under my eyes, the engine of the tractor stopped. Presumably it had reached its destination, which could not be far away.

"Still more Africans are following. They sing like the Dwarfs in Snow White going home. Now I understand why on our way up it sounded as though we were passing near crowded native villages."

"Anything else?"

"Nothing else. We have been transmitting the 'Return of the Sawmill Workers'. This is Mount Kenya Broadcasting Corporation. Good night, everybody."

The show over, the road became deserted once again. The shades of evening stole across the silent landscape. We were able to wait no longer.

We descended to the river, crossed it, filled our water bottles for the last time and were soon on the road bearing the imprints of the tractor and many footprints, of human beings at last. It was a delight once more to feel under our feet a smooth man-made road, after two weeks of scrambling in the trackless wilds of the mountain.

After a short while the road became level and we guessed we had reached the top of the hill on which the sawmill was situated. The air was damp and hot. The golden quarter of the moon was low in the western sky but cast enough light to allow us to be seen.

As we reached a house built in European style we stopped and agreed that it would be safer to wait until the occupants had gone to bed. Presently we heard voices inside and women's laughter. It was only eight o'clock.

"Just a little more patience," we admonished ourselves, and made for a small cypress wood. I was so exhausted that as soon as I sat down I was overcome by a strong desire to sleep. I slipped into my sleeping bag and fell asleep immediately.

A sensation of damp clammy cold awoke me. The moon was

still in the sky. It was only 9.00 p.m. but I felt I could wait no longer. It was too nerve-racking just to sit there and shiver, and at a quarter-past nine we went on again. The house was now dark and silent and we were grateful to its occupants for having gone to bed early.

We followed the road, walking so closely in single file that I could hear Enzo's half-repressed nervous giggling only a pace behind me. Why he giggled God only knows. Perhaps he thought that we must have looked funny, like children playing at being a train or a centipede.

The track was covered with sawdust but it was not the same one as that which we had struck on the way up. I wondered if we should be able to find the other that would enable us to follow an easy well-known path, or whether we should get held up again in some blind alley. For the moment I felt neither hunger nor weariness. Adventure still beckoned; still I felt the marvellous excitement of the unforeseen. It might be the last time I should experience it, before becoming a prisoner again, but it *was* thrilling.

Presently Enzo signalled me with a hiss.

I stopped. "What's the matter?" I whispered, strongly suspecting one of his typically improbable proposals.

"I should carry the ice axes at the slope," he said.

"Why?"

"The locals would think we were marching with rifles and might think twice before troubling us."

The idea did not seem unreasonable and was put into effect.

"Bravo!" I said, as we "sloped arms".

We reached a broad open square with native huts on all sides. A few huts had their doors open and people were going in and out. We heard chatter, laughing and the noise of musical instruments. A man passed some thirty feet from us but I could not tell whether he had noticed us or whether, frightened by Enzo's device, he pretended not to have seen us. Anyhow, without bothering us he went on his way.

If a few years hence a legend, not of a Nandi-bear but of a new sort of monster with six legs and two spikes should come to light among the Africans inhabiting the lower slopes of Mount Kenya, and if fertile native imagination adds that the monster has actually been seen devouring Kikuyu children on moonlit nights, I beg game wardens and scientists not to bother about sending expeditions to try to obtain a specimen for the British Museum or for some American zoo, because the monster will already be in a cage and – at least so I hope – well preserved. Scientists may gather further details about the beast merely by asking A.D.P.W., P.O. Box 4000 Nairobi about the movements of Prisoners of War 762, 41303 and 41304 on the night of February the 9th, 1943.

The square widened further. A layer of mist the height of a man made it difficult to see anything. I followed the marks of the tractor plates with my feet, and marched with my head stuck out like a tortoise. In spite of all these precautions, I avoided bumping into the tractor, simply left standing in the middle of the sawmill village, by a matter of inches only.

As we no longer had the "spoor" of the tractor to follow we were at a loss where to go, nor could we wait for Bwana Tumbo to see us out of his realm. Thus I steered due west, towards the setting moon, and soon I found under my soles another tractor trail; older this time as it was bounded by ridges of dried mud. I followed this and in due course it led us to the entrance of a road running between two buildings. Here the traces ended and we were faced by the opening of a track leading into the forest again.

Now that we needed light badly, the moon had just sunk below the horizon. Still, we had had luck in passing through the sawmill village unnoticed as we had now emerged on the far side of it.

Our track forked and we took the right branch. The left would have taken us too far westwards and Nanyuki, we reckoned, was due west-north-west.

The road we had chosen was so little used that presently it became a mere path, which, I feared, might at any moment end at some felling site inside the forest. Feeling my way with my ice axe I moved on. We did not like to use Enzo's torch, the last we had which was still working, while we were so near to the village.

Once again the forest close around us seemed alive with a hundred voices as we marched on in inky darkness, but now I had no fear. I even tried to enjoy it as I thought, this is the last time I should have the opportunity of listening to these sounds in freedom.

A fallen tree barred the way and for a moment we used the torch in order to pass the obstacle.

How narrow the track seemed in the fitful light!

Fortunately the path kept more or less north-north-west, as I observed by taking my bearings on Rigel of Orion.

We moved quickly.

We did not know how much time had elapsed since we had left the village but we did know that before dawn we should have to be prisoners once again if we wished to avoid one more day of starvation.

Perhaps my pace became too fast for Enzo for he asked and even begged for a halt, if only for a very short rest. I forced myself to be adamant. I quite realised that if I myself felt utterly "down," he would certainly feel still worse since he had not gone into training for the trip, was poorly equipped and had been ill for long. Even so I did not dare delay while we were still not at all sure that we should be able to reach the camp before daybreak.

"We shall have an hour's sleep after leaving the forest behind us," I promised him at last.

On we went.

Almost imperceptibly we started to descend while the path broadened again into a track, or perhaps it had joined a track and we had not noticed where and when.

Enzo insisted that we should at least slacken our speed, which we did.

Suddenly we were marching on level ground. How long it had taken us to reach this point I do not know, for we dared not show a light and I had not been able to look at my watch; but at any rate we had reached the plains.

On our right the forest still showed like a black wall, but to the left it opened out into broad glades. Presently on the horizon we saw the lights of Nanyuki township and the red light of the airport. By taking our bearings with the aid of the latter we knew that we should be able to locate the camp exactly.

We thought that it would be dangerous to follow the track any further. Indeed, even now we could see the lights of a motor car approaching. We stopped behind a shrub and watched them coming nearer and nearer. They had a strange fascination for us.

The car did not reach us as it turned southwards and rapidly disappeared. We waited a little longer in case it should return but nothing happened. The darkness remained undisturbed, and in the meantime Enzo had fallen asleep.

We got him up with some difficulty and walked straight on toward the red light of the airport, still more than ten miles away, as it seemed to us.

The grass was breast-high and I pushed it aside with my ice axe, feeling for holes with my feet. Enzo followed mechanically. I myself felt near collapse. The red light danced before my eyes and often it seemed to be completely obliterated by grey shades. Once more I felt a stinging pain in my stomach.

Presently Enzo drew a long breath and stammered: "You promised . . . once we were out of the forest . . ."

I was only waiting for an excuse before taking a rest, which I needed badly, and "Right you are," I said, dropped the rucksack, sat down and fell asleep.

Wednesday, February 10

When I awoke I saw from the stars that it was long past midnight. Probably we had only a few hours of darkness left.

I waited a little longer, however, as I had not the heart to rouse my companions from their peaceful slumber. As I lay there looking at the stars the sky was so clear that one could see stars and more stars down to the very horizon. Where but on the Equatorial highlands can one enjoy such a spectacle?

At last I performed my mournful duty by shaking Giuàn and Enzo and we again set out, slowly and painfully. Marching in high grass is a wearisome business even in daylight and under normal conditions. Now and then dark clumps of trees showed like islets in the sea of elephant grass. Under one of those olive trees somewhere not far from here we had spent our first night "out". It seemed to me that this had happened seventeen years ago, not merely seventeen nights.

We dragged ourselves along through the grass. Often one of us fell and immediately the others took advantage of this by sitting down as well, in order to enjoy a few moments' rest. I wondered if we should be able to reach the camp at all, but suddenly I saw something that raised my hopes.

"Giuàn!"

"Hm," he grumbled.

"Do you see that high dead tree?"

"Yes."

"Do you remember the one we took as a landmark during our butterfly hunt?"

"Yes. If that is the one there should be some native huts on our left."

"Exactly. We shall soon see if we are right."

We *were* right as presently we heard dogs barking on our left. Another dog answered from far away on the right. A neighing horse joined in the concert.

Near the big dead tree we had met a mongoose on our memorable preliminary trip. Then the grass had been high and had concealed many ditches and holes, but now we noticed with relief that it had recently been burnt and our progress accordingly became far easier.

I do not remember how far we walked on the pitch-black burnt soil but at last we sighted a dark strip of trees, perhaps a mile away.

"It's the wood near the church," I announced, very pleased at finding another well-known landmark as on this flat terrain we could no longer see the red light of the airport.

Had my head been less heavy, my stomach a little less empty and my knees not as uncertain as they were, it might have been a real pleasure to walk on the short burnt grass after the hours of toil in the elephant grass. But it was no pleasure, in spite of the fact that we now had a good landmark by which to steer.

Once I fell into a hole, and before I had scrambled out on the far side Enzo, automatically following in my footsteps, fell in on top of me, landing on my rucksack. I got angry:

"Can't you look where you put your feet? Didn't you see me

falling in here? If you want to fall in a hole you might at least choose another one, and not the one I'm still occupying!"

"I didn't see anything," he murmured plaintively and immediately started to go to sleep where he lay. Giuàn and I pulled him out and on to his feet, but after a few hundred yards he fell down again and refused to get up or to attempt to walk at all.

"I can't," he said. "Leave me here. You go on to the camp alone. Someone can bring me in tomorrow."

I was exasperated: "Haven't we marched together for eighteen days? Do you think we should leave you now, a few miles from the camp? Get up. We shall return together, as we started."

It was useless to appeal to his pride and sportsmanship. He was almost crying, like a child: "I can't bear the weight of my rucksack any more."

"That's your affair. I don't care. You march, and if you don't we shall kick you or even beat you with our ice axes."

"I'll march. But the rucksack . . ."

"If you can't carry it on your shoulders, carry it on your head."

The idea appealed to Enzo's sense of oddity and after he had balanced his load we marched on again.

The wood by the church did not seem to get any nearer. I was kept awake merely by the responsibility of leading the way. Had I been in the place of Enzo or of Giuàn I do not know if I should have been able to go any further at all.

When we were fairly near to the wood, we struck a barbed wire fence, which compelled us to make a long detour before reaching the main road.

This we crossed, Enzo still carrying his rucksack on his head – a strange picture of misery and exhaustion to anyone who might have seen us. But nobody was there to enjoy the scene.

During the whole of the time that we were passing through the strip of land between the road and the railway, at least one of us was sitting or lying on the ground. It was torture.

Carefully we crossed the rails and then we had a long rest before the final effort.

As my cooking pot, hanging outside my rucksack, might reflect even the light of the bright stars, I put it into the bag I had made for this purpose. We checked over our rucksacks carefully in order to fasten securely anything which might rattle or clink while we were moving and then, summoning all our energy, we approached our ultimate goal – the camp.

First we walked slowly and then we started crawling on the ground. Now the sentry towers along the double barbed wire fence rose over the near horizon, followed by the silhouettes of the dreary tar-painted barracks.

Holding our breath we crawled across the broad space, which formed the outer boundary of the camp gardens. This space was patrolled regularly by day and was supposed to be patrolled also by night, so far as we knew. Even if the sentries were not too conscientious in the performance of their duties at night the terrain over which we were crawling was always within easy range of the sentry towers.

Thorns pierced my hands and knees, already bruised and battered. Every yard seemed a mile, but we managed even this last endurance test, reaching the gardens without having provoked either shots or alarm whistles.

We were safe, but prisoners again.

Easily, in spite of the darkness, we located the hideout where we had spent the afternoon of our first day of freedom. The next thing was to ascertain whether our friends had left food and water for us according to plan.

We felt around with our hands, we even dug, but found nothing. Only when we met our friends did we learn what had happened. On the twelfth day after our escape they had brought a bottle of water and a box of ration-biscuits. By the next day both had disappeared, and since we had not reported back they had evidently not been taken by us. They brought another bottle and another box of biscuits only to find that by the following day unknown hands had once more removed the provisions. Thus they had carried on till the fifteenth day, when they had no more biscuits left. They wondered if the hideout was being watched, and in any case they resented the idea of providing food for somebody who had not even the courtesy to leave a note thanking them for the gift.

This was why on the eighteenth day after our escape we, to our grief, found nothing.

While Enzo fell asleep immediately, Giuàn and I buried, in a spot easy to describe and to identify, our most precious and "dangerous" belongings: compass, binoculars, sketches and diary.

As we finished, a cold wind blowing from the east told us that dawn was near, and we lay down near Enzo in order to have a short sleep.

The end of our adventure, which, with mixed feelings, I had seen approaching nearer with every step during the last few days, had unmistakably arrived. But at the very end I felt neither sadness nor relief, only complete, utter exhaustion.

CHAPTER VI

The Wind

*In which is related how captivity redoubled
and other consequences of our adventure.*

The next morning we awoke late, noticing with disappointment that a sentry was performing his duty, walking slowly up and down along the outer boundary of the vegetable gardens and over the open spaces across which we had crawled a few hours before. Every three or four minutes he passed some thirty feet from our hideout.

While his back was turned I managed to slip out and mingle with other prisoners working in the vegetable gardens, being dressed like them in P.O.W. shirt and shorts.

One of them recognised me and spoke to me as though I were a ghost:

"You? What are you doing here? Aren't you at Mogadishu?"

"Yes, it's me, but why on earth should I be at Mogadishu?"

"People thought that you would never come back, that you had told your friends you were going to climb Mount Kenya merely in order to lead the authorities astray . . . "

"As you see, here I am."

Two hours later Giuàn, Enzo and I entered the main gate of the camp with a working party, three members of which had kindly agreed not to re-enter the camp for lunch. I do not remember how they got back into the camp that evening but they managed it.

The same day our rucksacks, climbing suits, boots and ice axes came into the camp concealed in a lorry among bags of turnips and cabbage. Furthermore, a friend went out into the gardens with the afternoon working party and retrieved our buried treasure.

We were "in" once more.

*

First we devoured our mail, and then we tried to eat in one afternoon enough food to compensate for the meals we had missed during the past week.

We were rather coldly received by the majority of our fellow prisoners who had been subjected to some restrictions – soon lifted – because of our escape. Many of them did not believe that we had been on Mount Kenya and made the most silly remarks.

We hid during the evening roll-call, had our hair cut and slept blissfully in our bunks.

Next morning we put on clean, freshly ironed clothes and only then reported cheerfully to the British Compound Officer. "Good morning!" we said.

We were put in a cell and meticulously searched.

The *East African Standard* of February 20 related the story of how our flag had been found. It was a funny story indeed containing not only untrue but also contradictory statements, as the reporter – a member of the climbing party which retrieved our flag – stated it had been *"flying* upside down," while a photograph showing the colours *spread out on the rock* was headed "the improvised flag in the position in which it was found."

Well, all this is a petty chronicle of facts more or less resulting from feelings and ill-feelings connected with war and the P.O.W. mentality, and is concerned neither with the main story of our adventure nor with its main consequences in so far as these affected us three who had experienced it.

After all it is these consequences which are of importance to us and that is why I have written the whole story.

Thus, happily, we entered our cells.

Life was truly sybaritic.

*

Fig. 18. The English press relates the adventures of the three Italians

I shared a cell with Giuàn. Enzo was with another man who had been sentenced to twenty-eight days for trading with locals; if I remember rightly he had been selling them wooden suitcases he had made himself.

We had been sentenced to twenty-eight days as we had expected, but actually spent only seven in the cells as the Camp Commandant was very kind to us and had, as he put it, "appreciated our sporting effort". Only later when the affair of our flag on Mount Kenya had got unmerited advertisement by press and wireless were we sent to a camp where "bad people" were segregated.

In the cells it was rather hot as the roofs and walls were built of corrugated iron and there were lots of fleas, but at first we did not notice this as we only slept and ate, ate and slept. Our friends had "arranged matters" so that we got two or three times the quantity of food issued in the ordinary way.

We were allowed neither books nor cigarettes, but during our

263

exercise hours, from 7.00 to 8.00 a.m. and 5.00 to 6.00 p.m. our friends found it possible to circumvent this regulation. As a matter of fact I read Knut Hamsun's *Vagabonds*, thoroughly enjoying it, and as far as cigarettes are concerned we had so many of them that we distributed them not only to other fellow-prisoners in the cells but even to our African sentries.

At this time P.O.W. Camp 354 suffered from a water shortage during the dry season, and queues for drinking and cooking water started before dawn. There was not enough water for washing linen or for bathing in the compounds, but this did not apply to us happy inmates of the cells. Owing to the layout of the pipes of the camp water supply, the taps in the little cell-compound provided water enough for shower-baths and for the washing of linen, although prisoners who had not misbehaved as we had could not enjoy these privileges.

When inspections were made they started at the far end of the cells, and we knew from the noise made by the Askaris and from the sound of slammed doors what was happening. We had plenty of time to bury cigarettes, matches and books in a prepared hole in the earth floor and to clear away ash and cigarette ends.

To cut a long story short I shall merely remark that the memory of those seven days in the cells is almost as pleasant a recollection as that of our trip on the mountain.

Last but not least of the advantages of our cell life was the sight we could enjoy from the little iron-barred window. What we could see was intimately connected with us and was the primary reason for our being in the cells: Mount Kenya.

One night it seemed to me that a strong wind was blowing. This sensation became mingled in my dreams.

At first it was as though I were at home and the winter winds

264

were blowing icy from the Julian Alps and highlands, lashing the sea, rattling window shutters and whistling in the chimney in the old homely way.

Then it was as though I were again on the summit of Lenana, watching and following the turbulent track of the wind through the blanket of clouds at my feet.

It started rustling the gleaming, silvery leaves of the old olive, sighed through the mysterious abode of the elephants and reached the odd world of dry bamboo culms, clattering like dry bones.

In the heath belt it played heavenly harp music through the branches and needle-thin leaves of the giant heather, then it roared up the moss-and-senecio-covered upper valley of the mountain, and rippled the surface of the silent tarns.

At last, grown to the violence of a mountain gale it charged Lenana's summit and, flinging wide the colours of our country, opened our minds to new life and understanding.

As I awoke the cell was filled with eerie moonlight. A strong cool wind was actually blowing. The corrugated iron roof of the prison rattled.

I sat up on the wooden board that was my bed, trying to disentangle dream from reality.

A rat drifted noiselessly across the shadow of the iron window bars, neatly etched by the moonlight on the earth floor.

Giuàn was peacefully asleep.

I got up, and leaning my elbows on the window frame I gazed through the grid. I was uncertain yet whether it was real or whether I was still dreaming.

There on the far horizon lay Mount Kenya, its crystal white glaciers gleaming in the glorious moonlight, a halo of stars around Batian Peak that we had not conquered.

The mountain looked exactly the same as it had on so many

occasions before our outing. Slowly a doubt crept into my mind: Is it true? Have we really been there? Has not everything been a dream, a wonderful dream?

And then it seemed as though the wind brought me an answer from the mount of our dreams, murmured in a language that only I could understand:

"It is as you think. Only in dreams can humans approach me; only in dreams are they allowed a fleeting glimpse into my dearest secrets.

"You, then, only dreamt that you had seen my miracles of sheerest beauty: the emerald-green tarns, the infinite horizons, the ever-changing mountains of clouds, the unbelievably dark sky and the stupendous yellow walls of my north-east face, the icy water drunk through the hole in the ice, the weird music of harps and the chime of bells in the mist, the unearthly shape of lobelias and giant groundsels, the glamour of helichrysums, the legendary form of the *Flying Dutchman*, the mysterious dwelling of the elephants, the play of light and shade in Batian's shadow, the strange voices of night in the forest, the smell of bivouac fire and of heath resin, the feeling of utter independence of man and the inhabited world, the fullness of life and action, the sure knowledge that adventure is still a challenge and beauty still a reality for those who care, even for those degraded from man to a mere number in a camp.

"In your dream you did not conquer me, but you have reconquered yourselves.

"You shall live again encompassed by barbed wire, guarded by the bayonets of black sentries, among the people each with a black patch on the back of his grey shirt, people with shaken nerves jaded by war and captivity and dreadful news from home, petty and vindictive, silently suffering without reason to hope and yet maddeningly hopeful. But you shall be as children living in a dream world among grown-ups busy with the grim reality of life.

"You shall no longer share their misery, for in my world of solitude you have seen the shadow of eternity.

"I have given you riches which can never be confiscated even by the most exacting searchers – self-reliance and a sense of proportion.

"The hard present, which at first you feared and then tried to overcome, is neither everything nor nothing; it is only a part of Time, and this you will realise later.

"The time will come when your years of captivity will influence your lives to an extent which today you cannot yet grasp. Captivity will have been, paradoxical as it may seem to you now, a necessary part of your experience, as without darkness there can be no light."

Thus, it seemed, spoke the wind of the mountain, seeking me out in my prison cell.

And it was as if I had found something that I could not find on that last evening, meditating while watching by the river.

And the Wind seemed to add:

"The dream you dream shall live in your memory, a delight that never will stale; it will be your inspiration in the bitter years to come. But be careful! For what you have gained you have paid in full measure, but it is meant for you only. Keep my precious secrets to yourselves and reveal nothing to anybody."

I, obstinate as I am, have written a book about it.

July 10, 1946, P.O.W. Camp 366 – GILGIL (Kenya)

CHAPTER VII

The Unknown

In which a short historical postscript reveals
the depths of our ignorance.

Mountains, like men, have their history.

They too are born, grow old, decay and die.

"Do they also love?' a character from Mosca [1] might ask. No, of course they don't love. But they are loved, and with what love!

As knights of old crossed perilous seas, fought fiery dragons and even each other, for the love of their princesses, so nowadays mountaineers armed with ice axes and ropes, crampons, and pitons, make dangerous and wearisome journeys and endure every hardship for the sake of their mountains. And in winning their beloved many of them lose their lives.

To love our mountains even more, we desire to know everything.

We who loved our mountain so passionately, because it represented the goal, the very essence of our escape – finding ourselves again – we knew nothing at all about our mountain.

All that we know now we have since learnt from books, those books which, in the end, were the closest companions of our long sojourn behind barbed wire and the armistice period of day-release when we worked at jobs of all kinds in Kenya until the longed-for day when we could go home again. Unlike our other companions, they rarely disappointed us, often comforted us, helped us to forget and some (it seems impossible, doesn't it?) even made us think.

Thanks to these books I have been able to add to my love for Mount Kenya, born out of an allure that held me in its spell, an "intellectual" love, a love inculcated by books, agreed, but love all the same. I hope that for the sake of this love I may be forgiven if some things seem to the reader merely second-hand pseudo-learning.

Before us, other men, white and black, were fascinated by the beauty of the mountain. It is only right that they should be remembered, however briefly, and that their impressions are recounted, wherever possible, in their own words.

The sign of miracles

Before white men with the unquenchable desire to become acquainted with the massif of Mount Kenya ever set foot in the depths of Africa, the tribes that lived beneath it thought of it as a shrine that nobody dared enter: it was the throne of the gods.

According to the Kikuyu version of Genesis – as told to us by Jomo Kenyatta[2] – Mogai, the founder and organiser of the universe, created Kere-Nyaga ("Mountain of Brightness") as a place of rest for himself and a sign of his miracles for men. As soon as he had created Kikuyu, the father of the tribe, Mogai took him up to the highest peak and showed him the beauties of the land he had granted him. Before dismissing him, he told him that if ever he, Kikuyu, should have need of him, he should lift his hands to the Mountain, and he, the Lord of Brightness, would come directly to his aid. (Hadn't we, wretched prisoners that we were, also raised our hands towards the Mountain, to ask her to give us back to ourselves?)

According to the Mwimbi tribe, who live on the eastern slopes of the mountain, evil spirits known as *ngoma* populate the rivers, forests and rocks and kill the cattle that have strayed onto the mountain. Whenever they come across a man they enter his body, leaving him prey to terrible convulsions. The chief of all the *ngoma* is Ngai, the deity who lives on the highest peaks, beyond the reach of men, and implacably punishes anyone who dares enter his kingdom. This holy terror of the mountain is not yet completely extinguished among the local tribes: in 1924, a Kikuyu chief who accompanied a South African mountaineer up into the foothills of the mountain, kept asking him to remain absolutely silent in order not to disturb Ngai, who would rain down avalanches of rocks and snow from the peaks until he had killed the whole ungodly party.

The Meru, who live to the north of the mountain, have a legend rich in significance, collected by an Italian missionary, claiming that the origin of all human races lay there. The first men were created black and only God was white. Women, ashamed of their dark skins, envied him. They fretted so much that in the end they persuaded their men to pray to him to let them become white like him. In his infinite goodness, the Creator replied: "Go to the Mountain and bathe in that little lake at the edge of the glaciers and the inaccessible rocks." Those few who were willing to face such a perilous climb seized their spears, bows and arrows, and after infinite pains reached the miraculous lake. They dived in and did indeed emerge white from the icy waters. Their example spurred on others, but when they bathed in the lake, they found the waters still murky and returned to their huts no longer black, nor completely white, but brown. When at last even the idlest reached the lake, they found only a small muddy pool that, as soon as they touched it with their hands and feet, dried up completely. The first group were the ancestors of the Europeans, the second the forerunners of the Indians, and the third remained black, although, as is well known, the palms of their hands and the soles of their feet are white.

The mountain also plays an important role in the mythology of the Masai, who still fifty years ago would advance as far as its northern slopes. They worship the supreme goddess Ngai or Eng-ai, who dispenses rain and good weather from the height of the peaks. Eng-ai is black. To them, black is a sign of goodness, in contrast to Europeans, who might talk of "black moods", "a black day", "black sheep", and so on. Eng-ai is black and good, whereas a demigod called Neiterkop, who also lives on the peaks of Mount Kenya, is red and bad; and it is noteworthy that for the Masai, as for other African tribes, we Europeans are not white, but red . . .

The Masai call the mountain Ol-Donyo-Eibor, the White Mountain, or Ol-Donyo-Egere, the Speckled Mountain; the Samburu call it Ol-Donyo-Lorgenai, the Mountain of Black Stones, and the Rendile Ol-Donyo-Burgos, the Mountain with the White Collar. Each tribe uses the name most suited to the appearance that the mountain presents to those who look up at it from their pastures.

One curious name for the mountain is used by the Meru: Kelemara or Kelema-ya-mara, the Mountain of Intestines. When Father Mario Chiabrera, the chaplain of my prison camp, who, as a missionary of the Consolata of Turin, had spent some years among these peoples, once asked a Meru why his tribe had given the mountain that strange name, the man stretched his hand towards Mount Kenya, glowing white and red in the setting sun, and asked: "Don't you see, Father, that those snow-rimmed rocks look like the insides of freshly slaughtered oxen?"

The official name Kenya seems due to the fact that the man who discovered the mountain, the German Protestant missionary Dr Krapf, heard it called this the first time by the Wakamba. The Wakamba have adopted Kikuyu words but the letters "r" and "g" are not pronounced in the Kamba language; this explains how from the Kikuyu Kerenyaga (Mountain of Splendour) is derived the name Ke-enya-a – in other words, Kenya.

The mystery of the equatorial snows

Classical literature is full of references to equatorial mountains covered in eternal snow and ice: Aeschylus mentioned Egypt "fed by snows", Aristotle spoke of the "mountains of silver where the Nile is born", Ptolemy wrote that the Nile had its source in two great lakes nourished by the "Mountains of the Moon", and the image of the Nile "fed by eternal snows" was used by Tibullus, Horace, Ovid and Statius.[3]

It seems that the ancients believed in the existence of such mountains because it was the only way they could explain what was the most fascinating geographical mystery for many centuries: the source of the Nile.[4] Whether they had in fact learnt of the existence of such peaks from accounts by merchants and slaves, we unfortunately have no way of knowing.[5]

Arab geographers of the Middle Ages also mentioned snow-capped equatorial mountains, which we cannot easily identify: the Gebel Kmur (the Blue Mountain) and the Gebel el Qamar (Mountain of the Moon). Although Portuguese navigators occupied the coast in the sixteenth century, they did not go inland. It was the Spanish navigator Enciso who gave the first account of Kilimanjaro: "To the east of Mombasa rises the Mount Olympus of Ethiopia, which is very high, and even further inland are the Mountains of the Moon, which contain the source of the Nile." The great mystery of this source was still unsolved when sculptor Gian Lorenzo Bernini, in his "Fountain of the Four Rivers" in the Piazza Navona in Rome, depicted the Nile as an old man with his face covered with a veil.

The first European to actually discover a snow-covered equatorial peak was the Lutheran missionary Johannes Rebmann, who, having travelled inland from Mombasa with nothing but an umbrella for equipment, saw a huge white panettone-shaped mountain which to his awestruck eyes seemed like a strange cloud. Moved by the sight, he knelt and recited a psalm to the glory of the Lord. He had discovered Kilimanjaro. It was May 11, 1848.

He went closer to the mountain and questioned the inhabitants who lived on its slopes. They told him that the white substance covering the peak turned to water when carried to the plain in containers, and that some men who had climbed to the summit had come back with their hands and feet frozen. It could only be snow, and it was of snow that he spoke, bravely, in his account published in the *Church Missionary Intelligencer*.

He was not believed! There simply could not be such things as snow and ice on the Equator: the British geographer Desborough Cooley, in his *Inner Africa Laid Open* of 1852, claimed that Rebmann's discovery rested "much more on a 'delightful mental recognition' than on the evidence of the senses" and that the story of the frozen Africans was a mere fable. What the classical tradition had accepted without having any means of proving it, the rationalistic nineteenth century rejected outright.

And the controversy was to grow more bitter with a subsequent discovery, that of Mount Kenya.

At the time of Rebmann's discovery, the Savoyard Capuchin Léon des Avanchères, companion of the then Monsignor Massaia[6] in the lands of the Galla, heard about a "mountain of snow called Obada", which can be identified as Ebar or Eibor, the Masai name for Mount Kenya. Léon des Avanchères was also in correspondence with the Italians Cecchi and Chiarini before they left Let Marefia in the Scioa in 1878 on their dramatic journey to the south-west, to ascertain if "the great peaks of Kenya and Kilimanjaro form a knot or chain between the sloping shores of the Indian Ocean and the plateau of the great lakes, and if they extend in an arm – the Spina Mundi of the ancients – towards the Abyssinian Alps".[7]

It does not seem, though, that the information gathered by Father Léon was known to Rebmann's colleague and compatriot, Dr Johann Ludwig Krapf, who had been expelled from his mission in the land of the Galla, when he left Mombasa in 1849 with the intention of reaching the source of the Nile and "those surviving Christian groups on the equator" of which he had heard in the Scioa.

On December 3, 1849, having pushed even further inland than Rebmann, to Kitui, in the land of the Watamba, he saw another mountain also covered with what he cautiously called a "*white substance*": "There stretched from north to south a gigantic wall, on whose summit rose two towers of such a grandiose and majestic aspect that they gave rise to sublime thoughts in my mind": Mount Kenya with the peaks Batian and Nelion.

He discovered that this "white substance" constantly emitted water and resembled flour; sometimes it moved in great blocks, making a fearful noise. "It could be nothing else but snow and ice," he concluded in his book *Reisen in Ostafrika 1847–55*.

If Krapf was believed in France, where he and Rebmann were awarded a gold medal by the Société Géographique, the controversy continued in England and was echoed in Germany, because the naturalist J. M. Hildebrandt, who had left in 1877 to confirm his fellow countrymen's discoveries and had stopped in Kiti for several weeks, was unable to see Mount Kenya even once because of the continued bad weather. The thorough exploration of Mount Kilimanjaro subsequently undertaken by Baron von der Decken was to fully justify Rebmann, but Krapf had to wait . . .

Joseph Thomson

Almost thirty-five years had passed since Krapf's undervalued discovery when the young Scottish naturalist Joseph Thomson was given the task, by the President of the Royal Geographical Society, Baron Aberdare, of exploring a route that would lead from the coast to Lake Vittoria and of "examining" Mount Kenya. In his book *Through Masai Land*, published in 1885, in which he quoted his motto "He who goes gently, goes safely; he who goes safely, goes far", he recounted his adventures and discoveries in a lively, sometimes moving, sometimes poetic manner.

One morning, in the forest of the mountain chain he called Aberdare, he was following a leopard, rifle in hand, when "through a rugged and picturesque depression in the range rose a snow white peak with sparkling facets, which scintillated with the superb beauty of a colossal diamond. It was, in fact, the very image of a great crystal or sugar-loaf.

"At the base of this beautiful peak were two small excrescences, like supporters to a monument. From these, at a very slight angle, shaded away a long glittering white line, seen above the dark mass of the Aberdare range like the silver lining of a dark storm-cloud. This peak and silvery line formed the central culminating point of Mount Kenia.

"As I stood entranced at this fulfilment of my dearest hopes, I drew a great sigh of satisfaction; and as I said to Brahim 'Look!' and pointed to the glittering crystal, I am not very sure but there was something like a tear in my eye."

Today we read these lines of Thomson's with emotion and feel a bond of brotherhood with this young man who was the first European to fall under the spell of our mountain.

"But now, even while I stood and gazed, a moisture-laden

breeze touched the peak, wove a fleecy mantle, and gradually enshrouded the heaven-like spectacle. In a few moments there but remained a bank of clouds over the wooded reach of Settima. But I had beheld a vision as if from the Unseen to lure me on."

He wanted to go closer to the mountain, but a serious plague of cattle was attributed by the local people to the malign presence of the white man and he was only able to continue with flattery, promises, endless discussions, and constant dangers. He had reached the plane of Nanyuki then inhabited by the Masai (Nanyuki itself is a Masai name: it means "reddish-brown", perhaps from the colour of the river's waters after the rains) when he was forced to turn back.

"The sun set in the western heavens, and sorrowfully we were about to turn away, when suddenly there was a break in the clouds far up in the sky, and the next moment a dazzling white pinnacle caught the last rays of the sun, and shone with a beauty, marvellous, spirit-like, and divine, cut off, as it apparently was, by immeasurable distance from all connection with the gross earth.

"The sun's rays went off, and then, with 'a softness like the atmosphere of dreams', which befitted the gloaming, that white peak remained, as though some fair spirit with subdued and chastened expression lingered at her evening devotions.

"Presently, as the garish light of day melted into the soft hues and mild effulgence of a moon-lit night, the 'heaven-kissing' mountain became gradually disrobed, and then in all its severe outlines and chaste beauty it stood forth from top to bottom, entrancing, awe-inspiring – meet reward for days of maddening worry and nights of sleepless anxiety.

"At that moment I could almost feel that Kenya was to me what the sacred stone of Mecca is to the faithful who have wandered from distant lands, surmounting perils and hardships that they might but kiss or see the hallowed object and then, if it were God's will, die."

If, as in the passages quoted, Thomson lets himself be drawn by his poetic vein, adorned with Shakespearean quotations, this does not detract from the fact that he also examined the mountain with the eye of a scientist.

"This peak . . . without a doubt represents the column of lava which closed the volcanic life of the mountain, plugging or sealing up the troubled spirits of the earth. The crater has been gradually washed away.

"The sides of this upper peak are so steep and precipitous that on many places the snow is quite unable to lie, and in consequence the rocks appear here and there as black spots in the white mantle. Hence its Masai name of 'Donyo-Egère' (the Speckled or Grey Mountain)."

"Snow," Thomson wrote without any shadow of a doubt: it had taken more than thirty years for Krapf to obtain satisfaction!

Notwithstanding Joseph Thomson's importance in the history of our mountain, his name is not remembered in a peak, a lake, a glacier or a valley, as is the case with others who have bequeathed their names to the exploration of the mountain. There does exist a Point Thomson, a needle between Lenana and Nelion – that stone arm aspiring to the shape of a sausage – but it was given this name by Mackinder in honour of one John Thomson, a photographer from the Royal Geographical Society.

The coincidence of names has merely perpetuated the injustice, which is hardly unique, either in geography or in history.

The pioneers

The third European to see Mount Kenya was the German doctor G. A. Fischer, who, in his *Preliminary report on the expeditions in search of Doctor Junke*, mentions having fleetingly glimpsed "the snowy southern point" in 1885–86. It is not clear if by southern peak he meant Lenana, but his reference to snow definitely supported Krapf.

In 1887, there followed the scientific expedition of the Hungarian Count Sámuel Teleki de Szék, which led to the discovery, on the southern borders of Ethiopia, of Lakes Rudolf and Stefanie, so called in honour of the son and daughter-in-law of Emperor Franz Josef – a curious link between the remote corners of Africa and the tragedy of Mayerling.

Only one other European accompanied the Hungarian explorer, Ludwig von Höhnel, a lieutenant in the Austro-Hungarian Navy, who drew up a map of all the territory explored, a map that Gregory considered "probably the best ever prepared by an African traveller".

After many vicissitudes, Teleki and Höhnel reached the western foot of the mountain. Falling ill, Höhnel had to remain alone at the base camp to keep the threatening Masai at bay; Teleki began the ascent just with local people.

Having found the belt of bamboo "almost impassable", Teleki entered the "kingdom of moss" and on October 22 attained the highest point he would reach: 15,354 feet. At the head of the valley that today bears his name, he identified the crater of an extinct volcano, and on the highest peaks the rim of the crater itself. He observed that the limit of the eternal snows on Mount Kenya is lower than on Kilimanjaro because of its more continental position.

Meanwhile Höhnel was experiencing some difficult times. Teleki, the great "white witch doctor", had promised rain and the rain had not come. Teleki being gone, the Masai were angry with Höhnel. Things were threatening to take a nasty turn when Höhnel had an idea: "Where can the great white witch doctor have gone," he said, "if not to the Kelemara (Kenya) to speak with Ngai?" The Masai withdrew their threats.

It was in Höhnel's account that I found what I assume is the oldest description of Lenana: "The wall of the crater still rises to the north-east and forms a lower, more rounded peak."

The names of Teleki and Höhnel are remembered in various ways on the mountain: there is a *Senecio Telekii* and a *Helichrysum Höhnelii*, which, if I am not mistaken, is a shrub found on the lower heights. And there is the Teleki Valley, where he thought he had identified the crater of the extinct volcano.

In 1889, J. R. W. Piggott, administrator of the British East Africa Company, was the first to go up the river Tana and reach the eastern foot of the mountain. His name is recalled in the great northwestern shoulder of Batian, Point Piggott.

The same year, the German Johann Peters saw Mount Kenya from the west: it made such an overwhelming impression on him that he estimated its height as 23,000 feet.

A further step in the exploration of the mountain was taken by the British East Africa Company in 1891. This company, which then administered the territory that would later become the colony of Kenya, entrusted the direction of the expedition to the English officer W. Bird Thompson. Another participant was the civil servant C. W. Hobley, known for his ethnographic and geological publications. They approached through the forest to the south but never succeeded in getting any higher than 10,000 feet. The names

Fig. 19. The Nanyuki Valley with Lakes Oblong and Hausburg seen from Hausburg Col

of Hobley and Thompson were given, respectively, to the lakes and the valley to the south-east of Lenana.

The following year, Teleki's companion Höhnel decided to try again. He was accompanied by the American traveller William Astor Chanler, but was no luckier than the first time. He saw Mount Kenya only from a distance and almost bled to death after being charged by an angry rhinoceros. Owing to a mutiny by the porters, the expedition disbanded, and the Europeans were lucky to get back to the coast alive, which they did only after many vicissitudes.

A few years later, in 1897, the fate that had almost befallen Höhnel struck another explorer of the mountain, the German doctor and naturalist Georg Kolbe. He had climbed the mountain as far as the area of alpine vegetation, taking what are probably the first photographs of it. In a hunt between Marsabit and the Ewaso

Nyiro, he missed a rhinoceros, and the animal charged him and killed him. Lord Delamere, who was in the vicinity with his caravan from Somaliland, got there as fast as he could, but was only in time to attend Kolbe's funeral.

The name of Kolbe was given to the glacier, no longer in existence, to the north-east of Lenana.

In the meantime, the first mountaineer had appeared on the scene: J. W. Gregory.

In 1893 he had landed with a large caravan near the mouth of the Jubba with the intention of reaching Lake Rudolf, which had only been discovered a few years earlier, from the east. As a result of an agreement with the Italian authorities in Somalia, he was accompanied by the Italian G. Lovatelli. The enterprise, however, came to nothing because of difficulties with the porters, and the party disbanded. Gregory then organised an expedition himself, going further south. He first climbed to the peak of Mount Longonot, and then attempted Mount Kenya.

It was not an easy undertaking. Crossing the bamboo belt, the porters were so scared by this unaccustomed environment that they refused to continue; some, in fact, wept "like children". More difficulties arose when, having gone higher, they noticed one morning that the water "was all bewitched: it was white and would not shake".

Gregory established base camp in the high Teleki Valley and, accompanied only by the porter Fundi, reached a glacier that he named Lewis, after an American glaciologist. He urged the porter to follow him onto the glacier, but in vain.

"No farther, master," he said, "it is too white," and he knelt to thank Allah for having preserved his life thus far.

Gregory continued alone, and was the first man to set foot on the much-debated ice seen by Krapf. He climbed the Lewis Glacier to what is now the beginning of the normal route to Nelion, but a sudden storm forced him to turn back.

A subsequent journey led Gregory to the western parts of the massif, where he discovered and named the Darwin, Tyndall, Heim and Forel glaciers after various European scientists. He tried to reach the fork dividing Point Piggott from the north-west ridge of Batian (our ridge), but another storm prevented him from continuing.

He abseiled down over rocks covered with fresh snow.

When, after a difficult march, he reached the place where the base camp had been, he discovered to his astonishment that it had vanished. What had happened? During Gregory's absence, the cook, the only person on the expedition who could write, had forged an order to move camp lower down. The porters, who had been shivering with cold all day long, had not needed to be asked twice. Now Gregory, after his first attempt to climb Mount Kenya, had to start looking for his own camp, which he found at last on the edge of the forest. The cook's order had been carried out with great enthusiasm!

Joseph Gregory accurately defined the geological structure of the mountain. That Mount Kenya was an old volcano nobody had questioned, but unlike Teleki, he demonstrated that the hypothesis put forward, from a distance, by Thompson was correct: the highest peak was indeed "the column of lava which closed the volcanic life of the mountain, plugging or sealing up the troubled spirits of the earth".

In 1917-18 the English scientist G. St. J. Orde-Brown tried to confirm Teleki's hypothesis, but as soon as the war was over, Gregory, then already a celebrity, a university professor and president of the Geological Society of London, made another inspection of the mountain, at the request of the governor of Kenya, and unequivocally reasserted his own theories on the structure of the mountain.

In tribute to the governor, he named the northernmost glacier on the mountain Northey.

The conquest of the summit

The first expedition with both mountaineering and scientific intentions was organised in 1899 by the Scotsman Halford Mackinder (later knighted) and the naturalist and photographer Campbell B. Hausburg, who was to take some of the first-ever colour photographs on the Mount Kenya massif. Two other scientists, E.H. Saunders and C. F. Camburn, went with them. Looking for the Alpine guides indispensable for such a difficult enterprise, Mackinder turned to the Italian Vittorio Sella. It was Sella who introduced two Italians from Courmayeur in the Val d'Aosta whom he trusted absolutely and who were soon to achieve worldwide fame: the guide César Ollier and the then porter Giuseppe Brocherel.[8]

The expedition began under inauspicious circumstances and was to be confronted with every kind of obstacle and danger.

Landing in June in Mombasa after making a stop in Zanzibar to recruit porters, they first ran up against a smallpox epidemic, but for the moment this had no other consequence than a long quarantine. There followed a rail disaster from which they emerged unscathed. They arrived at the railhead on the plateau around which the current capital Nairobi[9] was coming to birth, only to find that the smallpox epidemic had spread there, and that they could neither purchase supplies nor gather information about the area. The best thing to do was to leave as soon as possible.

The caravan that began the painful march on July 28, in the

middle of the rainy season, was composed of a hundred and seventy people: six Europeans, sixty-six Zanzibarians and Swahili from Mombasa, ninety-six Kikuyu recruited in Nairobi as naked as the day they were born, and two Masai guides. They crossed broken terrain and thick forests under the relentless rain. Soon the porters recruited on the coast could no longer bear the cold and began to desert in dribs and drabs.

Mackinder had rationed the provisions, hoping to be able to purchase more on the way, but the Kikuyu and Masai they encountered not only did not have any because the area had been hit by a terrible famine, but welcomed the caravan as an unexpected source with which to supply themselves! There began a series of ambushes: some porters were killed in a treacherous night attack and others wounded. Mackinder himself escaped almost by miracle: a poisoned arrow narrowly missed him and fell at his feet.

The march went on for nineteen days in these conditions until they reached the foot of the longed-for mountain. But new dangers awaited them: on more than one occasion, the caravan was charged by a rhinoceros. The Masai guides were replaced by the Italians, and in fact Ollier and Brocherel, whom Mackinder never tires of praising as "woodmen as well as icemen", led the way with such a sense of direction that in a single day the caravan got through the forest and emerged at about 10,000 feet into the Höhnel Valley, where they established base camp. Things seemed to have taken a turn for the better.

But such was not the case. Having come back from a first reconnaissance of the glaciers, Mackinder and the two guides had to struggle all afternoon with a fire in the grassland, set off by a match thoughtlessly thrown by a member of the party (Mackinder's account tactfully omits the name of the culprit). Acting as firemen, struggling with flames and smoke, their clothes singed, their

287

eyes swollen and their hands covered in sores, the climbers managed with difficulty to save the base camp and the supplies.

The following morning, they were again on the move, looking for a suitable place for an "advance camp". On their return to the base camp, a new problem awaited them. Hausburg, who had gone back down to try to buy provisions from the inhabitants at the foot of the mountain, had been attacked and two of his porters had been killed. There was no point even talking about provisions, and the remaining porters were more scared and discouraged than ever.

Mackinder then sent another team, led by the naturalist Saunders, to Naivasha, some sixty miles as the crow flies, to ask for supplies directly from the British Administrative Officer. In the meantime, he would increase the pace and the very next day would attempt the summit with Ollier and Brocherel.

Having passed across the Lewis Glacier at the southern base of the massif, the roped party tackled the great rocky ridge dividing the Lewis from the Darwin. Beneath the precipice of the peak, which Mackinder called Nelion, they were forced to bivouac, a not very pleasant experience at 16,400 feet when the night lasts exactly twelve hours. They set off again at first light, but the rock was powdery, and an impassable crevice in the ridge persuaded them not to continue from that side. They turned back.

At the beginning of September, in order to find a new line of attack, Hausburg went around the whole massif with the two Italians.

He concluded that there was no point in making an attempt from the north (just where we were to end up!). This was the occasion of the first ascent of an easy point, half ice, half rock, which was named Lenana. At the top, Hausburg erected that little stone figure that we were to find intact forty-three years later.

Meanwhile, at the base camp, Mackinder was using all his

288

energy and prestige to try to calm the porters, who were becoming ever more menacing because of the cold, the hunger, the fear of marauders and the wrath of Ngai, which might be unleashed at any moment.

The team sent to Naivasha more than two weeks earlier had not returned, nor was there any news of them. Tirelessly, Mackinder swept the valleys below with his telescope: no sign. He was gradually forced to conclude that he could no longer handle the situation, and sent a note to Hausburg at the advance camp: if by September 7 Saunders's team had not returned from Naivasha, they would all try to retreat there. He no longer dared expect anything more.

Having received the ultimatum, Hausburg decided to make another attempt. It seemed possible to climb the peak from the south, and only from the south. At the first attempt on rock they had been defeated: they now tried on ice. It was exhausting work, but Hausburg and the two guides from Courmayeur set off up the steep Darwin Glacier. I do not know if they were aware of an observation of Gregory's that while the snow is more powdery on Mount Kenya than in the Alps, the ice on Mount Kenya is much harder; be that as it may, by evening they were exhausted. To make matters worse, they were struck by a fierce storm and would certainly have perished if they had had to bivouac there. In the last light of day, Ollier got the group back safely: as the great guide that he was, he had "sniffed out" a way over the glacier to the ridge where their first attempt had come to an end. Moving across rocks they knew well by now, they got back to the camp after nightfall. They were almost at the end of their tether, and what awaited them was the not very happy prospect of having to set off again the following morning, defeated and with minimal rations, in order to try to reach Naivasha . . .

Instead of which, two hours before their return to camp, the long-awaited caravan of supplies had arrived. Saunders was accompanied by the young Administrative Officer from Naivasha, Edmund H. Gorges, who for his help had gained Mackinder's eternal gratitude: in tribute to him he would name the largest valley on the eastern slope Gorges Valley.

Mackinder then arranged for Hausburg to leave with most of the caravan for Naivasha, along with Gorges, who was anxious to get back to his post. This was an excellent opportunity to get rid of the more recalcitrant porters (and they were the majority) and to take the scientific collections to safety: because some boxes had already been looted. He, Mackinder, along with the two Italians, would make a final attempt to conquer the summit and then join the others on the march.

On September 12, 1899, they set off for the crucial attempt. It was now or never.

Having gone back over the rocky ridge from the first attempt, they bivouacked on that same ridge in a Mummery tent. At dawn on September 13, they crossed to the highest tongue of the Darwin Glacier, which they had reached at their second attempt, and climbed it as far as a large rib of rock which falls sheer from Nelion to the west. In a difficult climb, they went up the rib to the height of the small glacier that hangs between the Batian and Nelion peaks. Ollier and Brocherel had calculated that in twenty minutes, work with the pickaxe, they would be able to overcome this final obstacle, which was no more than 130 feet long. But the ice was so hard that it took three hours to cross it. Not much more than thirty feet an hour! Mackinder called the glacier "Diamond", and with good reason. Like a diamond, it glitters as if mounted there beneath the rocks of the highest peak.

The final rocks were crossed without difficulty and at noon

the summit of the peak, which Mackinder named Batian, was touched for the first time by a human foot. They had won.

Brocherel and Ollier returned seven years later to Mount Kenya, and saw from a distance the giant they had tamed, but they did not approach it again. They were on their way to other victories: with the Duke of the Abruzzi and Giuseppe Petigax, they were to conquer the previously untouched peaks of the Ruwenzori.

The names of the members of the victorious party remain linked to Mount Kenya: the valley to the north of the highest peaks was named Mackinder, that to the north-west (where we established our base camp) Hausburg and the two branches of the horseshoe glacier César and Giuseppe. But why César and Giuseppe rather than Ollier and Brocherel? It's a mystery, although perhaps not such an impenetrable one.

Masai history: Batian and Lenana

Mackinder gave the main peaks of Mount Kenya the names Batian, Nelion, Lenana and Sendeyo. They are names of Masai chiefs, and he himself explained his choice at a meeting of the Royal Geographical Society in 1921 in this way: "The Masai, although cruel, were a fine race. They thought of their God as dwelling on the peaks of Kenya and I felt it was right that a memorial of the noble savage should there go down to history."

Then he added: "We took with us two Masai, and they carried Lenana's knobkerry by way of a passport in case we met any Masai out on the warpath."

The first Europeans to provide solid information about this race feared for its ferocity were, as we have seen, Joseph Thomson and G. A. Fischer.

Of Hamitic-Nilotic origin, basically herdsmen and warriors, the Masai despise any form of cultivation of the soil as the work of an inferior race. Even today the Masai tribes recognise no other wealth apart from cattle. Cattle take the place of money. Not that there is anything new about this. In ancient Rome it was virtually the same. It is from *pecus*, "cattle", that the word *pecunia* derives: the oldest Roman coins depicted an ox and were nothing but tokens for heads of cattle.

The political importance of a Masai tribe is measured in the number of heads of cattle it possesses, and it is with heads of cattle that young men, having finished the period of their military posting, buy their wives. They live only on meat, milk and warm blood drawn from the carotid arteries of the living animals. They have splendid physiques and proud characters. The particular politico-military organisation of the young men allowed, and partly still allows, the Masai to carry out attacks and raids with surprising speed and courage. They were not accustomed to taking prisoners: enemies captured in combat were killed with spears then and there, and the women were killed with clubs the morning after their capture.

It is hardly surprising, then, that at the time of Thomson and Fischer the mere name Masai had spread terror well beyond the territories where they lived.

But this all happened fifty or seventy years ago. Today they have even met Italian prisoners of war.

A sapper from Rome who had worked on a road in the Masai reserve told me that he had greatly appreciated the beauty of their women, the *Massaie*, as he called them, and, clicking his tongue, kept saying "They're good, the *Massaie*, really good!"

What happened to two Italian officers, Ettore Formento from Aosta and Corrado Corradino from Venice, is even more significant.

Fig. 20. "Chief Lenana", the great Masai chief with British officials in 1898.

Having been given permission by the commandant of their camp in Nairobi to make a "brief" Sunday excursion (this was during the armistice period), but having gone on a long march into a territory rarely visited by the British, they were suddenly surrounded by some twenty athletic Masai with warlike demeanours, armed with shields, bows, spears and clubs, completely naked but painted white and ochre. The two Italians did not like these people's wild air, but pretended that nothing was wrong. After a while, someone who seemed to be the chief stepped forward, spat on the ground as a mark of respect (which is their custom) and greeted them with "Italians *mzuri* (good)", adding in a booming voice: "*Porca miseria!* (Holy smoke!)".

No, decidedly, the wild and mysterious Africa no longer exists. Let us go back half a century and more.

The Masai do not usually bury their dead, because they do not want, as they put it, to defile the soil: apart from the great chiefs, the dead are abandoned to hyenas and vultures. I have referred to their religious beliefs above, speaking of Mount Kenya and the Kikuyu: they invoke Ngai to send rain and to "protect the uplands and lowlands of the vast country that belongs to our god".

The supreme religious and political authority of the Masai is the *ol-oibohi* or *laibon* for short, the great chief.[10] This office is the exclusive privilege of the Kidongi family of the Aiser tribe, and goes back more than three hundred years, because the story I am about to tell mentions nine generations. One of the basic tasks of the *laibon* is to predict the future, when the needs of the tribe require it. This operation can be done either through examining the innards of a freshly killed ox, just as our ancestors did, or drawing from an ox's horn two special stones (which, in 1904 when Hollis was writing, no European had been allowed to see), speaking in an intoxicated state produced by an abundant libation of mead, or even illustrating his own dreams in parables, which those present repeat in chorus.

"Now, of all the medicine-men who lived in olden days Mbatian was the greatest.

"It is said that formerly, before Europeans ever came to these countries, he prophesied that white people would arrive.

"Again, before he died he told the people to move their grazing grounds, 'for,' he said, 'all the cattle will die. You will first of all see flies which make hives look like bees, then the wild beasts will die, and afterwards the cattle.'

"Both of these prophecies have come true: the Europeans have arrived, and the cattle died.

"Mbatian himself died while the cattle plague was raging (*circa* 1890).

"When on the point of death, he called the elders of Matapato, the sub-district in which he lived, and said to them: 'Do not move from your country for I am about to die, and I will send you cattle from heaven. If you move, you will die of small-pox, your cattle will all perish, you will have to fight with a powerful enemy, and you will be beaten. I wish my successor to be the son to whom I give the medicine-man's insignia. Obey him.'

"The elders said: 'Very well,' and left.

"When they had gone, Mbatian called his eldest son Sendeyo, and said to him: 'Come tomorrow morning for I wish to give you the medicine-man's insignia.'

"While this was taking place, Lenana, who had hidden himself in the calf-shed, overheard the conversation. He arose early in the morning and went to his father's hut. On his arrival he said: 'Father, I have come.'

"Now Mbatian was very aged and he only had one eye. He therefore did not see which of his sons was before him and gave to Lenana the insignia of the medicine-man (the iron club and the medicine horn, the gourd, the stones, and the bag), at the same time saying: 'Thou shalt be great amongst thy brothers and amongst all the people.'

"Lenana took the medicine-man's insignia and went away.

"Sendayo then went to his father, but was told that his brother had already been there and been given the medicine-man's insignia. When he heard this, he was very angry and said: 'I will not be subject to my brother; I will fight with him until I kill him.'

"Mbatian died and was buried near Donyo Erok.

"When he was dead, some of the people proclaimed Lenana principal medicine-man, 'for,' they said, 'Mbatian told us that he would give the insignia of his office to whichever of his sons he wished should succeed him.' They therefore remained with Lenana.

"But others said: 'We will not acknowledge this man for he is a cheat,' and they threw in their lot with Sendeyo.

"Now disease broke out amongst Sendeyo's people, many of whom died, their cattle all perished, and they were defeated by the Germans; whilst those people who remained with Lenana did not fall ill, and they obtained cattle, as Mbatian had predicted.

"The two rivals waged war for many years, and eventually Sendeyo was beaten. He came in 1902 to beg his brother to allow him to live with him, and peace was concluded between the two parties."

This is the story, frankly Biblical in flavour, of Batian and Lenana, which the Masai passed on by word of mouth and which was collected by Hollis.

Nelion is none other than a corruption of Neliang: the brother of MBatian, according to Dutton, the son of MBatian and therefore brother of Lenana and Sendeyo, according to Hollis.

It was a genuinely original and praiseworthy idea of Mackinder's, not devoid of a certain poetry, to call the highest peaks of Mount Kenya by the names of great local chiefs rather than more or less famous European figures who had never set foot in Africa.

Those strange names, Batian, Nelion and Lenana, still cling to the peaks of Mount Kenya, in memory of those leaders with their iron clubs, around whom a great primitive people closed ranks before undertaking a lightning raid or before moving pasture in the "lowlands and uplands" of their "vast country" so rich in herds.

Contemporary history

Let us get back on track after this digression and resume the history of our mountain.

For thirty years Batian resisted all attempts. Six times between March 1909 and August 1920, the Anglican missionary Dr J. W.

Arthur, twice Major E. T. A. Dutton with Dr J. D. Melhuish, and an indefinite number of times others, known and unknown, failed in their attempts to repeat the triumph of 1899.

But their work was not in vain. The mountain was studied from every point of view: the topography was established with remarkable accuracy, the characteristic flora and fauna were classified, the glaciers, the most important minor peaks, and many of the numerous lakes were noted and named. Mount Kenya was photographed, filmed and described in noteworthy publications, including the account by Dr Arthur read to the Royal Geographical Society, with subsequent commentary by Mackinder, and the oft-quoted volume by Dutton.

Then, in 1929 an outstanding English mountaineer came on the scene: Eric E. Shipton, whose name would for ever be linked to the solution of some of the principal climbing problems of Mount Kenya and who would become one of the greatest names in mountaineering, not just in Britain but around the world. He would be the first person to climb Kamet (25,446 feet), Kellas Peak (23,179 feet), Kartaphu (23,687 feet) and other extraordinary undertakings in the Himalayas, the Alps, and the Americas; he would take part in the Everest expeditions of 1933 (in which he would reach without oxygen), 1936 and 1938.[11]

In short, from a technical point of view, he was a champion, and – more importantly – he was also a fine writer on mountaineering matters, being a man with a profound feeling for mountains.

Now he was tackling Batian. He was accompanied by P. Wyn-Harris, who on the 1933 Everest expedition would reach 27,500 feet with Smythe and find the pickaxe of Mallory and Irvine, who had disappeared on their tragic climb in 1924.[12]

*

Fig. 21. Shipton's Cave.

The initial idea of the two mountaineers was to find a "direct route" so as to avoid the ups and downs of the Mackinder route. So they turned first to the great north-east wall (misguidedly called north by some and east by others) which seemed to have the most inclined slope and would therefore provide the most direct access.

This magnificent wall is intersected by two huge parallel canyons: they chose the one on the right. Wyn-Harris was at the head, and the rope party quickly gained height.

"Gradually the climbing became more difficult," writes Shipton. "Each new step demanded a more determined effort. Gully, ice slope and ridge were mastered ever more slowly and we began to get worried about the time. At last we reached a great slab, about two hundred feet below not excessively steep, but above it was a great bulge, which ran the whole width of the face and ended in the gloomy overhanging gully under the Gate of the Mist. We had seen this bulge through field glasses from our camp, but we had greatly underestimated its size. Moreover it had appeared to be split by a vertical crack, but this turned out to be no more than a shallow groove as smooth as the rest and overhanging in its lower portion. It did not take us long to recognise that we had arrived at a hopeless impasse; but we continued to gaze at it in silence, each hoping that the other would find some miraculous solution, each waiting for the other to pronounce the verdict he knew only too well."

The following day brought another failed attempt; this time by the south-eastern face of Nelion. But as they retreated, Shipton continues, "We looked towards the east and saw there a great circle of rainbow colours, sharp and clear, framing our own dark silhouettes. It was the Spectre of the Brocken – the only one I have ever seen. Mountains have many ways of rewarding us for our pilgrimage, and often bestow their richest treasures when least expected. For my part, all disappointment, all care for the future were drowned in the great joy of living that moment. We climbed slowly down the ridge and crossed the glacier back to camp."

Shipton and Wyn-Harris, however, were not the kind of men to be disheartened by two failed attempts. On January 6 they once again approached Nelion from the south-east: "We climbed to a little recess at the end of the ridge. Behind this was a smooth wall some 60 feet high. But in its lower part there were some tiny holds, and balancing on these I started climbing, hoping to find more holds higher up. But before I had got 15 feet up they petered out. I managed to make a little progress to the left, but without gaining height, and there I clung until my fingers and feet were aching painfully. Working my way back above the recess I tried to the right and here found a narrow sloping ledge that led round a corner out of sight. It was an airy place above a sheer drop whose depth I did not bother to estimate. But before I had got far round the corner I found a shallow crack that split the surface of the wall above me. It was obviously the only line of possibility and I took it, though I was not at all happy. The crack was not wide enough to wedge my foot in it, and the only holds were smooth and sloping outwards. My progress was painfully slow, but soon the prospect of beating a retreat was even more repugnant than climbing on up. At length I reached the top of the crack and found myself on a fairly wide, platform above the wall. I felt rather ashamed of myself for wasting so much time on a fool's errand.

"But Wyn, when he joined me on the platform, was jubilant, though what there was in our situation to be pleased about I could not see. For the next hundred feet or so the ground was certainly easier, but above that the upper cliffs of Nelion frowned over us in a fearsome overhang, which, even in my somewhat desperate frame of mind, I could not imagine myself attempting.

"We climbed on until we were directly under the overhang. From here a wide gully ran steeply down to the right and plunged out of sight. By climbing a little way down this it seemed that we could cross to the buttress on the other side, which formed our skyline in that direction. But if we could get round this it would only bring us out on to the terrific precipice of the eastern face of Nelion. However it was the only way, and Wyn led off down and across the gully. The full length of the rope was stretched taut across the gully before he found a suitable stand and I could join him. Then we climbed diagonally up the buttress. Before it disappeared round the corner, I looked back and saw that we were already above the overhanging part of the southern face of Nelion. We crossed the crest of the buttress, expecting to be faced with a smooth perpendicular cliff. Instead, to our incredulous delight we found that easy broken rocks led on upwards. We could not see the summit, but it was clear that we were above the great wall of the east face and that there was nothing now to stop us. This sudden change from hopelessness to the certainty of success was among the most thrilling experiences I have known. There followed only a swift joyous scramble and we were there, on the hitherto untrodden summit of Nelion.

"By now the cloud was all about us, though we could still see the Lewis glacier below. Gustav had been watching the summit through field glasses. He saw us now and let out a tremendous shout that came faintly to our ears. Across the gap, filled with swirling mist, we could see dimly the rocky dome of Batian.

"After a short rest we started down the ridge towards the Gate of the Mist. Our first attempt to reach it failed, but by cutting steps down a hard snow slope on the northern side of the ridge we turned an overhanging pinnacle and got down to the floor of the gap. Thence we reached the summit of Batian."

They built a stone figure and started their descent towards the Gate of the Mists, as Mackinder had named the fork between Nelion and Batian, going around a precipice to the north with a notably steep crossing over snow. From the Gate itself they passed to the left of the Grand Gendarme and reached the peak of Batian at 1.45 p.m.

They found no traces left by Mackinder and his companions, but the place was perfectly recognisable from the photograph taken by the first climber; only one or two stones seemed to have been moved, perhaps by lightning.

Batian had been conquered for the second time and Nelion (16,998 feet) for the first.

Two days later, Shipton wrote thus about his own ascent: "Kenya is a tough nut to crack and stands up in comparison with climbing any of the highest peaks of the Alps. I would say that the difficulty of our route is pretty much similar to that of the Meije in the Dauphiné Alps, although shorter."

In December 1929, Shipton, accompanied by Pat Russell, repeated the ascent for the third time.

With these repetitions, the Shipton-Wyn-Harris route or "Nelion route" was destined to become the common route up Batian, so much so that a shelter, known as "Top Hut", was built near the Lewis Glacier opposite the opening, and another halfway up from Chuka, in Urumandi territory, at the upper limit of the forest (around 10,000 feet).[13]

All the preliminaries had been established to make Mount Kenya accessible, but neither the common route nor, less still, the Mackinder was entirely satisfactory, because they made use of a foreign body, Nelion, only the last few feet being on Batian itself.

In August 1930, therefore, Eric E. Shipton, who had rented a farming concession in Kenya at Turbo near Eldoret, returned to the fray to find a direct solution to the problem on the northern slope.

His companion this time was another champion of world mountaineering: H. W. Tilman, who, again with Shipton, was to conquer the Kellas Rock Peak (23,179 feet) in the Himalayas in 1932, and in 1936 to reach, along with the American Odell, the highest peak yet scaled anywhere in the world, Nanda Devi in the Garhwal Himalayas (25,656 feet). Later, at the head of the 1938 Everest expedition, he was to miraculously escape an avalanche.[14]

Of the north face of Mount Kenya Shipton had written the year before: "The northern side is amazingly complicated and the problem of forcing a route up any part of it is very difficult indeed.

"A very sharp and almost level ridge starts just below the summit of Batian and runs N. for some distance; then it divides into two parts, one descending to the W., the other to the N.E.

"The W. Ridge runs down to the col between Point Piggot and Batian and is quite continuous. It is very long and serrated and in places tremendously steep.

"The N.E. ridge is not so well defined, and is broken up into a series of huge pinnacles, somewhat resembling a ridge of Chamonix Aiguilles. Two glaciers have their origin in the face enclosed by these two ridges: one is the Northey Glacier; the other has two branches names the 'César' and the 'Joseph', after Sir H. Mackinder's two guides – César Ollier and Joseph Brocherel. Between these two glaciers two detached peaks rise: one is Point Peter – a fine rock spire; the other appears to have no name – it is the higher though the less imposing. Neither has been climbed."

And Shipton and Tilman climbed both of them in 1930.

About Point Peter (16,010 feet) Shipton comments that it is: "a short, though rather difficult climb". The higher (16,108 feet) was given the name of Major Dutton. It is "directly in front of the N. face, and commands an extremely fine view both of that face and of the W. Ridge from the Northey Glacier, or of gaining it from higher up the N. face. These were the last alternatives to attacking the W. Ridge direct from the col."

We escaped prisoners were to have a different impression: the very alternative rejected by Shipton and Tilman as "hopeless" was to constitute our actual line of attack, and the facts I think bore us out . . .

The north-east ridge presents two obstacles to an approach from the Col: the first is a donjon that Shipton called Petit Gendarme because it reminded him of the needles of Chamonix; the second, which appeared even more formidable, towered even higher and was named Grand Gendarme.

To examine whether or not it was possible to go around the

Petit Gendarme from the south, that is from beyond the Col, Shipton and Tilman made a reconnaissance of the Col and found a small ledge that seemed to go around the Petit Gendarme in the required direction and provide a starting point for a possible crossing. From their vantage point they could see no further and they also dismissed the plan to climb towards the top of Point Piggot to gain a better view of the traverse round the Petit Gendarme. "Had we done so," notes Shipton, "I doubt whether we should have attempted it." Already from the Col, as he honestly confesses, he had been "somewhat daunted by the appearance of the ridge".

By eight in the morning of August 1, 1930 the two climbers were already on the Col, having used many of the steps cut the day before. They sat down to catch their breaths, their feet dangling over the Tyndall Glacier, overwhelmed by the imposing appearance of the West Wall covered by the overhanging glaciers Heim and Forel: "a single wall of ice".

They then tackled the Petit Gendarme, following the venous ledge from the previous day, until they managed to get a look "round the corner".

"It was not good," says Shipton. The whole south face of the Gendarme seemed clad in green ice and covered in unstable-looking snow.

"A rib of iced rock prevented our seeing more than a rope's length ahead. This rib was gained after some labour and we were confronted by the same prospect. So it went on – I forget how many times. Sometimes the ice was too thin for steps, and a large area had to be chipped away before hold could be found in the smooth slabs beneath; at others the snow was in a dangerous condition and had to be cleared to the ice or rock beneath."

More than once, the two mountaineers debated whether or not

Fig. 22. Tyndall Glacier.

to turn back, but they carried on in the hope of finding something better behind the next rib. In this way they reached a gorge that led to the fork situated above the Petit Gendarme. The gorge, also covered in ice, was not easy work, but it was conquered.

By 11.40 a.m. the two were at the fork. A brief rest, then they tackled the hot dry rocks on the north slope of the Grand Gendarme.

The initial crossing was not difficult, but in some places the rock was crumbly. A difficult wall led to a ledge directly beneath the peak of the Grand Gendarme. Here they had to tackle a crevice that ended in a precipice. Tilman wedged himself into the crevice beneath the precipice and behind him Shipton hoisted himself up and got past the critical point.

More crumbly rock followed, over on the right, until they

reached the ridge. Fog had risen.

Four pinnacles on the ridge constituted the next obstacles. The worst was the second, which could only be tackled with another human pyramid and provided very small footholds higher up. Shipton considered this point the most difficult of the entire climb. Having got past the third and fourth pinnacles, they reached the point where the north-east ridge joins the final ridge. It started to snow. Easy stretches alternated with genuinely difficult patches. They had to descend by abseiling down a groove, cutting steps on a very thin ridge of ice, then tackling another pinnacle, which reminded Shipton of the Grépon both because of the nature of the rock and the difficulty of the climb.

Now, past a final spur of rock, there was difficult ice just below the summit. "This simply had to 'go' and we attacked with great eagerness," says Shipton. By 4.20 p.m. they were at the summit. They had achieved the first ascent of Batian entirely on Batian.

They began their descent by the "common" route, well known to Shipton because it was "his" and he had done it twice. But they were tired, and Shipton was starting to feel ill from having eaten a tin of rotten meat essence. What made things worse was the fact that the mountain on the southern slope was in winter conditions.

Since Mount Kenya is almost exactly on the Equator, its north and south slopes present an interesting phenomenon, one which is of vital importance for mountaineers. When the sun is in the northern hemisphere (European summer), the north slope is in summer conditions: dry rock, very little ice and not much snow, while the south slope is in winter conditions: icy rock covered in snow. Conversely, when the sun is in the southern hemisphere (European winter) the north slope is in winter conditions and the south in summer conditions.

In order to have a chance of succeeding on the north-west

ridge, Shipton and Tilman had chosen August, which in Europe is a summer month, when the new route they were trying on the north slope would present easier summer conditions, and the descent on the south slope more difficult winter conditions. (We, in our ignorance, went north in February, in winter conditions – as if things were not already difficult enough!)

The winter conditions were another reason why the descent was a nightmare. They had to scramble down in complete darkness, Shipton was suffering from stomach cramps, and Tilman did not know the way. Both already had behind them twelve hours of difficult climbing, done without planting a piton. The moon rose and the descent continued all night. The dawn of August 2 found them on the Lewis Glacier, walking towards the shelter, without having bivouacked. The "great crossing" from north to south had been accomplished in twenty-four hours.[15]

*

The "north-west" was the fifth ascent of the Batian.

The sixth was accomplished on November 22, 1936 by R. J. Irens and Ed. Sladen. The seventh, on January 31, 1937, was that of Piero Ghiglione from Turin with Dr Ed. Wyss-Dunant from Geneva. They traced a new route up Nelion, one noticeably more direct and difficult than the common route. I shall not bother with the details of this undertaking, which is well known from the two mountaineers' own publications.[16]

The eighth ascent, and the first by a woman, was carried out on the normal route on March 5, 1938 by Miss Una Cameron with the guides Edoardo Bareux and Eliseo Croux, who, like Mackinder's guides, were from Courmayeur. Days earlier, with the same men, Miss Cameron had climbed five of the main peaks of the Ruwenzori. The ninth, done the following day by E. Sladen and his sister Miss G. Sladen, was the last before our attempt.[17]

Conclusion

There was so much, then, of which we had not the faintest idea!

All we knew was what had been written about the fauna and flora by Lieutenant Colonel Stockley, that mention by an anonymous British major about the approach to the northern glaciers that ended in storms and buffaloes, the story of the papal cross placed on Lenana, and Giuseppe Brocherel's exclamation, "It's worse than Mount Kenya."

Far too little, really!

Of Batian we knew only the name and the terrible northern rock faces seen through binoculars; Lenana we had only seen in photographs and we did not even know where exactly it was; we did not dream that there was a shelter; we did not know that Nelion even existed, nor did it ever occur to us that via its peak lay the common route to Batian.

The names Batian and Lenana, however strange and harmonious, suggested nothing to us of the affairs of a fierce, indigenous race of warriors and herdsmen doomed to inevitable decline. We had no idea that Lenana, like another Jacob, had cleverly stolen from his brother Sendeyo the club of command, which can now be admired in a display case in the museum in Nairobi.

We had no idea that Krapf, Teleki, Gregory, Mackinder and his guides from the Val d'Aosta had devoted their energies to learning about the Mountain – nor Shipton, nor Wyn-Harris, nor Tilman. As far as we were concerned, none of them had even existed!

"As everyone knows," says Lammer, "successors have ten times easier a life"; but we, in our complete ignorance, didn't even know to what extent we were successors! For us, the mountain might well have been virgin territory, as if it had been touched only by the wind, the snow and the clouds. For us, it had just been created.

From one point of view, it seems to me today that it was madness for two grown men, out of training for eight years, having spent twenty months in prison, debilitated by a backbreaking flight of nine days, by the weight of impossible rucksacks, and by a lack of food and sleep, having left from an irrationally distant and low base camp, to be prepared to go, in winter conditions, where mountaineers like Shipton and Tilman, vastly superior to them in technical terms, well trained, well nourished and aided by porters, had not wanted to go in summer conditions of their own free will.

"We didn't know and we couldn't have known," is our one excuse.

But looking at it from another point of view, a different consideration comes spontaneously to mind. Never perhaps have lovers of mountains approached the mountain of their dreams in conditions like ours, at least in this century, which has turned information into an industry.

Materially, our ignorance meant that we were gravely, irredeemably inferior; from a purely spiritual side, however, which matters more to a true mountaineer, our ignorance was a genuine godsend.

Every step was a discovery, a new beginning. We were back at the dawn of time, before places had names; everything we saw aroused thoughts of awe, gratitude and reverence. We were, as Pascoli said, like Adam.

NOTES

1   Giovanni Mosca (1908-1983), Roman journalist and satirical writer, had particular success among the young before the war with his column in the weekly paper *Marc'Aurelio* (later suppressed by the regime) entitled "Whether or not you have any doubts, gentlemen, ask me and I will answer you."

2   Later first President of Kenya.

3   Ptolemy, *Geography* VI; Aeschylus, *The Suppliants* 559; Aristotle, *Meteorology* I; Tibullus, *Elegies* I, 7; Horace, *Odes* IV, 14; Ovid, *Metamorphoses* II, 254/255, *Ars Amandi* III, 6; Statius, *Silvae* III, 5.

4   In Lucan's *The Civil War* (X, 188), Caesar exclaims: "If I could be sure of seeing the source of the Nile, I'd abandon the civil war." The tomb in London's Westminster Abbey of the explorer David Livingstone (1813-1873), who devoted his life to the search for the source of the Nile, bears the following inscription: *Tantus amor veri, nihil est quod noscere malim quam fluvii causas per saecula tanta latentes.*

5   The archaeologist Leakey's discovery at Nakuru in Kenya of beads made in Egypt or the Middle East proves there was communication in ancient times between the Mediterranean basin and equatorial Africa. It would be difficult, I think, to prove scientifically that the communication also went the other way, because the only goods exported from equatorial Africa up until a century ago were ivory and slaves.

6   See Ettore Cozzani, *Vita di Guglielmo Massai*, Vallecchi, Firenze, 2 volumes.

7   At Let Marefia, near Ancober in Central Ethiopia, at an altitude

of about 10,000 feet, there was from 1876 to 1882 an Italian geographical station founded and directed until his death by Marchese Orazio Antinori, who also asked to be buried there. Giovanni Chiarini (born in Chieti in 1849) and Antonio Cecchi (born in Pesaro, also in 1849) were kept prisoner for two years by the Galla on the borders of Kaffa province. Chiarini died there in October 1879 either of malaria or poisoning, some months after their companion in misfortune Father Léon, and Cecchi, having reached the goal of their adventurous journey, returned to Italy after many vicissitudes. He was later appointed consul in Aden and then in Zanzibar. Given the task of beginning trading negotiations with the Somali sultan of Gheledi, he died in an ambush near Mogadishu.

8　Natives of Courmayeur, they were Italian – not Swiss, with all due respect to Dutton (*Kenya Mountain*, pp. 55, 108 and 209), Rev. Arthur (*Mount Kenya*, p. 10), the writers Elspeth Huxley (*East Africa*, p. 40) and Vivienne de Watteville (*Speak to the Earth*, p. 269), or French from Chamonix, as maintained by the Swiss aviator Walter Mittelholzer (*Kilimanjaro Flug*, p. 41). Nor were they brothers, whatever Eric Shipton may say (*Upon that Mountain*, p. 46), although they did indeed share many climbing triumphs.

9　A Masai word meaning "cold".

10　The English translation medicine-man or German *Medizin-mann* is etymologically more accurate, because *ol-oiboni* derives from *ol-aibon* "medicine". But since the function of the *laibon* goes far beyond his medical activities, I have preferred to translate it as "great chief".

11　In 1951 he was the first to reach the southern slope of Everest, in the valley he named Western Cwm (Western valley; the word *cwm* is Welsh) [*translator's note*: other sources say it was named by Mallory in 1921] and which, as he predicted, was the key to the victorious assault on the summit later made by the Hunt expedition led by Hillary. The fact that Shipton was excluded from the expedition caused astonishment in British mountaineering circles. When he died at the age of seventy in London in 1977, the press called him one of the greatest mountaineer-explorers of the century.

12 P. Wyn-Harris was a Colonial official, and the last British governor of the Gambia. Until an advanced age, he was a daring yachtsman. He died in 1979 after a long illness, at the age of seventy-five.

13 After the Second World War the mountain was declared a national park above the height of 11,000 feet (about 3,500 metres) and largely thrown open to tourism.

14 During the war he was among other things the British liaison officer with Italian partisan groups in the Belluno region and gave a lively account of his exploits in the book *When Men and Mountains meet* (Cambridge University Press, 1946).

15 It was repeated, after a failed attempt in August 1947, by A.H. Firmin and P. Hicks on January 23, 1948 (*Alpine Journal*, vol. 57, p. 94) and in summer conditions on August 5 and 6, 1962 by Walter Welsch and Leo Herncarek with a descent down the north wall (*Mitteilungen des DAV*, XIV 1962, p. 202).

16 I consider it unnecessary to remind the reader of this late-lamented Italian academic who pulled off one mountaineering triumph after another around the world and who died in a car accident on October 10, 1960. But I will mention the detailed and fitting account of his character and his exploits in the *Rivista Mensile del CAI*, 1961 (p. 83) and the special issue (no. 10) of the *Journal of the Swiss Foundation for Alpine Exploration* (Zurich, 1961).

Dr Edouard Wyss-Dunant of Geneva was among other things head of the Swiss Everest expedition of 1952, whose members Raymond Lambert, the guide from Geneva with the deformed toes, and Sherpa Tensing, setting off from the Nepalese valley explored the previous year by E. Shipton, reached an altitude of 28,215 feet on the eastern shoulder. Their route was largely followed and continued up until the first conquest of the summit on June 26, 1953 by Tensing and (Sir) Edmund Hillary of the Hunt expedition. Wyss-Dunant, born in 1897, died on April 30, 1983.

17 The top of Nelion was reached during the armistice period after September 8, 1943 by other Italian parties. It was climbed on January 5, 1945 by Lieutenant Colonel Gennaro Sora – who as a captain had skied from Spitzbergen to search for the survivors of the Nobile polar expedition – Lieutenant Colonel Olimpio Gabrioli and the Kikuyu guide Ali Muceti. On January 21, they were followed by a party from the civilian camp in Nyeri consisting of Carlo Barassi, Ugo Ferrero, Belisario Lolli and Antonio Varenna. Gabrioli returned to the same peak, by a new route, on March 12, 1946 with Giuseppe Cogorni (who while bivouacking on the descent was fatally struck by a volley of stones) and on July 17, 1946 in winter conditions with Felice Micheli.

After the war, the peak of Batian was reached – sometimes by new routes – more than forty times, before and after the parenthesis of the Mau-Mau rebellion, when the area of the mountain was inaccessible and the shelters were damaged: the parties were mainly British, but there were also many South African parties, one French, and one German from Munich.

I also know of these Italian ascents to the highest peak of

Mount Kenya: the repetition of the Mackinder route and a new route on the south-west ridge, in January 1958 by Lorenzo Marimonti, Romano Merendi and Giorgio Gualco (who gives an account of it in his book *Olimpo nero*, Ceschia, Milan, 1960. See also *Rivista Mensile del CAI* 1959, p. 13), and a repetition of the normal route in January 1961 by Guido Monzino and Piero Nava with Jean Bich and Pierino Pession (see *Rivista Mensile del CAI* 1961, pp. 116–18).

In the whole of 1965 there seem to have been fourteen fatalities on the entire Kenya massif: too many in relation to the number of ascents!

Translation of *credi tu ancora?*

do you still believe?

do you believe
in armchairs
in rugs in furnishings?
in nice beds for one or two people?
do you still believe in armchairs?

do you still
believe in Campari
in Ramazzotti in Cora
and in that strange jester story
about fragrant beer?
do you still believe in Campari?

I no longer believe
in Roman-style lamb
in Livorno-style fish stew
or in that other fake and ugly subject of
suckling pig on a spit
I no longer believe in Roman-style lamb

gnocchi?
Chianti and Barbera?
cherries and apricots?
not one of these is real!
tales for fools
Chianti, Barbera
gnocchi!

women?!
do you really still believe skirts exist?!
only Kikuyu exist. early in the morning
befuddled or sleepless
you're still dreaming about women!

Sicelio

Translated by Howard Curtis

PICTURE CREDITS

FELICE BENUZZI was born in Vienna in 1910 and grew up in Trieste, beginning his early mountaineering in the Julian Alps. He studied law at the University of Rome and represented Italy as an international swimmer from 1933–35. He served in the Italian Colonial Service in Abyssinia until his imprisonment in 1941. Following the conclusion of the war he worked as a diplomat, including with the United Nations. He died in Rome in 1988.